CHANGING COURSE

PRINCETON STUDIES IN

INTERNATIONAL HISTORY AND POLITICS

Series Editors
Jack L. Snyder and Richard H. Ullman

———————————

CHANGING COURSE

IDEAS, POLITICS, AND THE SOVIET
WITHDRAWAL FROM AFGHANISTAN

Sarah E. Mendelson

PRINCETON UNIVERSITY PRESS PRINCETON, NEW JERSEY

Library of Congress Cataloging-in-Publication Data
Mendelson, Sarah Elizabeth.
Changing course : ideas, politics, and the Soviet withdrawal from
Afghanistan / Sarah E. Mendelson.
p.   cm. — (Princeton studies in international history and politics)
Includes bibliographical references and index.
ISBN 0-691-01677-1 (alk. paper)
1. Soviet Union—Foreign relations—1985–1991.   2. Soviet Union—
Politics and government—1985–1991.   3. Soviet Union—Foreign
relations—Afghanistan.   4. Afghanistan—History—Soviet occupation,
1979–1989.   I. Title.   II. Series.
DK289.M467   1998
327.47—dc21   97-18082   CIP

This book has been composed in Caledonia

http://pup.princeton.edu

Printed in the United States of America

10   9   8   7   6   5   4   3   2   1

For Margaret Algie Mendelson
and in Memory of Myer Mendelson

Contents

Acknowledgments

SEVERAL institutions have provided me with research support. I gratefully acknowledge assistance from the Institute for the Study of World Politics, the Harriman Institute at Columbia University, the Variable Term Program of the American Council of Teachers of Russian, the Peace Studies Program at Cornell University, the Center for International Security and Arms Control at Stanford University, the Joint Committee on Soviet Studies of the Social Science Research Council, the American Council of Learned Societies, the Center of International Studies at Princeton University, and the State University of New York at Albany. I must thank especially the many wonderful people at both the Peace Studies Program and the Center for International Security and Arms Control for making me feel so welcome and for providing happy and supportive environments for working.

Many people read and commented on this project, and special thanks go to several. Jack Snyder consistently read in an attentive, insightful and rarest of all, timely fashion. His questions and comments were both interesting and inspiring. Ned Lebow took me on as a student making no distinction between me and his Cornell students. I thank him for this and for his helpful advice and unstinting support over many years. Janice Gross Stein and Kimberly Marten Zisk gave the manuscript a close read and valuable comments. Elizabeth Valkenier, Robert Jervis, Richard Betts, and John Hazard all provided helpful criticism. Lynn Eden pushed and praised at all the appropriate moments. David Dessler always had insightful and encouraging comments. Nina Tannenwald was a great reader and colleague and a wonderful friend. George Breslauer read a shorter and earlier version of this argument and provided many helpful comments. I thank Peter Katzenstein for some well placed and valuable comments. I thank Irina Vasilieva for putting in endless hours carefully transcribing the interviews. Toward the final stages, the manuscript was sharpened considerably by the expert editing of Teresa Lawson. I have mainly used the Library of Congress system of transliteration except in a few cases.

I thank Clinton Ely for being brave enough to take twenty-seven seventeen-year-olds to the Soviet Union in 1979 and for including me among them.

Many friends provided encouragement along the way. Wallace Sherlock proved a great friend. Thanks also go to Elizabeth Cousens, Renée DeNevers, Mike Elleman, Chrystia Freeland, Judy Gillespie, Gavin Helf, Bobby Herman, Christine Ingebritsen, Riina Kionka, Mike McFaul, Donna Norton, Scott Sagan, and Alex Wendt.

A special of word of appreciation goes to John Harvey. It's hard to imagine what it would have been like to finish this book without him.

My father and mother, Myer Mendelson and Margaret Algie Mendelson, gave me more support—emotional, intellectual, and financial—than any child deserves, for which I am grateful.

Washington, D.C.
January 1997

Preface

Encounters with a Declining Power

The Sea of Faith
Was once, too, at the full, and round earth's shore
Lay like the folds of a bright girdle furled.
But now I only hear
Its melancholy, long, withdrawing roar,
Retreating, to the breath
Of the night-wind, down the vast edges drear
And naked shingles of the world.
        (Matthew Arnold, "Dover Beach")

THE "melancholy, long, withdrawing roar" that, as Matthew Arnold suggested, accompanies the collapse of empires has been heard recently from the East. In many ways, it began in Afghanistan—when the Soviet Union withdrew its troops in 1988 and 1989. Then the roar grew almost deafening as it rumbled through Eastern Europe in 1989 and 1990 and through the Baltic states, Ukraine, Moldova, the Trans-Caucusus, and the states of Central Asia in 1991. In the mid 1990s, its echo still reverberates as many in Russia, incredulous over events, speak of reassembling the empire.[1]

I came face to face with the "melancholy, long, withdrawing roar" of Soviet power in the course of researching this book, interviewing Soviet (and later, former Soviet) decision makers regarding the dramatic shifts in foreign policy that occurred in the 1980s. The puzzle for me was to understand how the new thinkers had won out over the old thinkers. I was particularly interested in the war in Afghanistan, and my reasons for wanting to meet these people

---

[1] See, for example, the editorial by Russian presidential candidate and head of the Communist Party of the Russian Federation, Gennady Zyuganov, "'Junior Partner'? No Way," *New York Times,* February 1, 1996: "We see the restoration of the union of the former Soviet peoples . . . as a historical necessity dictated by Russia's needs and those of world security." The Russian Parliament overwhelmingly voted to denounce the Belovezhsk accord that led to the break-up of the Soviet Union. Michael Specter, "Russian Parliament Denounces Soviet Union's Breakup," *New York Times,* March 16, 1996.

were straightforward: these were the men who had run the war and who had gotten the withdrawal on the political agenda.

By 1990, when I conducted most of the interviews in Moscow, *glasnost* had effectively broken down the barriers that had earlier prevented people from directly speaking or writing critically on the topic of the war in Afghanistan. New thinking in foreign policy had eroded the norm against discussing such topics with Westerners, especially with Americans. Nevertheless the war in Afghanistan, particularly after the withdrawal from Eastern Europe in 1989, remained a particularly sensitive issue for Soviets. The sentiments were not unlike those that surrounded the American war in Vietnam for American policymakers. Although the Soviet Union was less engaged in Afghanistan than the United States was in Vietnam, the aftermath of Afghanistan was even more dramatic. It was as if, following the U.S. withdrawal from Vietnam, first NATO and then the whole of the United States had collapsed. The subject of the war in Afghanistan was difficult to approach, both individually and collectively as a nation, but once confronted, it seemed just as difficult to set aside.[2]

During several months, as the Soviet Union came apart and after, I found myself facing the men who had run the war in Afghanistan. The circumstances of my interviews with two of the top military men involved in Afghanistan serve to highlight the enormous changes that occurred in the late 1980s, and provided a glimpse into the personal drama that many in the Soviet elite experienced following the collapse of the empire.

In early January 1991, during the last days of the Soviet empire, I padded along the quiet halls of the Kremlin, accompanied by a KGB escort, on my way to meet Marshal Sergei Akhromeev, who had been chief of the General Staff from 1984 to 1988 and then Gorbachev's main military advisor from 1988 to 1991. The marshal, in full military uniform, sat talking about the war in Afghanistan over tea, cookies, and chocolates of a quality I never saw in stores. He presented himself as a military reformer, and claimed to have been on the side of those who wanted to get out of the war. Although in his sixties, he characterized himself as genuinely sympathetic with the Gorbachev gen-

---

[2] Comparisons of the Soviet war in Afghanistan with the U.S. war in Vietnam must make clear the different levels of engagement. Three million U.S. military personnel served in Vietnam, approximately 50,000 U.S. personnel died, and at the peak of the war, over 500,000 soldiers were deployed. In the Soviet case, half a million military personnel served, approximately 15,000 Soviet personnel died, and at the peak of the war, 115,000 were deployed. In Afghanistan, the Soviet Union only used approximately 2.1 percent of its force, compared to 21 percent in the U.S. case. See Bruce D. Porter, "The Military Abroad: Internal Consequences of External Expansion," in Timothy J. Colton and Thane Gustafson, eds., *Soldiers and the State: Civil-Military Relations from Brezhnev to Gorbachev* (Princeton: Princeton University Press, 1990), 293–294; Alexander Alexiev, "The War in Afghanistan: Soviet Strategies and the State of the Resistance," P-7038 (Santa Monica, Calif.: RAND, November 1984), 2; Alexander Alexiev, "Inside the Soviet Army in Afghanistan," R-5627-1 (Santa Monica, Calif.: RAND, May 1988) 7.

eration. Yet, only months later, I would hear of his suicide following his participation in the failed August 1991 putsch. What had happened to this man who had expressed sympathy for the reforms, and only a short time later was involved in attempts to stop them? It would seem that the melancholy that accompanies collapsing empires literally overwhelmed him.

When I returned to Moscow in July 1993 to continue interviewing, the Gorbachev cohort was no longer in the Kremlin and a team from the International Monetary Fund—in town to advise on market reform—had set up an office in what had been the Central Committee. On this visit, I met with former Soviet advisors in their homes, or in buildings that the Yeltsin government had given to members of the old government, a form of professional courtesy unprecedented in Russian or Soviet history.

I met Valentin Varennikov, former head of the ground forces in Afghanistan and later deputy defense minister, while he was under house arrest—until the Russian parliament granted an amnesty in February 1994—for his involvement in the August 1991 putsch.[3] Instead of in the Kremlin, with cookies and chocolates, I sat with this once-powerful man in the common room of his apartment building under the not-so-watchful eye of his dozing bodyguard as he answered my questions about the war in Afghanistan. He spoke at length about various military maneuvers. He ranted about Eduard Shevardnadze, the former Soviet foreign minister, whom he claimed had "cut a deal" with the Americans in Afghanistan and undermined the Soviet military. Any question about the war was welcome, as long as I did not ask about Varennikov's involvement in the August putsch. I agreed to his conditions; I was writing about the war in Afghanistan and not about the putsch. But I agreed for other reasons as well; I felt that to understand the events of August 1991 as well as the collapse of the Soviet Union, it was necessary to go back first to when, like "the sea of faith," the Soviet empire seemed to be expanding rather than collapsing. Then it was necessary to look at how the new thinkers had prevailed over the old thinkers and how the "melancholy, long, withdrawing roar" had begun. This book details that story.

[3] Varennikov refused the amnesty—claiming his innocence—and the military collegium of the Russian Supreme Court that reopened the case in June 1994 acquitted him. Julia Wishnevsky, May 11, 1994, Radio Free Europe/Radio Liberty; Vera Tolz, June 21, 1994, Radio Free Europe/Radio Liberty.

Abbreviations

ANSSSR	Academy of Sciences of the Soviet Union
CC	Central Committee
CCID	Central Committee International Department
CDSP	Current Digest of the Soviet Press
CPSU	Communist Party of the Soviet Union
DRA	Democratic Republic of Afghanistan
FBIS	Foreign Broadcast Information Service
GDR	German Democratic Republic
GS	Soviet General Staff
IMEMO	Institute of World Economics and International Relations
IMF	International Monetary Fund
INF	Intermediate Nuclear Forces Treaty
ISI	Inter-Services Intelligence Directorate (Pakistan)
ISKAN	Institute of USA and Canada of the Soviet (later Russian) Academy of Sciences
IVAN	Oriental Institute of the Soviet (later Russian) Academy of Sciences
NGOs	Non-governmental organizations
PDPA	People's Democratic Party of Afghanistan
SAMs	Surface-to-air missiles
SDI	Strategic Defense Initiative
TsKhSD	Center for the Storage of Contemporary Documents

CHANGING COURSE

CHAPTER ONE.

Introduction: How the New Thinkers
Beat the Old Thinkers

THE ARGUMENT

The roar of the collapsing empire caught most who studied international relations and the Soviet Union by surprise. Scholars in these fields had focused for several decades on stability, both in the international system and in the Soviet Union. Many Western critics of Soviet foreign policy considered any retreat impossible. The continuation of the war in Afghanistan, for example, was viewed by most observers as fundamental to Soviet national interests.[1]

While many fault scholars for their failure to predict such changes, this obscures the main puzzle.[2] Observers were not necessarily wrong in their perceptions. Change in Soviet foreign policy and the withdrawal from Afghanistan occurred in spite of the fact that many decision makers continued to hold on to traditional Soviet conceptions about the international system. The interesting question is not why we failed to see all the changes coming. It is rather: how did they happen? How did policy makers and their advisors bring about such dramatic reversals of foreign policy as the withdrawal from Afghanistan? How did ideas that starkly challenged conventional wisdom—that were in fact "misfits"—become policies? In short, why did certain ideas win out over other ideas?

After the initial shock following the end of the Cold War and the collapse

---

[1] For the standard treatment of stability in the international system, see Kenneth N. Waltz, *Theory of International Politics* (New York: Random House, 1979). Typical of comments by Sovietologists is Elizabeth Kridl Valkenier: "It is simply unrealistic to expect this 'new thinking' on the part of the Soviet Union to result in its unconditional withdrawal from Afghanistan. . . . Clearly, Moscow would not capitulate to that extent. Gorbachev would be committing political suicide if, in addition to hectoring his compatriots about domestic shortcomings, he were to start divesting the Soviet Union of its few geostrategic outposts." Valkenier, "New Soviet Thinking about the Third World," *World Policy Journal* 4, no. 4 (Fall 1987): 671. Or see Jerry F. Hough: "It is inconceivable that the Soviet Union can make even small retreats under open public pressure that humiliates it. It is inconceivable that the Soviet Union can abandon allies under pressure unless the pressure is an unstoppable invasion." Hough, *The Struggle for the Third World: Soviet Debates and American Options* (Washington, D.C.: Brookings, 1986), 272.

[2] For an example of blame over the failure of social science to predict the collapse, see Theodore Draper, "Who Killed Soviet Communism?" *New York Review of Books*, June 11, 1992, 7–14.

of the Soviet Union, scholars began sifting through the rubble and testing out various explanations. These efforts have spawned a debate—still in the early stages but likely to go on for many years—over various explanations of change in Soviet foreign policy and the end of the Cold War.[3] Several approaches stress the role of ideas or lessons about the international system and superpower conflict. None of these approaches deal adequately, however, with what evidence shows to be the motivation for change: domestic political responses to economic and social conditions within the Soviet Union. In addition, messages from the international system were, at best, ambiguous: for many decision makers, they reinforced rather than challenged traditional conceptions of Soviet foreign policy. Other approaches that place the reasons for change within the state, stressing the role of needs and interests generated by domestic political considerations and the institutional changes that arose from these considerations, provide little sense of the importance of reformist thinkers and their ideas in influencing these changes.[4] Yet the real story is one of both politics and ideas.

I argue that the withdrawal from Afghanistan and other subsequent reversals of foreign policy resulted because the Gorbachev coalition gained control of political resources and placed what had been misfit ideas about both domestic and foreign policies squarely on the political agenda. The Gorbachev coalition shifted the internal balance of power in favor of reformists and "new thinkers" through a series of political strategies previously unused by Soviet political elites attempting reform.[5] Specifically, they actively encouraged the growth and empowerment of new constituencies pushing reformist, accommodationist beliefs, and simultaneously disempowered old constituencies advocating status quo agendas. They used new reformist constituencies to alter traditional institutions, such as the Communist Party, and to create new ones, such as a critical press. The leadership's mobilization of ideas and experts changed the internal balance of power and created the conditions necessary and sufficient for change in foreign policy, including the withdrawal from Afghanistan.

---

[3] See, for example, Richard Ned Lebow and Thomas Risse-Kappen, eds., *International Relations Theory and the End of the Cold War* (New York: Columbia University Press, 1995).

[4] For an example of a learning approach, see Robert Legvold, "Soviet Learning in the 1980s," in George W. Breslauer and Philip E. Tetlock, eds., *Learning in U.S. and Soviet Foreign Policy* (Boulder: Westview, 1991), 684–732. For a systems-based argument, see Daniel Deudney and G. John Ikenberry, "The International Sources of Soviet Change," *International Security* 16, no. 3 (Winter 1991/1992): 74–118. For an example of a domestic politics approach, see Jack Snyder, "The Gorbachev Revolution: A Waning of Soviet Expansionism?" *International Security* 12, no. 3 (Winter 1987/1988): 93–131.

[5] James G. Richter, *Khrushchev's Double Bind: International Pressures and Domestic Coalition Politics* (Baltimore: Johns Hopkins University Press, 1994); and George W. Breslauer, *Khrushchev and Brezhnev as Leaders: Building Authority in Soviet Politics* (London: George Allen and Unwin, 1982).

I test existing explanations for change in Soviet foreign policy and the decision to withdraw from Afghanistan against my competing explanation by looking at new evidence gathered from my interviews with the men who ran Soviet foreign and domestic policy, and from archival documents of the Central Committee of the Soviet Communist Party and the Kremlin.[6] I use this evidence to look at three time periods (1979–80, 1982–84, 1985–89) during each of which conditions in the international system were fairly static, but domestic conditions were highly varied. Between 1979 and 1989, there were four different leaders of the Soviet Union, and the ability of expert communities to influence policy making varied. The different time periods function as separate case studies.[7] I find that there was no withdrawal from Afghanistan when the crucial cause, reformists changing the internal balance of power in their favor, is absent. For example, in 1979–80 and 1982–84, the war in Afghanistan began and continued despite the desire of some influential members of the leadership to withdraw troops; this was because the internal balance of power continued to favor the old thinkers. In the third period, however, 1985–89, the internal balance of power shifted in favor of the reformers with the help of the expert communities; one result was the Soviet withdrawal from Afghanistan.

The mobilization of ideas and the change in the internal balance of power have implications that go beyond the changes in Soviet foreign policy. This explanation makes clear an important aspect of the end of the Cold War and the collapse of the Soviet Union: specific changes within the Soviet Union ultimately drove structural changes within the international system. Without an understanding of the domestic dynamic underlying the breathtakingly historic end of the Cold War, explanations are bound to be inaccurate; without the shift in the internal balance of power within the Soviet Union, few, if any, of the changes inside and outside the Soviet Union would have occurred.

[6] The majority of the interviews were conducted in Russian in Moscow in 1990–91 and in the summer of 1993. I also had the occasion to interview various Russian policy makers who visited Cornell University and Stanford University. All the interviews were tape-recorded; several native Russian speakers transcribed the interviews, and I then translated the interviews from this written record. I thank Mark Kramer, Matthew Evangelista, Andrew Bennett, and the National Security Archives for assistance in acquiring a set of the most pertinent documents from "Fond 89," particularly notes from Politburo meetings. Fond 89 refers to a special collection of declassified documents, mainly from the Presidential archives, now stored at TsKhSD (Tsentr Khraneniia Sovremennoi Dokumentatsii [Center for the storage of contemporary documents]). The archivists assigned the number 89; there are over 100 such "Fonds" or collections.

[7] On the merits of comparisons within cases, see Gary King, Robert O. Keohane, Sidney Verba, "Increasing the Number of Observations," in *Designing Social Inquiry: Scientific Inference in Qualitative Research* (Princeton: Princeton University Press, 1994); Jack Snyder, *The Ideology of the Offensive: Military Decision Making and the Disasters of 1914* (Ithaca: Cornell University Press, 1984), 34–35 and 219; Harry Eckstein, "Case Study and Theory in Political Science," in Fred Greenstein and Nelson Polsby, eds., *Handbook of Political Science* (Reading, Mass.: Addison-Wesley, 1975), vol. 8.

This story also has implications for international relations theory in general. International relations scholars have looked at how ideas become institutionalized and change public policy, but few have looked at how ideas that challenge conventional wisdom or entrenched elites and institutions become public policy.[8] In a world that is trying to reconstruct itself following the collapse of the old order, there are valuable lessons about the possibilities and the limits of, for example, democratization, or any endeavor that has as its goal the institutionalization of ideas that challenge deeply-entrenched patterns of thinking and behaving. The importance of new ideas and of domestic constituents who can alter the internal balance of power and make these previously unacceptable ideas become policies will be crucial as democrats struggle to institutionalize concepts such as "the rule of law" and "free and fair elections" in previously communist states.

The rest of Chapter 1 develops the argument about the mobilization of ideas and change in the internal balance of power. Chapter 2 discusses competing theories and hypotheses about the role of the international system and conditions inside the Soviet Union in explaining the great change in Soviet foreign policy in the 1980s. Chapter 3 explores the first case period, outlining the incremental decision making in 1979 that led to the escalation in Afghanistan. Chapter 4 details Gorbachev's initial mobilization of reformist experts in the second case period, 1982–84, as the war continued in Afghanistan. The third case, in Chapter 5, focuses on the way in which the Gorbachev coalition altered traditional institutions of power and created new ones with the help of reform-minded experts in the years 1985 through 1989. It highlights how the withdrawal and other reformist ideas finally got placed on the political agenda after the internal balance of power had shifted in favor of the reformers. Chapter 6 explores further conclusions from this case and implications for other cases.

DEFINITIONS

In this story, the focus on politics is largely internal to the state. "Politics" includes not only power-consolidating strategies and coalition building but also the role of reformist ideas and the empowerment and legitimation of policy entrepreneurs in the policy process. The roles of experts and ideas are considered in terms of the political environment in which they existed. The tim-

---

[8] On how ideas that "fit" become policy, see Kathryn Sikkink, *Ideas and Institutions: Developmentalism in Brazil and Argentina* (Ithaca: Cornell University Press, 1991); Judith Goldstein, *Ideas, Interests, and American Trade Policy* (Ithaca: Cornell University Press, 1993); and Peter A. Hall, ed., *The Political Power of Economic Ideas: Keynesianism across Nations* (Princeton: Princeton University Press, 1989).

ing and nature of experts' advice given to the leadership partly explain changes in policy.[9] But without the convergence of interests and the diffusion of ideas between the specialist network and the leadership, there would be no story at all. Ideas about reform would still be circulating in institutes in Novosibirsk, Moscow, and Leningrad with little impact on policy were it not for the strategies implemented by Gorbachev and his advisors for getting the ideas on the political agenda. What follows then is an examination of the interplay of the ideas, the people who voiced the ideas, and the political processes through which the ideas were institutionalized and the people empowered.

The political process by which the leadership selects and promotes ideas and policies is one main determining force in this story. Here it involved coalition-building, personnel change, and various other power-consolidating strategies inside and outside traditional institutions that the leadership used to alter the internal balance of power. Ideas—that is, the knowledge, values, beliefs, and expectations that a network of specialists empowered by the leadership brought to bear on the political agenda—are the other determining force; neither the ideas alone nor the political process independently determined policy changes. It was the combination of the reformist ideas and the political strategies that brought about the change in Soviet foreign policy.

New ideas about domestic and foreign policies threw into relief various problems inherent in old decisions. Domestic reform could not be seriously undertaken as long as the Cold War continued as it had, when the priority of the old thinkers had been to wage competition with the outside world. The war in Afghanistan was a symptom of such competition. The urgency of domestic reform and the consequent need for better relations with the external world made, therefore, the need to withdraw from Afghanistan salient.

The state of the internal balance of power in the Soviet Union directly determined the leadership's ability to get issues placed on the political agenda as well as others' ability to keep issues off the agenda: power involved both the ability to get things done and the ability to prevent things from being

[9] My focus on the timing and nature of specialist advice draws on Peter H. Solomon Jr., *Soviet Criminologists and Criminal Policy: Specialists in Policy Making* (New York: Columbia University Press, 1978). See also Thane Gustafson, *Reform in Soviet Politics: Lessons of Recent Policies on Land and Water* (Cambridge: Cambridge University Press, 1981). On specialist advice, see also the comparative study of American and Soviet policy making in the early 1960s by Zbigniew Brzezinski and Samuel P. Huntington, *Political Power: USA/USSR* (New York: Viking Press, 1963). I modify these indicators and apply them to a foreign policy case. As Solomon notes, such a test provides the analyst with independently verifiable criteria with which to compare the role specialist advisors played in policy making across different countries and different issue-areas.

done.[10] For ideas that did not fit previous conceptions of either domestic or foreign policy, the state of the internal balance of power had particular relevance. The political possibility for change would not increase until after: (1) the mobilization of members of reformist expert communities that occurred before Gorbachev came to power; (2) massive personnel changes in the Central Committee, the Politburo, and other main institutions that took place after Gorbachev came to power; and (3) the empowerment of specific members of the expert communities as an alternative source of political support, once Gorbachev had consolidated his power inside traditional institutions. Reformers helped alter political institutions so that, eventually, new thinking could fit onto the policy agenda.

The relationship of power between the leadership and the experts flowed two ways; this is fundamental to understanding how policy changed in the Soviet Union in the 1980s and led to additional policy changes in the 1990s. Gorbachev needed and cultivated the support of the specialist network, because it helped him legitimize and publicize the multitude of economic and social pressures bearing down on the Soviet Union. Many of the ideas that Gorbachev endorsed and promoted in the late 1980s including specific ideas regarding Soviet–Third World relations and change in foreign policy, originated with the specialist advisors years before the ideas became policy.[11]

In order to win battles against the old order, reform-minded experts had to have access to resources, that is, to a base from which to wage battles. In this sense, the relationship of power and knowledge flowed the other way as well. Many of the specialist advisors benefited from contact with the leadership by being given or by acquiring public platforms from which to articulate and disseminate their ideas.[12] In addition, following the elections to the Congress of People's Deputies in March 1989, several members of the specialist network gained independent voices as deputies in the Supreme Soviet. Some went on to run as deputies in the first parliamentary elections in Russia in December 1993. With anonymity cast aside, these men and women changed the climate of ideas. By the early 1990s, thanks to the changed environment and various

---

[10] Peter Bachrach and Morton S. Baratz, "Two Faces of Power," *American Political Science Review* 56, no. 3 (September 1962): 947–952. For a discussion as it pertains to a Soviet case, see Gustafson, *Reform in Soviet Politics*, 86–95. For a more recent overview of different definitions of power and balance of power, see William Curti Wohlforth, *The Elusive Balance: Power and Perceptions during the Cold War* (Ithaca: Cornell University Press, 1993), 3–8.

[11] Nodari Simoniia, *Strany vostoka: puti razvitiia* (Countries of the east: paths of development)(Moscow: Nauka, 1975). Simoniia was a researcher at the Oriental Institute (hereafter IVAN) and is now deputy director of the Institute of World Economics and International Relations (hereafter IMEMO).

[12] These platforms came in the form of new Moscow institutes (Tatyana Zaslavskaya, National Center for Public Opinion), governmental positions (Leonid Abalkin, deputy prime minister), senior party posts (Alexander Yakovlev, Politburo member), and publications (Vitaly Korotich, editor of *Ogonëk*).

new institutions (such as a critical press and a nascent legislative branch of government), advocacy and access to resources in the Soviet Union were no longer exclusively controlled by the leadership. One result was that reform spun out of the control of the leadership and became, in essence, a revolution.

ALTERNATIVE EXPLANATIONS

The most frequently iterated answers as to why Soviet foreign policy changed, and specifically why the Soviets withdrew from Afghanistan, emphasize the role of external determinants such as ideas or lessons about the international system that Soviet leaders learned as a result of U.S. policy. The evidence gathered in this book, however, shows that U.S. policy in Afghanistan did not cause the withdrawal of Soviet troops. For example, the infamous "Stinger" missiles supplied by the United States to the Afghans who were fighting the Soviets became operational long after many in the Soviet leadership had already decided that troops should be withdrawn, but just as these reformers were struggling politically at home against old thinkers to get this issue on the political agenda. This tells us useful things about the larger process of change: actors in the international system made it more difficult and not easier for the new thinkers to get their accommodationist ideas turned into policies. The Gorbachev coalition was successful in its efforts to change foreign policy despite and not due to the fact that the rhetoric and policies of the United States in the early 1980s confirmed the perceptions of the most confrontational old thinkers in the Soviet Union.

To understand how the Gorbachev cohort was able to get controversial ideas on the political agenda I examine ideas in relation to the political context in which they existed and attempt to assess the conditions under which ideas influenced this political context. The case of Soviet reform in the 1980s and particularly the withdrawal from Afghanistan suggests that the role of ideas in policy making is highly complex and nuanced. Ideas function in different ways at different times. Sometimes they simply justify the actions of policy makers.[13] In this case, sometimes they became weapons in domestic political battles. This case will show, however, that sometimes ideas truly guide and shape policy.[14] During the period 1985–89, for example, reformist

---

[13] For a critical discussion of "rationalist" approaches that treat ideas exclusively as convenient hooks for the real motivations of various competing elites, see Judith Goldstein and Robert O. Keohane, "Ideas and Foreign Policy: An Analytical Framework," in Judith Goldstein and Robert O. Keohane, eds., *Ideas and Foreign Policy: Beliefs, Institutions, and Political Change* (Ithaca: Cornell University Press, 1993), 4.

[14] See Audie Klotz, "Norms Reconstituting Interests: Global Racial Equality and U.S. Sanctions against South Africa," *International Organization* 49, no. 3 (Summer 1995): 451–478.

ideas about domestic policy guided leaders making domestic policy and were used to justify change in foreign policy.

My focus on expert communities in the Soviet Union in the 1980s departs in several ways from earlier works. Most important, I am assessing conditions under which ideas that do not fit previous constructs get put on the political agenda. This contrasts with earlier work where ideas get on the agenda because they in some way fit existing structures or old ideas.[15]

In addition, the conditions under which expert communities are likely to be influential arise more explicitly from domestic political conditions than in earlier works.[16] Earlier work has emphasized the international or "transnational" aspect of "learning" from expert communities.[17] Because of the opaque nature of the Soviet Union during the Cold War, I focus on identifying conditions under which expert communities are likely to affect policy in their own country rather than the conditions under which they influence policy in other countries. I find that the implementation of ideas and the influence of expert communities were highly dependent on access to the political leadership and the salience of the ideas to the leadership. In situations where ideas severely challenge the status quo—where ideas are misfits—the ability of the political leadership to muster political resources is especially important.

These conclusions affect our understanding of the end of the Cold War. Specifically, domestic politics and not international actors were decisive in changing Soviet foreign policy, and eventually, in altering the international environment. These conclusions contrast with expectations that arise from

---

[15] See, e.g., Sikkink, *Ideas and Institutions*; and Goldstein, *Ideas, Interests and American Trade Policy.*

[16] Scholars often refer to these groups as "epistemic communities." I prefer the terms "expert communities" and "specialist networks." These refer to groups of experts from various academic fields (the natural and social sciences as well as the humanities) who share common understandings and beliefs about certain issues, as well as some ideas of how to implement their beliefs. On epistemic communities, see Peter M. Haas, ed., "Knowledge, Power and International Policy Coordination," special issue of *International Organization* 46, no. 1 (Winter 1992). For a slightly different version of the epistemic communities argument, see Ernst B. Haas, *When Knowledge Is Power* (Berkeley: University of California Press, 1990).

[17] The standard work on this is Haas, ed., "Knowledge, Power, and International Policy Coordination," the special issue of *International Organization*. On a Soviet case, see Matthew Evangelista, "The Paradox of State Strength: Transnational Relations, Domestic Structures, and Security Policy in Russia and the Soviet Union," *International Organization* 49, no. 1 (Winter 1995): 1–38; Jeffrey T. Checkel, *Ideas and International Political Change: Soviet-Russian Behavior and the End of the Cold War* (New Haven: Yale University Press, 1997); and Robert Herman, "Identity, Norms and National Security: The Soviet Foreign Policy Revolution and the End of the Cold War," in Peter J. Katzenstein, ed., *The Culture of National Security: Norms and Identity in World Politics* (New York: Columbia University Press, 1996). In the post-Soviet era, transnational campaigns are certainly more common, but scholars have yet to clarify how they have influenced policy making.

neorealism, the dominant approach in the American school of international relations. Neorealists would expect changes in global polarity to shift as a result of changes in the external balance of power, that is, in the balance of power between states.[18] Yet, in this case, changes in global polarity arose from a shift in the *internal* balance of power in the Soviet Union. Power shifted not only from old thinkers to new thinkers but from the Party apparatus to governmental institutions. Ultimately, this shift was so decisive and uncontrollable that the Party, and indeed, the empire collapsed.

METHODS OF ANALYSIS

To test causal hypotheses about how change in Soviet foreign policy and the withdrawal from Afghanistan came about, this study uses a controlled comparison. Using a "process-tracing" procedure, I identify links between the causal variables—the reformist ideas challenging the status quo, and the political strategies for altering the internal balance of power such as changes in personnel and the empowerment of specialists—and the outcome to be explained; that is, change in foreign policy and the withdrawal of Soviet troops from Afghanistan.[19]

I hypothesize, based on actual case comparisons and counterfactual arguments, that if the internal balance of power had not shifted in favor of reformers—if the reformist leadership's political strategies had failed—the Soviets would not have withdrawn troops from Afghanistan beginning in 1988.[20] This statement is supported by the fact that during periods when important members of the leadership recognized the need to withdraw, but the balance of power was not in the reformists' favor, Soviet involvement not only continued but escalated. Even with the shift in the balance of power, reformist decision makers battled those leaders who favored staying in Afghanistan up to the very last troop withdrawal.

The most decisive factors in shifting the internal balance were specific

---

[18] Waltz, *Theory of International Politics*.

[19] On structured focused comparison and process tracing, see Alexander George, "Case Studies and Theory Development," Stanford University (manuscript, Fall 1982). Some might argue that these independent variables—ideas and strategies for shifting the internal balance of power—are contingent on other outcomes, but this is true of most agents of causation. See James D. Fearon, "Counterfactuals and Hypothesis Testing in Political Science," *World Politics* 43, no. 2 (January 1991): 192. Fearon writes, "A variable may help explain one outcome and still itself be explained by the action of other variables. In large-N work this pattern is commonly found in structural equation models, in which a dependent variable in one equation may be an independent variable in another equation."

[20] On the importance of using counterfactuals to strengthen causal claims for small-N research designs, see Fearon, "Counterfactuals and Hypothesis Testing in Political Science": 181–182.

leadership strategies that involved expert communities. Gorbachev and his cohort worked both inside and outside traditional institutions because of past failures of reform efforts. That is, the specific way in which reform was carried out appears to have been a response to previous failed attempts. Gorbachev and his advisors understood the problems of reformist strategies that did not include an extensive base of support.[21] When decision makers in the 1960s had only empowered actors inside—and not outside—the traditional power structure, their bids for reform had failed. And when decision makers mobilized the specialists in the early 1980s, but had not yet changed the internal balance of power, reform was stymied. The Gorbachev cohort believed that if the intelligentsia and society were strengthened and the Party weakened, participation and the desire for reform would increase, making possible policies even as controversial as the withdrawal from Afghanistan.

I show how ideas and the internal balance of power affected first the political agenda and then actual policies by tracing the influence of the expert communities and the coalition-building strategies used by Gorbachev and his circle inside and outside traditional institutions. To assess the influence of the specialist network and its various layers, I examine a number of issues.[22] For example, I look at the types of issues specialists were called upon to analyze. What did Gorbachev consider to be the most important issues? Were issues in any way linked to one another, e.g., were there foreign policy implications embedded in the advice given by domestic policy experts? Second, I consider the character of the advice. Was there criticism of existing policies, suggesting that ideas had real influence, or just a repetition of what the leadership wanted to hear, suggesting that ideas were simply rationales for policies reached for other reasons? Third, I look at the level of the advice. What kinds of specialists had the most access to the leadership? Did foreign policy specialists, for example, have more access to the leadership than, for example, sociologists or economists focusing on issues internal to the Soviet Union? This would suggest that issues related to the international system were principally driving reform efforts.

The timing of advice—not only what people were saying but when they were saying it—is an important measure for assessing the influence of experts on the policy making process. Did advice come before the "preliminary" decision, or the "final" decision? This, again, would suggest that ideas were guid-

---

[21] To this extent, key members of the leadership appear to have learned, but this stemmed from domestic politics, not the international system. See Richter, *Khrushchev's Double Bind*; Breslauer, *Khrushchev and Brezhnev as Leaders*.

[22] Here I draw on the work of Soviet experts Peter Solomon and Thane Gustafson. In their studies, both came to the conclusion that Soviet specialists played a much more active role in various aspects of domestic policy than had been previously thought. See Solomon, *Soviet Criminologists and Criminal Policy*, 4–7 and 107–125; Gustafson, *Reform in Soviet Politics*, 83–95.

ing policy.[23] Or were specialists brought in after a decision that had been initiated from above was announced, and then, only to mobilize public support.[24]

Finally, I consider the extent to which specialists themselves were used to build coalitions within the Party and other institutions in order to change the internal balance of power. Gorbachev had ties with many members of the expert community. I consider to what extent certain specialists were empowered by the leadership in a formal sense. Did these experts move from being outside to inside the policy process, and thus have greater impact on decision making?

Ultimately, I address whether the experts and their ideas merely legitimized or actually guided policy. If they only legitimized policy, then the role of ideas was minimal. If they were also guiding policy, and helping to shift power in favor of reform, then they played a crucial role in helping new thinkers win out over old thinkers. To answer this critical question, in addition to the information on the timing and nature of advice, I trace the coalition building that occurred after Gorbachev came on the national political scene in 1982 and through 1989 when reformers were successful in getting the withdrawal turned into policy. For example, when Andropov came to power, he put Gorbachev in charge of personnel changes within the Central Committee. This position allowed Gorbachev to build the ranks of reformist-minded regional party secretaries, and to ease the task of getting reforms on the political agenda.[25] This observation leads me to consider how the Gorbachev coalition's strategies for power consolidation inside the system corresponded to the empowerment of the expert community inside and outside the system. How did these factors influence the adoption of reformist platforms, especially the withdrawal from Afghanistan?

The answers to these questions reveal much about the importance of both the specialist network and the power-consolidating strategies in understanding and explaining change in policy. Using evidence from interviews with observers and participants in foreign and domestic policy, from recently declassified archival material, from behavior, and from secondary sources, I show that the network participated in the policy making process before the preliminary decision to withdraw from Afghanistan was reached in July 1987 and again before the final decision was reached in February 1988. The roles of

[23] I define a preliminary decision as an acceptance in principle of a policy proposal, which I argue occurred in the summer of 1987 in the case of the withdrawal from Afghanistan. I define a final decision as the formal announcement of the proposal (February 1988) or the formalization of the decision (April 1988). For a discussion, see Solomon, *Soviet Criminologists and Criminal Policy*, 113–114.

[24] See Brzezinski and Huntington, *Political Power: USA/USSR.*

[25] On personnel changes, see Thane Gustafson and Dawn Mann, "Gorbachev's First Year: Building Power and Authority," *Problems of Communism* 35 (May–June 1986): 1–19; Jerry F. Hough, *Russia and The West: Gorbachev and the Politics of Reform* (New York: Simon and Schuster, 1990).

ideas and of power consolidation inside and outside traditional Soviet institutions emerge as central in describing and explaining the dramatic changes in Soviet foreign policy in the late 1980s, as well as the end of the Cold War.

SOURCES

Scholars conducting research in the Soviet Union in the late 1980s and early 1990s and following the collapse of the Soviet Union encountered unprecedented opportunities for data collection. I was able to conduct interviews with policy makers and Gorbachev's advisors in the Kremlin and the Central Committee of the Communist Party, with academics in foreign policy institutes in Moscow, and with journalists and editors from many of the country's main newspapers and magazines. I was able to explore the story behind the stories: for example, how controversial articles on the war in Afghanistan had been published just as *glasnost* began to touch on issues of foreign policy, and how military leaders felt about the political leaders' policies of new thinking.

My interviews focused on evidentiary issues: the policy making process and specific actions taken by specific leaders. I needed to piece together the story, and I wanted to avoid anecdotal and impressionistic accounts. But I was also interested in interpretive questions: the relationship between Gorbachev and the military, the military response to the withdrawal, the relationship of the leadership to advisors. To control for biases and faulty memories, I have in most cases used only information from interviews that is corroborated by at least one other source.

I also rely on Kremlin archival material declassified after the collapse of the Soviet Union. This material details the discussions surrounding the decision to escalate in Afghanistan and the decision to withdraw troops. These documents are supplemented by diplomatic cables that passed between Kabul and Moscow and that were reprinted in the Soviet press. Memoirs of those involved in the decision making process, such as Sergei Akhromeev and Anatoly Chernyaev, are also valuable sources. With new opportunities, however, came some old restrictions. I could only get one of the *zapiski* (written reports) of specialists sent to the Central Committee and none of the various policy reports that Gorbachev solicited from policy intellectuals in the early 1980s.[26]

Very little has been written about the withdrawal from Afghanistan. Studies have been done on the decision to intervene, but very little discussion has

---

[26] Andrei Kokoshin claims that the *zapiski* were handed directly to Gorbachev. Author's interview with Andrei Kokoshin, then deputy director, USA/Canada Institute, November 11, 1991, Stanford University. My research also drew on Soviet leadership speeches and Soviet journals and newspapers for the years 1980–90, including *MEiMO, Narody Azii i Afriki, Kommunist, Aziia i Afrika segodnia, New Times, International Affairs, SSHA, Moscow News, Pravda, Izvestiia, Literaturnaia gazeta,* and *Ogonëk.*

appeared in print on the decision to withdraw Soviet troops.[27] The Western literature on the war is scanty.[28] On the intervention there are two excellent sources: Raymond Garthoff's *Détente and Confrontation* and Henry Bradsher's *Afghanistan and the Soviet Union*, on both of which I rely when exploring the early period of the war.[29]

There are many studies on the role of power versus knowledge in Soviet foreign and domestic policy making, but very little on the Afghanistan case or the time periods of this study.[30] There is good data collected on the politics of personnel change within the Party in the 1980s on which I rely gratefully in Chapters 4 and 5.[31]

CHAPTER SUMMARY

Chapter 2 is a systematic inquiry into the debate in international relations literature on explanations for change in Soviet foreign policy. I situate my ar-

[27] An important exception was a 45-minute television interview with Alexander Yakovlev on December 27, 1991, Central Television, First Channel; Foreign Broadcast Information Service–Soviet Union (hereafter *FBIS-SOV*), December 31, 1991, 3–5.

[28] For an excellent account that draws on firsthand experience negotiating the withdrawal, see Diego Cordovez and Selig S. Harrison, *Out of Afghanistan: The Inside Story of the Soviet Withdrawal* (New York: Oxford University Press, 1995). See also Amin Saikal and William Maley, eds., *The Soviet Withdrawal from Afghanistan* (New York: Cambridge University Press, 1989); Tom Rogers, *The Soviet Withdrawal from Afghanistan: Analysis and Chronology* (Westport, Conn.: Greenwood Press, 1992); and Richard Herrmann, "The Soviet Decision to Withdraw from Afghanistan: Changing Strategic and Regional Images," in Robert Jervis and Jack Snyder, eds., *Dominoes and Bandwagons: Strategic Beliefs and Great Power Competition in the Eurasian Rimland* (New York: Oxford, 1991), 190–219. There are several accounts of the war written by Soviet journalists, the best of which is available in English: Artyom Borovik, *The Hidden War* (New York: Atlantic Monthly Press, 1990).

[29] Raymond L. Garthoff, *Détente and Confrontation: American-Soviet Relations from Nixon to Reagan* (Washington, D.C.: Brookings, first ed. 1985, second ed. 1995); Henry S. Bradsher, *Afghanistan and the Soviet Union* (Durham, N.C.: Duke University Press, 1985).

[30] See, for example, Solomon, *Soviet Criminologists and Criminal Policy*; Gustafson, *Reform in Soviet Politics*; Thane Gustafson, *Crisis amid Plenty: The Politics of Soviet Energy under Brezhnev and Gorbachev* (Princeton: Princeton University Press, 1989); Oded Eran, *Mezhdunarodniki: An Assessment of Professional Expertise in the Making of Soviet Foreign Policy* (Tel Aviv, Israel: Turtledove, 1979); Elizabeth K. Valkenier, *The Soviet Union and the Third World: An Economic Bind* (New York: Praeger, 1983); Hough, *The Struggle for the Third World*; Franklyn Griffiths, "Images, Politics and Learning in Soviet Behavior toward the United States" (unpublished Ph.D dissertation, Columbia University, 1972). See also Griffiths, "The Sources of American Conduct: Soviet Perspectives and their Policy Implications," *International Security* 9, no. 2 (Fall 1984): 23–70.

[31] Jerry F. Hough, *Russia and the West: Gorbachev and the Politics of Reform* (New York: Touchstone, 1988); Gavin Helf, "Gorbachev and the New Soviet Prefects: Soviet Regional Politics 1982–1988 in Historical Perspective," in *Analyzing the Gorbachev Era: Working Papers of the Students of the Berkeley-Stanford Program in Soviet Studies* (Berkeley and Stanford, Calif.: University of California at Berkeley and Stanford University, 1989), 10–12.

gument about the role of ideas and politics in this debate. I derive hypotheses from several competing approaches including systemic and "learning" explanations. Systemic explanations, I argue, are ill-suited for explaining change in foreign policy because they provide little focus on how the international system interacted with the Soviet political scene; they obscure the politics that took place within the domestic context and make outcomes appear inevitable, when in fact the evidence suggests that outcomes were highly contingent. This approach cannot explain why misfit ideas won out over other, more traditional ideas, the question central to this study.

Variations of learning have been the most commonly used approach to explain change in Soviet foreign policy in the late 1980s. This approach hypothesizes that Soviet leaders received information that challenged their long-held beliefs, and that this is why they changed. However, my data suggests the opposite: the Soviet leadership was exposed to information that confirmed long-held beliefs about the United States and its role in the war in Afghanistan, but policies changed anyway. This evidence suggests that the learning approach is insufficient in explaining the events.

Chapters 3, 4, and 5 are organized chronologically and contain the case studies that test my hypothesis about the role of the leadership and experts in changing the internal balance of power and getting controversial ideas on the policy agenda. I begin in the late 1970s with the revving up of the Cold War. I then examine how a group of reformers worked inside and outside traditional institutions of power throughout the 1980s, gradually mounting a successful challenge to the old thinkers that had dominated Soviet politics and policy for decades. The process of mounting the challenge to the status quo that I describe and explain sets the stage for the later drama of the withdrawal and the collapse of empire.

The significance of the Soviet withdrawal from Afghanistan is best understood in contrast to the politics behind the intervention and escalation in Afghanistan, so in Chapter 3, using previously classified material, I examine in detail the incremental decision making behind the escalation. In 1979 and 1980, the internal balance of power was firmly in favor of the old thinkers and the decision making process was extremely centralized. The process of policy making at this time is a baseline against which to measure later decentralization; it is characteristic of the old thinking against which the Gorbachev coalition would later fight.

Specialist networks had existed in various forms in the Soviet Union before Gorbachev and his circle of progressive thinkers in the party apparatus tapped into them, mobilized them, and politicized them. In Chapter 4, I discuss in detail the early stages of these efforts, as well as the trajectory of the war in Afghanistan. Also during 1982–84, Gorbachev and other reform-minded members of the leadership began to implement strategies inside institutions that would ultimately shift the internal balance of power. I discuss, for example, how Gorbachev, having gained control over the personnel process inside the Central Committee, began to build up the ranks of the reformist-minded cadres.

The political constraints on Gorbachev when he came to power were considerable. In Chapter 5, I focus on the strategies the Gorbachev coalition used in 1985–89 to shift the internal balance of power and get the withdrawal from Afghanistan on the agenda. These strategies involved two tracks: on one track, members of the expert communities were given new resources and national platforms from which to raise reformist issues, giving them a power base outside traditional institutions. The second track involved more personnel changes in the Party, and power-consolidating strategies so that the main institutions of power were at least hindered from actively blocking reform.

In Chapter 6, the concluding chapter, I summarize my findings. The domestic arena, rather than the international system, emerges as the main domain of this drama. I compare the policy process surrounding the decision to escalate with the decision to withdraw and find that although in the later case, some centralization in decision making continued, experts and ideas had greatly affected the internal balance of power and thus the political climate in which policy was made.

I assess the theoretical contributions of an approach that stresses equally the role of ideas and the role of politics in explaining policy change, and consider the generalizability of the findings in light of work on the role of ideas in international relations. I address a case where ideas that did not fit traditional conceptions succeeded in getting onto the political agenda. Because they did not fit, the political strategies used to get the ideas in place were as necessary to the outcome as the ideas and the experts themselves.

The withdrawal from Afghanistan is an example of public policy change, and I discuss how conclusions here might be applied to a larger universe of cases of public policy changes beyond international relations. In all such cases, I argue, attention must be paid to the political mechanisms involved in advancing ideas as well as the ideational frameworks themselves.

Finally, I consider how the political dynamics detailed in this book manifest themselves in post–Cold War, post-Soviet Russia. The plethora of new ideas regarding democracy and markets that have been pouring into Russia and other post-Soviet states for nearly a decade and which do not fit with any previous intellectual or institutional structures points to the need to develop political constiuencies who can use these new ideas to alter the balance of power domestically. Old thinking still exists and the internal battles that reformers have to fight in the 1990s are if anything as difficult as those faced by new thinkers in the 1980s.

CHAPTER TWO

Explaining Change in Soviet Foreign Policy: Three Competing Arguments

SEVERAL competing approaches drawn from international relations theory attempt to describe and explain to varying degrees the changes in Soviet policy in the late 1980s. Most explanations stress the role of the international system—either the specific nature of the system, or the influence of lessons learned from the behavior of specific states or from transnational groups of experts.[1] These explanations do not match the evidence drawn from Soviet sources; it shows that the role of the international system was indeterminant, and highlights the importance of political struggles between old thinkers and reformists inside the state. Explanations that do point to domestic politics and Gorbachev have not focused on the role played by experts and their ideas in altering the internal balance of power.[2] Without an understanding of how this balance of power changed in favor of the reformers, any explanation is incomplete.

New thinkers and their ideas played a central role in the success of the strategies that the leadership used to shift the internal balance of power. The leadership provided experts with resources. These experts helped legitimize a series of ideas that challenged conventional wisdom about a range of issues including foreign policy. They helped make the ideas fit by altering the political environment inside traditional institutions as well as creating new ones. Once altered, this environment was permissive to increasingly reformist policies, such as the withdrawal from Afghanistan.

In this chapter, I outline the main ideas involved in each explanation and derive hypotheses based on each argument. I then evaluate the explanation in terms of what it adds to an understanding of change in Soviet foreign policy, and specifically, the decision to withdraw from Afghanistan. Let me make clear: I am not arguing that events in the international system played no role

---

[1] Daniel Deudney and G. John Ikenberry, "The International Sources of Soviet Change," *International Security* 16, no. 3 (Winter 1991/92): 74–118; Robert Legvold, "Soviet Learning in the 1980s," in George W. Breslauer and Philip E. Tetlock, eds., *Learning in U.S. and Soviet Foreign Policy* (Boulder, Colo.: Westview, 1991), 684–734; Matthew Evangelista, "The Paradox of State Strength: Transnational Relations, Domestic Structures, and Security Policy in Russia and the Soviet Union," *International Organization* 49, no. 1 (Winter 1995): 1–38.

[2] Jack Snyder, "The Gorbachev Revolution: A Waning of Soviet Expansionism?" *International Security* 12, no. 3 (Winter 1987/88): 93–131.

in the withdrawal from Afghanistan or any other policy change associated with the end of the Cold War and the collapse of the Soviet Union. I am arguing rather that these events were indeterminate.

THE INTERNATIONAL SYSTEM AND CHANGE IN FOREIGN POLICY

Systemic Explanations

Neorealism, the most parsimonious structural theory of international relations, does not attempt to explain change in foreign policy. Instead, it explains patterns of international interaction over time, and specifically, the recurrence of balance of power.[3] Neorealism does not provide a satisfactory account for change, at least changes within states, nor does it concern itself with how interests are formed. Interests are particularly pertinent, however, to explaining how some issues get on the political agenda and others are kept off.[4]

Since the end of the Cold War, authors have used variations of systemic explanations to discuss the changes in Soviet foreign policy and the end of the Cold War. Works by Kenneth Oye, William Wohlforth, Daniel Deudney, and John Ikenberry point to the relevance of structural explanations in accounting for these phenomena.[5] These authors claim, with a considerable range of reliance on traditional structural realist variables, that the nature of the international environment allowed for, and to a certain degree, caused the accommodationist policies adopted by the Soviets in the late 1980s. Kenneth Oye and William Wohlforth try hardest to rescue realism (in Wolhforth's case, classical realism) from the failure of this approach to predict the changes that occurred in the international system in the late 1980s.

Oye examines the effect of the international system on change in foreign policy. He argues that the pacific nature of the system, and specifically, the

[3] The main example of this approach is Kenneth N. Waltz, *Theory of International Politics* (New York: Random House, 1979). His theory of structural realism assumes that states exist in an anarchic, self-help world in which gains are zero-sum. Interdependence exists only insofar as states band together for preservation. Change is explained as a state's response to structural shifts in the international environment. If a state fails to respond to the structural shifts, then it risks elimination.

[4] On the inability of neorealism to explain change, see John Gerard Ruggie, "Continuity and Transformation in the World Polity: Toward a Neorealist Synthesis," *World Politics* 35, no. 2 (January 1983): 261–285; and Joseph S. Nye, Jr., "Neorealism and Neoliberalism," *World Politics* 40, no. 2 (January 1988): 235–251, esp. 236–241.

[5] See Kenneth A. Oye, "Explaining the End of the Cold War: Morphological and Behavioral Adaptations to the Nuclear Peace?" in Richard Ned Lebow and Thomas Risse-Kappen, eds., *International Relations Theory and the End of the Cold War* (New York: Columbia University Press, 1995), 57–83; William Wohlforth, "Realism and the End of the Cold War," *International Security* 19, no. 3 (Winter 1994/95): 91–129; and Deudney and Ikenberry, "International Sources of Soviet Change."

absence of war and the presence of nuclear weapons, allowed "liberal" domestic arrangements to flourish. "A relatively benign international security environment fostered the development of more liberal polities and economies by weakening domestic groups and bureaucracies that might otherwise have blocked movement toward liberalization."[6] If there is war in the international system, then repressive domestic political environments flourish. With peace come liberal domestic environments. He argues convincingly that hegemonic wars have brought with them certain state actions that are in no way democratic and, in fact, distinctly not liberal. He notes, for example, that "America's sense of heightened insecurity contributed directly to the purges of State Department China hands and Alger Hiss, the witch hunts of the House Un-American Activities Committee, and the McCarthy hearings."[7]

Hegemonic peace, and in this case, "nuclear peace," however, does not correlate, let alone cause, liberal domestic reform as widely as Oye suggests. In fact, the Cold War brought with it a high degree of military preparedness on the part of both the United States and the Soviet Union. Quite aside from the issue of whether or not this emphasis on military security was appropriate, it came at the expense of other types of security for both Americans and Soviets. For example, in the United States, the military budgets in the 1980s reached over $300 billion. At the same time, Soviet military budgets may have been as large as 25 percent of the GNP.

Governments must make do with a finite amount of resources; as allocations for defense swell, allocations for education, health and housing (and in the Soviet case, consumer goods) shrink. The results in all societies with enormous defense allocations tend to be that those most in need of social welfare assistance—the elderly, children, and single mothers—pay the price. In this way, the "peace," or more correctly, the absence of hegemonic war, did not necessarily bring with it a liberal domestic environment but instead brought one in which national security was defined in a way that minimized the allocations to social welfare. Some may argue that this realization is what prompted Gorbachev to push for reform. Even if this were so, it tells us little about why he was *successful* at getting his conception of national security on the political agenda, particularly given the fact that the nature of the international system was deeply contested among the Soviet elite. Thus, real-

---

[6] Oye, "Explaining the End of the Cold War," 59. This argument bears some similarity to Fred Halliday, "International Society as Homogeneity: Burke, Marx, Fukuyama," *Millennium: Journal of International Studies* 21, no. 3 (1992): 435–461, where he argues that "international pressure for homogeneity destroyed the Soviet Union. . . . It was the T-shirt and the supermarket, not the gunboat or the cheaper manufactures that destroyed the legitimacy and stability of the Soviet system. Bruce Springsteen was the late-twentieth century equivalent of the Opium Wars" (437).

[7] Oye, "Explaining the End of the Cold War," 61.

ism is an inadequate explanation of the major changes in Soviet foreign policy of the late 1980s.

William Wohlforth's spirited defense of realism, or rather the resurrection
of classical realism and the grafting on of various auxiliary assumptions, is an
intellectual cousin to Oye's argument. Like other realist explanations,
Wohlforth argues that the great changes that occurred in the late 1980s—
from the shift in Soviet security policy to the bettering of relations with the
United States to the acceptance of the collapse of the Eastern European empire—are all the result of a shift in the international balance of power. "For
the purpose of evaluating realism, then, much post-1987 international change
can be defined as a single series of events, linked by a single generative
cause."[8] I disagree with him on the nature of that single generative cause.

Like other realist explanations, Wohlforth's emphasizes the importance of
the shift in the international balance of power. But for Wohlforth, there is an
additional "necessary precondition" for explaining the events of the 1980s:
"the perception of reduced capability to continue competing."[9] In the end,
the role of perception appears, however, more as a necessary and sufficient
independent variable—an agent of causation—than a "precondition."

The coupling of perceptual explanations with realism is problematic for a
number of reasons. While Wohlforth argues that realist theories "explain
much of the story," the role of perception in his argument further highlights
the limitations of the theoretical approach he is meant to be salvaging. He is
moving from the shaky ground on which realism exists, trying to explain post-
hoc the end of bi-polar stability, to the slippery patch of perception; perceptual explanations are laden with empirical problems, as evidence from the
Afghanistan case reveals. Below, I address at some length these problems in a
discussion of cognitive approaches. While Wohlforth is not in any strict sense
applying a cognitive explanation to events, much of the criticism generated by
this type of explanation applies equally to more limited perceptual arguments.

In their argument about change in Soviet foreign policy and the end of the
Cold War, Daniel Deudney and John Ikenberry incorporate economic and
socio-cultural variables "outside of the contemporary realist focus," but still
emphasize the structural characteristics of the international system.[10] Not
unlike Oye, they argue that the "pacific" nature of the international environ-

---

[8] Wohlforth, "Realism and the End of the Cold War," 95.

[9] Ibid., 96.

[10] Deudney and Ikenberry, "The International Sources of Soviet Change," 77, name eight
specific variables that they claim influenced the nature of the Soviet response including realist
understandings of power and global liberalist explanations of interdependence. These variables
include: 1) regime type of leading states in the system; 2) composition of military power; 3) distribution of military power; 4) economic resources of other states in the system; 5) economic stability of other states; 6) external appeal of various economic systems; 7) the strength of international organizations; 8) character of the global society and culture.

ment allowed and, to a certain degree, brought about Soviet accommodationist policies in the late 1980s.[11] While Deudney and Ikenberry attempt to extend the theoretical reach of both the realist and the liberal paradigms, their explanation of change in Soviet foreign policy in the 1980s is mainly systemic.

However, the systemic level of analysis used by Deudney and Ikenberry, as well as Oye and Wohlforth, is ill-suited for several reasons. First, to understand change in Soviet foreign policy one needs to understand how the international system interacted with the Soviet political scene. Without a specific understanding of the interaction, one is left with an overly deterministic picture of events in the Soviet Union in the 1980s, obscuring the politics and the human agency involved in change. The Soviet leadership in this explanation appears as a unitary actor and change in policies seem inevitable.

Second, systemic explanations are intrinsically underspecified when accounting for change in a specific nation's foreign policy. In fact, Soviet leaders had several different options for responding to the international system in the 1980s. One possible strategy, for example in dealing with the war in Afghanistan, certainly from the viewpoint of a Soviet hardliner, was escalation: to stop "imperialist aggression" in the region, as exemplified by U.S. aid to the mujahideen, the Soviets could have responded with counter-measures. Another strategy, put forth by Soviet reformers who looked beyond the Reagan arms build-up and the U.S. policy in the region, was withdrawal; the benefits of reform at home and economic cooperation abroad outweighed the costs associated with getting out or of staying in and engaging in tit-for-tat interactions.

Third, the international system was not as pacific, either empirically or according to certain Soviet perceptions, as the authors imply. For example, Deudney and Ikenberry do not account for the many conflicts waged "in the name of peace" around the globe where U.S. troops, guns or funds were deployed such as in Korea, Vietnam, Grenada, and Panama. Most important, many in the Soviet elite did not perceive the United States or the West as peaceful or non-offensive in nature. Wohlforth implicitly acknowledges that among the Soviet elite competing images did exist: reformers emphasized the underlying pacifism of the system, while old thinkers stressed the aggressive character of the capitalist states that dominated the system.[12] But unless we

[11] Ibid., 76–78, 117. While Oye, "Explaining the End of the Cold War," 79, does claim that his conception of "nuclear peace" contrasts with Deudney's and Ikenberry's emphasis (78) on the "pacific character" and "pacific tendencies" associated with the West, his conception does not do so in a way that makes the argument significantly different; both arguments emphasize the role of the pacific character of the international system in explaining change in Soviet foreign policy.

[12] Wohlforth, "Realism and the End of the Cold War." For a discussion of Soviet interpretations of U.S. foreign policy in the 1980s that highlights differences in perception, see Douglas Blum, "Soviet Perceptions of American Foreign Policy after Afghanistan," in Robert Jervis and Jack Snyder, eds., *Dominoes and Bandwagons: Strategic Beliefs and Great Power Competition in the Eurasian Rimland* (New York: Oxford, 1991), 190–219.

can account for why and how one perception affected the political agenda, we only have a part of the story.

In summary, several variables determine whether elements of the international system influence developments within states in the system. I concentrate for the moment on the absence of two that most pertain to the Soviet case in the late 1980s: the porousness of the state, and conditions within the international system aside from polarity.[13]

The porousness of the Soviet Union—that is, the possibility of free movement of people, indigenous and foreign non-governmental organizations, and information across borders—began to develop only after Gorbachev introduced reforms in the 1980s; it was a consequence and not a cause of reform.[14] Porousness may have greatly influenced if not caused the revolution in Eastern Europe, as East Germans flowed into a democratizing Hungary on their way to Austria. But this developed only after reform in the Soviet Union began. Moreover, porousness did not develop in any significant way until *after* the collapse of the Soviet Union.

If the character of the international system had been more extreme—either truly pacific or extremely aggressive—then perhaps it would have played a greater role in determining the nature of Soviet foreign policy. Conditions were, however, highly ambiguous and interpretations were hotly contested.[15] Auxiliary assumptions at a domestic level of analysis are needed to demonstrate how certain priorities came to dominate the political agenda and thus led to, among other changes, the withdrawal from Afghanistan.

Learning Explanations

For several years, international relations scholars and psychologists have been writing about a list of psychological variables that affect decision making and foreign policy, including definitions and models of learning and learning-

[13] On the growing body of literature concerning the ability of actors in the international system to affect policy within states, see for example, Thomas Risse-Kappen, ed., *Bringing Transnational Relations Back In: Non-State Actors, Domestic Structures and International Institutions* (Cambridge: Cambridge University Press, 1995); Audie Klotz, "Norms Reconstituting Interests: Global Racial Equality and U.S. Sanctions against South Africa," *International Organization* 49, no. 3 (Summer 1995): 451–478; and Kathryn Sikkink, "Human Rights, Principled Issue Networks, and Sovereignty in Latin America," *International Organization* 47, no. 3 (Summer 1993): 411–441.

[14] Suggesting different findings is Evangelista, "The Paradox of State Strength." He stresses the role of a transnational epistemic community of nuclear weapons experts in influencing Soviet responses to the Strategic Defense Initiative (SDI) and nuclear testing in the 1980s. Whether or not his analysis is correct, the ability of the group to affect change in the Soviet Union was ultimately, however, determined by domestic politics.

[15] For a similar argument, see Janice Gross Stein, "Cognitive Psychology and Political Learning: Gorbachev as an Uncommitted Thinker and Motivated Learner," in Lebow and Risse-Kappen, *International Relations Theory and the End of the Cold War*, 224–229.

related theories.[16] In this section, I focus on the most popular example of a cognitive learning approach used to explain the changes in Soviet foreign policy in the 1980s: complex cognitive learning. Studies using this approach stress the impact of lessons learned about the international system by those who make foreign policy decisions.[17]

Complex learning may be understood as a profound response to data, or in the words of George Breslauer, "a process of cognitive reevaluation."[18] Learning is complex in the sense that reevaluation occurs at basic levels of the belief system. This kind of change occurs in a chaotic, unsystematic way. Due to the nature of cognitive structures, the change is likely to be long-lasting.[19] Belief systems and perceptions are treated implicitly in the literature both as independent variables with causal force and as dependent variables or outcomes to be explained.[20] In the case of change in Soviet foreign policy and the withdrawal from Afghanistan, they are discussed as having a causal force.[21] The unit of analysis is usually the individual but may also be groups of people in similar circumstances.

One general theoretical hypothesis about complex learning would argue that individuals repeatedly exposed to conflicting information about a subject process the information alongside existing beliefs. Occasionally, individuals *can* process the information in such a way that leads to complex cognitive change. Changes in core parts of the belief system in turn lead to changes in goals, priorities, policies, and ultimately, in behavior. Not all experience or

---

[16] For one of the best overall critiques and synthesis of learning approaches, see Jack S. Levy, "Learning and Foreign Policy: Sweeping a Conceptual Minefield," *International Organization* 48, no. 2 (Spring 1994): 279–312. For a discussion of learning applied to Soviet foreign policy, see Philip E. Tetlock, "Learning in U.S. and Soviet Foreign Policy: In Search of an Elusive Concept," in Breslauer and Tetlock, *Learning in U.S. and Soviet Foreign Policy*, 20–61. A discussion of the many different definitions of learning runs throughout the Breslauer and Tetlock volume; see particularly George W. Breslauer, "What Have We Learned about Learning?" ibid., 825–856.

[17] Tetlock, "Learning in U.S. and Soviet Foreign Policy," 27–28. Examples include Richard K. Herrmann, "The Soviet Decision to Withdraw from Afghanistan: Changing Strategic and Regional Images," in Jervis and Snyder, *Dominoes and Bandwagons*; and Legvold, "Soviet Learning in the 1980s."

[18] George W. Breslauer, "Ideology and Learning in Soviet-Third World Policy," *World Politics* 39, no. 3 (April 1987): 432. The definition and description that I use combines elements of Tetlock's "cognitive content" and "cognitive structuralist" approach; Tetlock, "Learning in U.S. and Soviet Foreign Policy," 27–35.

[19] For a discussion of the nature of cognitive change, see Jennifer Crocker, Susan T. Fiske, and Shelley E. Taylor, "Schematic Bases of Belief Change," in J. Richard Eiser, ed., *Attitudinal Judgment* (New York: Springer-Verlag, 1984), 197–226; and Deborah Welch Larson, *Origins of Containment: A Psychological Approach* (Princeton: Princeton University Press, 1985), 24–65.

[20] Legvold, "Soviet Learning in the 1980s," 687, does state that "learning causes nothing; rather it sheds light on phenomena that are the real sources of altered behavior."

[21] See, for example, Herrmann, "The Soviet Decision to Withdraw from Afghanistan."

disconfirming evidence causes change; not all learning occurs in this way.[22] It is, however, the principal dynamic in complex learning.[23]

Scholars have used complex learning specifically to explain the decision to retreat from Afghanistan and in general to capture the larger change in policy. According to this approach, the Soviet image of the opponents—both the mujahideen and the United States—changed as a result of disconfirming and overwhelming information about the war and the international system.[24] This information resulted in a reordering of goals and preferences, and ultimately, convinced the Soviets of the necessity of withdrawing troops.

However, such an explanation does not fit well with the evidence: Soviet policy makers received evidence throughout the late 1980s that confirmed their Cold War view of the United States as an aggressive, hostile, "imperialist" force, particularly with regard to Afghanistan.[25] Indeed, after shipments of the Stinger heat-seeking anti-aircraft missiles reached Afghan rebels in the fall of 1986, there was much confirming information about U.S. aid to the mujahideen.[26] Georgii Arbatov, former director of the Institute of USA and Canada (hereafter ISKAN), claims that the arms build-up under President Reagan did much to fan the flames of the conservatives in the Soviet Union. American foreign policy in general, and specifically, toward Afghanistan,

---

[22] Indeed much of cognitive political psychology attempts to specify the conditions under which this does and does not happen. See Tetlock, "Learning in U.S. and Soviet Foreign Policy."

[23] There could be other types of cognitive explanations to explain the Soviet withdrawal from Afghanistan, where tactical lessons were learned but core beliefs were left untouched. For example, the anti-aircraft Stinger missiles could have raised the cost of staying in the war, thus altering military calculations of how to "win," or at least not lose the war. In this case, withdrawal would have been based on a reassessment of the costs of prevailing, with little or no change in overall beliefs about the nature of the international system or the adversary. I thank George Breslauer for bringing this point to my attention.

[24] See Herrmann, "The Soviet Decision to Withdraw from Afghanistan," for an example of this argument.

[25] Herrmann, ibid., 223, does not argue that U.S. policy caused a change in Soviet behavior, and he warns against "cold war motivational assumptions" underlying this argument. He does not, however, account fully for why Soviet threat perception of the United States would decrease when U.S. policy was aggressive.

[26] From top secret notes from Politburo meetings discussing Soviet policy in Afghanistan as early as March 1979 it is clear that Soviet decision makers thought the United States was supporting anti-government action in Afghanistan. See in particular Gromyko's comments on March 18, 1979, as cited in TsKhSD, Fond 89, Perechen' 25, Dokument 1, Listy 1, 17 (translation by the National Security Archives). From 1980 to 1984, U.S. aid to the rebels averaged $50 million per year. By FY (fiscal year) 1986, it was up to $470 million and by FY 1987, $630 million. See Olivier Roy, *The Lessons of the Soviet-Afghan War*, Adelphi Paper no. 259 (London: International Institute for Strategic Studies [IISS], Summer 1991), 34. Between September 1986 and August 1987, 863 Stingers and Blowpipes (British anti-aircraft missiles) were received by the mujahideen. Aaron Karp, "Blowpipes and Stingers in Afghanistan: One Year Later," *Armed Forces Journal*, September 1987, 40.

made it more difficult—not easier, he contended—for Soviet foreign policy to change in an accommodationist direction.[27]

In assessing the role of external determinants in bringing about change in Soviet foreign policy, the withdrawal from Afghanistan provides important evidence; Stingers were largely irrelevant to overall Soviet foreign policy. Certainly, the missiles appear to have altered some specific Soviet combat tactics.[28] Many inside the leadership believed that a withdrawal was necessary, however, long before the mujahideen received the Stingers; the issue of withdrawal began to appear on the political agenda before the Stingers became militarily effective in the spring of 1987.[29] Both critics and supporters of the "peace through strength" argument tend to agree that these surface-to-air (SAM) missiles did negatively affect the morale of the Soviet troops.[30] But assessments of the SAMs' tactical effectiveness are, at best, mixed. Stingers did not result in an increase in casualties. In fact, casualty rates actually decreased despite missile deployment.[31] Finally, some critics (and even some in the mujahideen) claim that the Stingers were not even particularly effective at hitting their targets.[32]

Continued Soviet aid of $300 million a month to the Kabul government long after troops returned home underscores the point that at least some "lessons learned" in Afghanistan had to do with what was politically feasible; relations with the West could be cooperative as long as Soviet *troops* were

---

[27] Author's interview, January 4, 1991. This view was also expressed by Andrei Kokoshin, then deputy director, ISKAN, November 11, 1991.

[28] While Soviet helicopter pilots generally flew at higher altitudes following the deployment of the Stingers, Soviet combat tactics had actually changed in 1986 before the deployment of the surface-to-air missiles. See Mark Urban, "Soviet Operations in Afghanistan—Some Conclusions," *Jane's Soviet Intelligence Review* 2, no. 8 (August 1, 1990): 366; and Roy, *The Lessons of the Soviet-Afghan War*, 20–23.

[29] The role of Stingers as well as troop levels and other aspects of the war on the ground are discussed in detail in Chapter 5. See also Roy, *The Lessons of the Soviet-Afghan War*, 23, 36.

[30] For a positive and a neutral account of the Stingers, see respectively "Army Lauds Stinger Effectiveness in Afghan War," *Defense Daily* 164, no. 3 (July 6, 1989); and David Isby, "Soviet Surface-to-Air Missile Countermeasures: Lessons from Afghanistan," *Jane's Soviet Intelligence Review* 1, no. 1 (January 1, 1989): 44. For critical assessments, see Ian Kemp, "Abdul Haq: Soviet Mistakes in Afghanistan," *Jane's Defense Weekly* 9, no. 9 (March 5, 1988): 380; and Urban, "Soviet Operations in Afghanistan."

[31] The highest casualties were sustained in 1984 with 2343 dead. Rates for the following years were: in 1985, 1868; in 1986, 1333; in 1987, 1215; in 1988, 759; and in 1989, 53. See V. Izgarshev, "Afganskaia bol'" (Afghan pain), *Pravda*, August 17, 1989, 6; see also Urban, "Soviet Operations in Afghanistan."

[32] Abdul Haq, the military commander of the Hizb-i-Islami, claimed that the impact of the missiles on the war had been exaggerated. "How could we stop all the Soviet aircraft because we have 25 or 30 Stingers? No, it is impossible." Kemp, "Abdul Haq: Soviet Mistakes in Afghanistan"; see also Urban, "Soviet Operations in Afghanistan."

home and in spite of Soviet *aid* sent to Kabul.[33] To a certain degree, when considered separately from the momentous events that followed the withdrawal, Soviet-Afghan policy after 1989 points to specific tactical lessons about what the international system would tolerate much more than it did a reconceptualization of world politics implied by "complex learning."

This last point about tactical learning raises one additional explanation for change in Soviet foreign policy that must be addressed: did the Soviets withdraw from Afghanistan simply because they were getting beaten? Was the Soviet retreat from the war a response to losing? And if so, is not this event quite separate from other changes in Soviet foreign policy?

In brief, no. The full weight of the Soviet military machine was not brought to bear in Afghanistan. Only approximately 2.1 percent of the Soviet force was deployed at the height of the war (compared to 21 percent of the U.S. military in Vietnam).[34] Certainly the Soviets were not "winning" the war, but that the Soviets were beaten in Afghanistan is inaccurate. Lt. General Boris Gromov, then the honored commander in Afghanistan although later widely discredited for his role in the war in Chechnya, claimed that after the summer of 1987 "we've managed to reduce the loss of life by approximately one and a half times and the loss of machinery by two-fold."[35] Moreover, that the pro-Soviet government held on for three years after the Soviet troops left attests to the fact that the Soviets had greatly influenced the consolidation of the government and the reconfiguration of about 90 percent of the Afghan military. The survival of the pro-Communist, pro-Soviet PDPA government during those three years must be seen in contrast to the belief that most participants and observers shared prior to the withdrawal, that there would be a bloodbath as soon as the Soviets began the withdrawal, and all remaining Soviets

---

[33] Reports on Soviet aid amounts in 1990 vary from $400 million a month to $250 million. See Riaz M. Khan, *Untying the Afghan Knot: Negotiating Soviet Withdrawal* (Durham, N.C.: Duke University Press, 1991), 88. Olivier Roy, *The Lessons of the Soviet-Afghan War*, 34, writes that the Soviets were sending "huge amounts of economic and military aid" through 1990. By the mid 1990s, Russia was once again a "significant arms supplier" to Afghanistan; John F. Burns, "The West in Afghanistan, Before and After," *New York Times*, February 18, 1996. Many observers speculate that given the seizure of Kabul by the Islamic Taliban movement in September 1996, Russian involvement in Afghanistan may once again become more overt. See Mark Huband, "Russia Warns of Afghan Intervention," *Financial Times*, December 18, 1996.

[34] See Bruce D. Porter, "The Military Abroad: Internal Consequences of External Expansion," in Timothy J. Colton and Thane Gustafson, eds., *Soldiers and the State: Civil-Military Relations from Brezhnev to Gorbachev* (Princeton: Princeton University Press, 1990), 293–294; Alexander Alexiev, *The War in Afghanistan: Soviet Strategies and the State of the Resistance*, P-7038 (Santa Monica, Calif.: RAND, November 1984), 2; Alexander Alexiev, *Inside the Soviet Army in Afghanistan*, R-5627–1 (Santa Monica, Calif.: RAND, May 1988), 7.

[35] As cited in Artyom Borovik, *The Hidden War* (New York: Atlantic Monthly Press, 1990), 245.

and any Afghans who had worked with the government would be killed.[36] In fact, Eduard Shevardnadze (then foreign minister) and Vladimir Kryuchkov (then head of the KGB) suggested that President Najibullah's family leave Afghanistan prior to the withdrawal for fear that they would be killed. On behalf of his family, Najibullah refused.[37]

Finally, the withdrawal from Afghanistan cannot be taken as an event isolated from the rest of the collapse of the Cold War. Not only did the "long, withdrawing roar" that accompanied the collapse of the Soviet empire begin in Afghanistan, but the process that brought the withdrawal onto the agenda was still in motion as young Germans leaped exuberantly over the Berlin Wall in October 1989 and Boris Yeltsin stood defiantly on a Soviet tank in front of the White House in August 1991. This was a process that entailed a radical reconception of security (in addition to other issues) as well as institution-building in order to provide the new thinkers with the resources to get their issues on the political agenda. Like the old joke, that the operation was a success but the patient died, this was a process that resulted in the unintentional unraveling of an empire, and indeed, of an international order.

Both complex learning approaches and systemic explanations tend to be underspecified because they have provided a poor sense of the influence of domestic politics on policy making.[38] Both, for example, could predict that, given the increase in U.S. aid to the rebels, no change in Soviet policy toward Afghanistan or the United States would occur. Yet they could equally well predict that change in Soviet decision makers' strategic beliefs led the decision makers to alter fundamental conceptions about their external conduct and ultimately led to the withdrawal of troops from Afghanistan. Without attention to the process of policy, and how different interpretations of events dominate policy making, any outcome can appear inevitable.

In the case of complex learning, underspecificity arises partly due to the fact that the building blocks of psychological approaches include slippery

---

[36] See Soviet and American comments in Elaine Sciolino, "Aides See Summit as 'Turning Point' for a Soviet Withdrawal from Afghanistan," *New York Times*, December 5, 1987; Alexander Yakovlev, Central Television, First Channel; Foreign Broadcast Information Service–Soviet Union (hereafter FBIS-SOV), December 31, 1991, 3–5; "Afghanistan: Soviet Occupation and Withdrawal," U.S. Department of State, Bureau of Intelligence and Research, Unclassified Special Report, no. 179 (1988), 1, as published in The National Security Archive, *Afghanistan: The Making of U.S. Policy, 1973–1990* (Alexandria, Va.: Chadwyck-Healey, 1990), item number 02245.

[37] Boris Pyadishev, "Najibullah, the President of the Republic of Afghanistan," *International Affairs* (Moscow), February 1990, 22.

[38] For additional critiques of learning approaches applied to Soviet politics in the late 1980s, see Jack Snyder, *Myths of Empire: Domestic Politics and International Ambition* (Ithaca: Cornell University Press, 1991), 233–237; and Matthew Evangelista, "Sources of Moderation in Soviet Security Policy," in Philip E. Tetlock, et al., eds., *Behavior, Society, and Nuclear War: Vol. Two* (New York: Oxford University Press, 1991), 254–354.

concepts such as "beliefs" and "perceptions." These concepts are not independently verifiable and are normative in nature. What appears to one observer as learning (positive) is pragmatism or adaptation (neutral or negative) to another.[39] Claims based on psychological approaches tend to be non-falsifiable and difficult to identify operationally.[40] Perhaps because of these limitations, psychological approaches are more and more being recognized as useful only when combined with another level of analysis. To a certain extent, although it was not couched in psychological terms, this is what Wohlforth did in grafting classical realism onto a perceptual argument.

While cognitive explanations in general may provide a partial antidote to the rationalist claims that underlie many systemic explanations, they exaggerate the intellectual and even the rational basis for change. They tend to ignore the confluence of disparate imperatives that tug at the decision maker in the form of needs, interests, and pressures from various domestic coalitions and policy groups. These competing imperatives were particularly strong in the case of Soviet reform. Like systemic explanations, cognitive learning approaches tend to reify the state by treating it as a unitary actor.[41]

In the Soviet case, underspecificity proves to be particularly problematic because change in foreign policy in the 1980s was an intensely political process inseparable from much of what went on domestically in terms of coalition building, and the acquisition of new and more prominent resources by critics of old policies. The focus on the international system comes at the expense of attention to national politics and to the process by which competing definitions of national interest were contested. Focus on the international balance of power neglects the internal balance of power. The result is that

---

[39] For a discussion of the difference between learning and adaptation, see Tetlock, "Learning in U.S. and Soviet Foreign Policy," 45–47. On normative aspects of learning, see Robert Darst, "Unitary and Conflictual Images in the Study of Soviet Foreign Policy," *Analyzing the Gorbachev Era: Working Papers of the Students of the Berkeley-Stanford Program in Soviet Studies* (Berkeley and Stanford, Calif.: University of California at Berkeley and Stanford University: 1989), 155–157.

[40] For a discussion of this problem, see Richard K. Herrmann, "Cognitive Models in International Relations Theory: The Cold War and Soviet Foreign Policy as a Case Study," paper presented at the conference on "The Transformation of the International System and International Relations Theory," Cornell University, October 18–19, 1991; and Herrmann "Conclusions: The End of the Cold War—What Have We Learned?" in Lebow and Risse-Kappen, *International Relations Theory and the End of the Cold War*, 273–274.

[41] For example, personnel change and generational change are political and sociological phenomena and not manifestations of learning. Yet several authors in the volume edited by Tetlock and Breslauer blur the distinction between change in an individual's beliefs and change in the "system's" beliefs. Breslauer and Tetlock, *Learning in U.S. and Soviet Foreign Policy*. Tetlock, "Learning in U.S. and Soviet Foreign Policy," writes: "learning is often so cognitively difficult, that it typically occurs only in the presence of massive personnel shifts." This observation leads him to question whether evolution rather than learning is the appropriate metaphor (p. 31). See Evangelista, "Sources of Moderation in Soviet Security Policy," 272, for a similar argument.

these studies offer little sense of the element of contingency that was inevitably involved in the policy process. While complex learning may or may not describe overall trends in changes in belief systems, neither systemic nor learning explanations can answer the questions surrounding the withdrawal from Afghanistan and the larger changes in Soviet foreign policy: how did certain ideas and specific constituencies win out over others? Why did they win out when they did and not earlier? A more nuanced approach is needed, and is offered in the next section.

IDEAS AND POLITICS

In recent years, much scholarly effort in the study of international relations has been devoted to assessing the impact of ideas and politics on policy making. International relations theorists have used a variety of methodological approaches to address the problem across issue-areas from U.S. trade policy to arms control to human rights policy.[42] Yet most work on the role of ideas in explaining change in policy has failed to address adequately the process by which some ideas win out over others.[43] At the same time, work that focuses on the political process of change has tended to ignore the role of ideas and knowledge in its explanations, or it has not made clear the way in which knowledge and process interacted and affected outcomes.[44] To remedy these shortcomings, the approach in this book explicitly links politics to ideas by focusing on the process by which some ideas are selected and others ignored.[45]

[42] See for example, Judith Goldstein, *Ideas, Interests, and American Trade Policy* (Ithaca: Cornell University Press, 1993); Kathryn Sikkink, *Ideas and Institutions: Developmentalism in Brazil and Argentina* (Ithaca: Cornell University Press, 1991); Sikkink, "Human Rights, Principled Issue-Networks, and Sovereignty in Latin America;" Judith Goldstein and Robert O. Keohane, eds., *Ideas and Foreign Policy: Beliefs, Institutions and Political Change* (Ithaca: Cornell University Press, 1993); Emanuel Adler, "The Emergence of Cooperation: National Epistemic Communities and the International Evolution of the Idea of Nuclear Arms Control," *International Organization* 46, no. 1 (Winter 1992): 101–145. For general reviews of the literature and different approaches, see Thomas Risse-Kappen, "Ideas Do Not Float Freely: Transnational Coalitions, Domestic Structures, and the End of the Cold War," in Lebow and Risse-Kappen, *International Relations Theory and the End of the Cold War;* and Albert Yee, "The Causal Effects of Ideas on Politics," *International Organization* 50, no. 1 (Winter 1996): 69–108.

[43] See, for example, Peter M. Haas, ed., "Knowledge, Power and International Policy Coordination," a special issue of *International Organization* 46, no. 1 (Winter 1992).

[44] See for example, Jack Snyder, "The Gorbachev Revolution: A Waning of Soviet Expansionism?" *International Security* 12, no. 3 (Winter 1987/88), as reprinted in Sean M. Lynn-Jones, Steven E. Miller, and Stephen Van Evera, *Soviet Military Policy: An* International Security *Reader* (Cambridge, Mass.: MIT Press, 1989), 71–109.

[45] For an earlier version of this argument see Sarah E. Mendelson, "Internal Battles and External Wars: Politics, Learning and the Soviet Withdrawal from Afghanistan," *World Politics* 45, no. 3 (April 1993): 327–360.

What sets this study apart from other work on ideas and politics is the fact that the ideas that make it onto the political agenda are ones that do not in any way "fit" with—and in fact explicitly challenge—previous conceptions.

Neorealist and various other rationalist approaches have little to say about any independent causal force for the role of ideas; this school sees ideas exclusively as hooks or justifications for larger, determining materialist interests. The issue of "when ideas matter" is not considered; ideas do not matter except as they are part of a larger story about power. Ideas, beliefs, and ideology are all seen as essentially tools to rationalize drives for power.[46]

Research has shown, however, that ideas that experts or policy makers espouse do not necessarily always derive from material interests. One of the most compelling examples of this is David Lumsdaine's work on foreign aid. In some cases, countries send foreign aid when there are few if any material benefits.[47] My research shows that a related dynamic also characterizes the case of the Soviet new thinkers in the 1980s. Certainly Gorbachev was pushing ideas of reform because he believed that they would "better" the Soviet Union in the sense of making it more efficient and productive. But Soviet foreign policy experts—Americanists and Third World specialists, for example— were essentially calling for a shift in perspectives and resources away from competing with the United States. In other words, the primary priorities that drove Soviet foreign policy, and which provided these experts with privileged status in the foreign policy elite, were being questioned. And once the priorities were questioned and abandoned, these experts (and their institutions) no longer held the same positions.

Many of the ideas that experts were espousing cut across materialist and corporate interests. Writing about American trade policy, Judith Goldstein notes that "entrepreneurs rarely know which policy idea will maximize their interests."[48] Ideas contain within them unintended consequences. This turned out to be quite profound for Soviet experts: ISKAN and IMEMO, the two largest and most important foreign policy think tanks in the Soviet Union in the 1980s, found themselves in post-Soviet Russia renting space to commercial firms in order to stay financially afloat. The collapse of the Soviet state brought with it the end of subsidies for universities and the Academy of Science that funded these institutes.

To assume that ideas always serve materialist purposes is to obscure the process by which ideas affect policy. More important, it blurs the politics behind the campaigns committed to getting certain ideas on the political agenda

[46] For similar critiques of the neorealist approach, see Goldstein and Keohane, *Ideas and Foreign Policy*; and Alexander Wendt, "Constructing International Politics," *International Security* 20, no. 1 (Summer 1995): 71–81.

[47] David Halloran Lumsdaine, *Moral Vision in International Politics: The Foreign Aid Regime, 1949–1989* (Princeton: Princeton University Press, 1994).

[48] Goldstein, *Ideas, Interests, and American Trade Policy*, 3.

and thus presents outcomes as inevitable. Ideas always matter; some idea always wins out over another. The question is: why do certain ideas win at some times and others do not? Why does nationalism reverberate in Yugoslavia or Chechnya at certain times and not others? Why do democratic ideals, such as multi-party elections and freedom of the press, take hold at certain times and not others? Why do new thinkers in the Soviet Union prevail in the 1980s and not at other times? Why do they prevail and not the old thinkers?

The other end of the analytic spectrum suggests that ideas are causal in and of themselves, that they themselves drive behavior. The question then of "when" do ideas matter is nonsensical; they always matter. Few scholars claim outright to follow such a straight ideational approach. The sociologist John Hall actively calls for avoiding the pitfalls of either extreme: "that human beings have values, but equally they are purposive calculators—suggests that we must stand somewhere between the false extremes identified."[49] These false extremes suffer from similar constraints; both purely ideational and purely materialist approaches obscure the process of how and why ideas matter. This obscuration is particularly salient in the Soviet case; ideas alone did not change policy, neither ideas about the international system and its "pacific" nature, nor ideas about the need to reform domestically.

This story is incomplete without a discussion of how decision makers provided resources for those espousing new and reformist ideas. Without an understanding of how decision makers shifted the internal balance of power in favor of reformers, we cannot understand why new thinkers and new thinking prevailed.

The majority of people addressing ideas, experts, and institutions usually find themselves somewhere in the middle of this spectrum. They claim, as I do, to tell a story of *both* ideas and politics. For example, Kathryn Sikkink is concerned with ideas about economic development in the Third World and how they evolve. She is very clear about the mix of ideas and politics, stressing the need for policy makers to support ideas and for the ideas to become embedded in institutions.[50] Judith Goldstein, looking at the development of U.S. trade and manufacturing policies, is very explicit about the relationship of ideas, the carriers of the ideas, and the political leadership. "Change is contingent upon the existence of a new solution, the realization by elites that some new policy is superior to the old, and their political savvy in being able to create political support for the new ideas."[51]

While their work acknowledges the political process in which certain ideas are more successful than others, the process and conditions they identify are somewhat different from the Soviet case in one important respect: in their

---

[49] John A. Hall, "Ideas and Social Science," in Goldstein and Keohane, *Ideas and Foreign Policy*, 43.

[50] Sikkink, *Ideas and Institutions*.

[51] Goldstein, *Ideas, Interests, and American Trade Policy*, 250.

work, ideas tend to get picked because of "fit." Goldstein writes, "just as new groups who enter government must comply with existing rules, so too must new ideas 'fit' and accommodate existing structures."[52] Sikkink writes that "new ideas are more likely to be influential if they 'fit' well with the existing ideas and ideologies in a particular historical setting."[53]

In contrast, new thinking and *perestroika* simply did not "fit" traditional notions of security or domestic policy. While access of experts to the leadership and the salience of experts' ideas to the leadership played large roles in the Soviet case, the ability of Gorbachev and his cohort to control political resources well enough to create institutions so that the ideas and the new thinkers (in both domestic and foreign policy) had a chance to make an impact was crucial.

John Ikenberry borrows from Max Weber the metaphor of ideas as "switchmen" and acknowledges the "fragility" of these "switchmen" in certain cases.[54] Fragility seems to be related to contingency. In the Soviet case, decision makers *made* the ideas fit, but it was a highly contingent and political process; they altered existing institutions and created new ones.[55] Because the new ideas challenged the status quo directly, the process by which ideas were selected and survived on the political agenda emerge as particularly salient analytically. If both ideas and politics were important in the Sikkink and Goldstein cases, they are even more so in this case.

While many claim to inhabit a middle analytical ground where both ideas and politics matter, in fact, few pay sufficient attention to either the political side of the story or to ideational claims that contrast with evidence pointing to the importance of politics. To be sure, it is difficult to find the mix that accurately describes and explains changes in policy. But, in much work, the role of ideas is privileged over that of politics in ways that are often contradicted by the evidence.

In making this argument, I focus briefly on the work of Emanuel Adler. While most studies looking at ideas and expert communities have focused on cases of international political economy, Adler, like me, addresses security is-

[52] Judith Goldstein, "The Impact of Ideas on Trade Policy: The Origins of U.S. Agricultural and Manufacturing Policies," *International Organization* 43, no. 1 (Winter 1989): 32; and Goldstein, *Ideas, Interests, and American Trade Policy*, 255.

[53] Sikkink, *Ideas and Institutions*, 26. Peter Hall's discussion of the viability of certain ideas is also related to this notion of "fit." See the conclusion to Peter A. Hall, ed., *The Political Power of Economic Ideas: Keynesianism across Nations* (Princeton: Princeton University Press, 1989), 371.

[54] G. John Ikenberry, "Creating Yesterday's New World Order: Keynesian 'New Thinking' and the Anglo-American Postwar Settlement," in Goldstein and Keohane, *Ideas and Foreign Policy*, 85.

[55] The efforts of Western non-governmental organizations (NGOs) to spread ideas about democratization and privatization in the newly independent states should provide important additional cases for the post-Soviet era regarding the issue of "fit."

sues. He considers how controversial ideas got on the political agenda in both the United States and the Soviet Union. Adler argues that the work of one "epistemic community" involved with strategic planning in the United States affected Soviet policy on the issue of the Anti-Ballistic Missile treaty through influencing the parameters of debate in the Soviet "epistemic community."[56]

The main causal force in Adler's explanation is learning at the collective level, where some ideas win out over other ideas. Politics is built into Adler's theory of "collective learning," as he emphasizes the process by which domestic institutions sponsor innovation. But, as in most learning arguments, politics takes a back seat to cognitive processes. Specifically, Adler's discussion of the selection of understandings, beliefs, and ideas does not convey the sense of contingency and struggle that are integral to policy making. We have no sense of who is battling whom or how some decision makers prevail over others. As Jack Levy notes, learning at the collective level and treating states as "organisms that have goals, beliefs, and memories is not analytically viable."[57]

In addition, while Adler claims the role of ideas is paramount in his discussion, his evidence speaks to the importance of politics. For example, the role of President John F. Kennedy in sponsoring the "whiz kids," the arms control specialists in the 1960s, was central to the ability of the specialists to change the U.S. policy agenda. As Adler himself notes, Kennedy built "a political coalition on their behalf."[58] Adler argues that the expert community convinced the American people of the need for arms control.[59] Yet were it not for the fact that the Kennedy administration was gripped by the issue, even given a liberal democracy where experts have access to media with which to influence public opinion, it is, at best, unknown how successful the specialists would have been. In the end, the administration helped institutionalize the community and provided a favorable intellectual climate for the ideas. Both the administration and the experts benefited from the relationship; the same is true of the Soviet experts and decision makers in the 1980s.

Ideas have complex and nuanced lives, sometimes guiding, sometimes justifying behavior. Indeed, some scholars have spent much time in classifying different types of ideas (e.g., world views, principled beliefs, causal beliefs).[60]

---

[56] See Adler, "The Emergence of Cooperation." For an alternative explanation regarding this case, see Coit D. Blacker, "Learning in the Nuclear Age: Soviet Strategic Arms Control Policy, 1969–1989," in Breslauer and Tetlock, *Learning in U.S. and Soviet Foreign Policy*, 429–468. For an argument related to Adler's that picks up the ABM story in the 1980s, see Evangelista, "The Paradox of State Strength."

[57] Levy, "Learning and Foreign Policy," p. 287.

[58] Adler, "The Emergence of Cooperation," 125.

[59] Ibid., 133, 140–141.

[60] For examples see Goldstein and Keohane, *Ideas and Foreign Policy*, 8–26; Goldstein, *Ideas, Interests, and American Trade Policy*, 11.

Equally varied are the types of inquiry into the life-cycle of ideas. Constructivists, for example, are interested in the framing of ideas, and particularly the social context in which ideas are framed.[61] Why, for example, did Gorbachev become a new thinker?

I take as given that ideas were framed the way they were. The area of inquiry explored here is, why and how did they affect policy making? It is important for the argument that I am making to understand that much of what drove reformist thinkers, including Gorbachev, was information that experts had about a variety of issues, the most important concerning conditions endogenous to the state.[62] But I am mainly interested in issues that lie further away from the inception of an idea.[63]

If one looks at earlier attempts at reform in the Soviet Union, and why they failed, for example, in the 1960s, much of the reason lies in the fact that decision makers did not mobilize support outside traditional institutions. Reformist ideas independent of successful strategies for shifting the internal balance of power were not enough. Equally, controlling the internal balance of power without reformist ideas is a failure; this is the story of stagnation in the 1970s under Brezhnev.

Traditionally, political process models that have coalition building as the independent variable paid little or no attention to the role of ideas.[64] An exclusively political explanation left little room for the possibilities of reform in the Soviet Union. This approach described what was thought to be an immutable system. Brzezinski and Huntington writing in the 1960s claimed that "newcomers to the Soviet national leadership are absorbed into the prevailing outlook, and new initiatives must overcome the inherent resistance of set patterns."[65] Given this scenario, the chances for reformers such as Gorbachev

[61] An important aspect that separates Emanuel Adler's work from that of others on ideas and institutions is that he is interested in how actors define problems. Adler's agenda is consciously constructivist in the sense that, for him, "the most important questions" revolve around "the framing of knowledge and ideas." Emanuel Adler, letter to the author, June 4, 1993. For a general theoretical statement on constructivism, see Wendt, "Constructing International Politics."

[62] For an argument that stresses the role of ideas exogenous to the state, see Jeffrey T. Checkel, *Ideas and International Political Change: Soviet-Russian Behavior and the End of the Cold War* (New Haven: Yale University Press, 1997).

[63] Sikkink argues that political and social context explains when and why some policies are accepted: "it was not until the convergence of détente, public disillusionment with Vietnam, and the initial successes of the civil rights movements that human rights ideas led to changes in American foreign policy in the mid-1970s"; Sikkink, "The Power of Principled Ideas: Human Rights Policies in the United States and Western Europe," in Goldstein and Keohane, *Ideas and Foreign Policy*, 140.

[64] Perhaps one of the most extreme examples of this tendency is the comparative study done at the height of the Cold War by Zbigniew Brzezinski and Samuel P. Huntington, *Political Power: USA/USSR* (New York: Viking Press, 1963).

[65] Ibid., 412.

to exist, let alone successfully mount a challenge to the status quo, would have been minimal.

Subsequent approaches, exemplified by the work of Matthew Evangelista and Jack Snyder, used ideas as intervening variables. Writing in the 1980s and focusing on the Soviet Union, both coupled the process of policy making with a focus on state structure and timing of modernization.[66] These studies attempted to make a domestic political structural argument and to account for the pressures and interests that were present in the Soviet policy process.

Jack Snyder's "The Gorbachev Revolution: A Waning of Soviet Expansionism?" is particularly pertinent. He also looked at changes in Soviet foreign policy in the late 1980s and argued that the character of domestic institutions determined foreign policy. Expansionist and zero-sum thinking in Soviet foreign policy had been a result of Stalinist domestic institutions. The underlying hypothesis of Snyder's argument was that, if the institutions were to change, then foreign policy would change. Snyder used the term "institutions," as I do, to refer both to physical entities like the military or the Party and to abstract concepts like the administrative command system and the market system.[67]

Where do knowledge, ideas, interests, values and expectations fit in this explanation? Snyder provided an excellent historical discussion of the origins of the atavistic institutions and ideas that needed to be replaced. He explicitly addressed the relation of changes in foreign policy to the reformist domestic agenda, but he did not develop a full explanation for why this agenda won out over others. "Gorbachev and his allies have propounded strategic concepts that facilitate[d] their own domestic program. . . . Because the military-industrial complex, the orthodox ideologies, and autarkic interests [were] in eclipse, images of unappeasable opponents and offensive advantage [were] also in eclipse."[68] He acknowledged that the policies tended to be "a response to a variety of domestic political pressures, identical to none of them individually, but caused by the need to manage all of them simultaneously."[69]

Snyder's treatment of interests resembled that of a rationalist conception of ideas as hooks; interests were tied to specific institutions.[70] Decision makers and policy specialists were expected to voice ideas based on institutional interests. Evidence from the Afghanistan case suggests, however, that the nexus of interests and ideas is not purely materialist. Policy groups should not always be expected to push for ideas or interests that represent institutional

---

[66] See Matthew Evangelista, *Innovation and the Arms Race: How the United States and the Soviet Union Develop New Military Technology* (Ithaca: Cornell University Press, 1988); and Snyder, "The Gorbachev Revolution," in Lynn-Jones et al. (see n. 44, above).

[67] Snyder, "The Gorbachev Revolution," in Lynn-Jones et al. (see n. 44, above), 74.

[68] Ibid., 95. See also Snyder, *Myths of Empire*, Chapter 6.

[69] Snyder, "The Gorbachev Revolution," in Lynn-Jones et al. (see n. 44, above), 107.

[70] Snyder, *Myths of Empire*, 52–53, 238.

affiliation. Chapters 4 and 5 detail many examples of individuals and policy groups that endorse ideas that run counter to institutional affiliation.

It would be difficult to address in detail the process of agenda-setting and the timing of change in an article-length study such as Snyder's.[71] These are, however, issues that must be explored in order to gain insight into the relationship of ideas and politics. I find that the best way to do this is to examine a specific issue, such as the withdrawal from Afghanistan. In the next three chapters, I show how experts' ideas were turned into policies. I address the coalition-building strategies that Gorbachev used within traditional institutions to bring about change and the empowerment of a dominant community of experts that helped ensure an alternative source of legitimacy and power for the reformist agenda.

Political process models and discussions of how "domestic politics" matter in foreign policy making have not adequately incorporated the role of ideas. The role of knowledge and experts does not exclude an emphasis on domestic institutions, already present in policy process models. These models have been developing in an ideational direction for the last ten years. Evidence from this Soviet case should encourage that tendency.

CONCLUSION

Tricky and somewhat slippery analytical problems remain. How can one distinguish between those ideas that catch on within institutions because they legitimize constituencies' plans and those that do so because they are innovative? As Philip Tetlock points out, expert communities may serve to justify rather than guide policy.[72] Further, how does "learning" explain the timing of events? Why did reformist ideas catch on in the early 1980s among some segments of the party elite in the Soviet Union? Why did new thinking take hold in the late 1980s and result in changes in actions and not merely words?

An approach stressing ideas and experts adds a critical aspect to any discussion of the end of the Cold War. Specialist networks in the Soviet Union played a central role in changing the political discourse and the environment in which policy was made. The role of ideas and experts cannot, however, explain completely why or how the political environment changed or the timing of the change. Successful strategies for shifting the internal balance of power that involved coalition building and the convergence of interests between the expert community and the leadership were instrumental in getting consensual knowledge on the political agenda and then changing policy.

In summary, the approach presented here marries ideas and politics; it is

---

[71] It should be noted that Snyder, *Myths of Empire*, aims to explain not why foreign policy changes but why superpowers over-expand.

[72] Tetlock, "Learning in U.S. and Soviet Foreign Policy," 47.

not purely ideational, nor does it rely only on the political strategies of decision makers to shift the internal balance of power. It is a multi-causal explanation that finds that both ideas and politics are necessary and sufficient variables for explaining the change in Soviet foreign policy in the 1980s and the Soviet withdrawal from Afghanistan. Inasmuch as these events are linked to the end of the Cold War, this type of explanation has much to add to the debate about the momentous events of the late 1980s and early 1990s, as I detail in Chapter 6.

CHAPTER THREE.

Escalation in Afghanistan, 1979–1980:
A Case of Old Thinking

As ONE policy maker in Moscow put it, "you have to understand the inter-vention if you are going to understand the withdrawal."[1] One could add, one needs to understand "old thinking" in order to appreciate the boldness of new thinking. The decision making process surrounding the intervention displays the conceptions of competitive security and the highly centralized policy process that characterized the old thinking against which the Gorbachev coalition would later fight. The Gorbachev cohort's emphasis on domestic re-structuring, international reintegration, and consultations with experts were direct responses to Brezhnev's policies that resulted in corruption at home and imperial overreach abroad, including the Soviet war in Afghanistan.[2]

New thinking and *glasnost* were still several years off during the Soviet es-calation in 1979, and this period remained obscured to Western scholars until the late 1980s and early 1990s. Accordingly, views on the war often revealed more about analysts' perceptions of Soviet foreign policy than about the for-eign policy itself.[3] In the 1980s, Western debate over the intervention cen-tered around whether it was an offensive move driven by expansionist ideol-ogy or a defensive reaction to systemic constraints.[4] The evidence that has recently become available suggests that ideology and systemic factors did play a role but were decisively mediated by domestic political constraints.[5]

[1] Author's interview with Vadim Zagladin, former Director, Information Department, Inter-national Department of the Central Committee (CCID), December 12, 1990.

[2] Chapters 4 and 5 explore how these responses got turned into policy and how new thinkers beat out old thinkers in setting the political agenda.

[3] "The arguments [about why the Soviets intervened in Afghanistan] . . . sometimes sounded more based on personal attitudes toward Soviet communism than on the case at hand." Henry S. Bradsher, *Afghanistan and the Soviet Union* (Durham, N.C.: Duke University Press, 1985), 160.

[4] On the offensive nature of the intervention, see Harry Gelman, *The Brezhnev Politburo and the Decline of Détente* (Ithaca: Cornell University Press, 1984). On the defensive nature, see Ray-mond Garthoff, *Détente and Confrontation: American-Soviet Relations from Nixon to Reagan*, 1st ed. (Washington, D.C.: Brookings, 1985).

[5] The second edition of *Détente and Confrontation* contains a detailed discussion of the in-tervention in Afghanistan. Raymond Garthoff, *Détente and Confrontation: American-Soviet Re-lations from Nixon to Reagan*, 2d ed. (Washington, D.C.: Brookings, 1995). (Citations hereafter to Garthoff, *Détente and Confrontation*, refer to the second edition unless otherwise specified.) The second edition incorporates much new material previously unavailable and as a result, paints a portrait of Soviet decision making that also highlights domestic political constraints. While

New evidence suggests that the increase in Soviet involvement in Afghanistan stemmed mainly from the way that certain decision makers bargained among themselves about the costs of inaction.[6] The costs of restraint were seen as high because they were embedded in the conception of imperial "internationalist" duty.[7] The process of bargaining among decision makers in 1979–80 was dominated by traditional notions of empire and confrontational conceptions of security. As we shall see, this contrasts with the 1985–89 period when domestic political actors bargained about withdrawal. The decisive factor then involved the advance of ideas that conflicted with traditional conceptions of security.

A notable feature of the bargaining about the regional situation in 1979 was the absence of expert participation. This absence contrasts starkly with the active involvement of experts in policy making about the war and other issues

---

Garthoff maintains that he has not changed his central analysis of the intervention, the new evidence he marshals does suggest a picture much more highly contingent on domestic politics than the original one.

[6] Thanks to *glasnost*, the Soviet withdrawal from Afghanistan and the collapse of the Soviet empire, more information on the intervention is available now than in the early and mid 1980s when the main works on the war were written. The analysis here draws on declassified Kremlin, Central Committee and Ministry of Defense archival documents about the war in Afghanistan. The documents largely consist of notes from Politburo meetings as well as Soviet cables sent in 1979 by Soviet representatives in Kabul to the political leadership in Moscow and the response from Moscow. For the most important published documents, see Lieutenant Colonel A. Oliynik, "Vvod voysk v Afganistan: kak prinimalos' reshenie" (The troops go into Afghanistan: how the decision was taken), *Krasnaya zvezda*, November 18, 1989, 3–4; D. Muratov, "Afganistan" (Afghanistan), *Komsomolskaya pravda*, December 27, 1990, 3; "Kak prinimalos' reshenie" (How the decision was taken), *Voenno-istoricheskii zhurnal* 7 (1991): 40–52. These top-secret documents were released and published apparently as part of a decision by the Ministry of Defense to examine the experience of the 40th Army in Afghanistan. Their appearance may also have had some connection with an investigation of the war carried out by the Supreme Soviet's Committee on International Affairs in the fall of 1989. The *Komsomolskaya pravda* material was published in December 1990 as "a war in the Persian Gulf [was] imminent." Another important source is the cables sent in 1979 from the U.S. embassy in Kabul to the U.S. embassy in Teheran, seized by Iranian students when they took over the embassy on November 4, 1979. The cables were published as *Documents of the Nest of Spies (Afghanistan)* (Tehran: Moslem Students Followers Imam, 1981), Vols. I and II. Other new sources include articles, published after the decision to withdraw was announced in 1988, which address the war in critical terms. Among the best retrospectives are interviews conducted by Artyom Borovik with several military participants, for example, his interview with General Valentin Varennikov, *Ogonëk* 12 (1989): 6–8, 30–31. Also see S. Pashev and V. Kazako, "Veterany i perestroika" (Veterans and perestroika), *Krasnaya zvezda*, March 4, 1989, 2; Igor Belyaev and Anatoly Gromyko, "Tak my voshli v Afganistan" (So we went into Afghanistan), *Literaturnaya gazeta*, September 20, 1989, 14.

[7] Costs and obligations to a client state, in this case, Afghanistan, are often components of what Jack Snyder has called the imperial myth. These myths usually involve belief in the necessity of expansion and even overreach to maintain the security of the empire. Challenges to client states are interpreted in terms of the imperial myth, making action by the patron state appear necessary. See Jack Snyder, *Myths of Empire: Domestic Politics and International Ambition* (Ithaca: Cornell University Press, 1991).

in the late 1980s. Indeed, two key conditions under which experts are more likely to be influential were absent in 1979: 1) access to the leadership, and 2) the salience of expert advice—that is, its political value—to the leadership. Additionally, the essential element that led to the withdrawal was absent in 1979: reformists had not been mobilized to shift the internal balance of power. In 1979, old thinkers dominated conceptions of security as well as the policy making scene.

It would be misleading to focus on one day or one decision as the beginning of the Soviet war in Afghanistan, just as scholars find it difficult to state precisely the date of the American intervention in Vietnam.[8] The intervention occurred gradually over many months in 1979 and 1980, involving many separate decisions. Two steps decisively increased the role of the Soviets in Afghanistan: 1) the decision to use KGB troops to overthrow the Hafizullah Amin government and to establish Babrak Karmal as head of the People's Democratic Party of Afghanistan (PDPA) in December 1979; and 2) the decision to permit Soviet troops to engage in offensive maneuvers against the Afghan resistance beginning in February 1980. These decisions were made against a background of other decisions, contradictory information and opinions, and bargaining among and between the Soviet and Afghan political elites. This background must be filled in to understand how the Soviets got involved in what would be the longest and most unsuccessful war in that country's history.

I briefly address alternative explanations for the intervention. Drawing on the new sources, I focus on a number of aspects central to the escalation, including who supplied what information, how the information was used and most important, the configuration of power among the key decision makers. While I evaluate the importance of the international system and superpower obligations in explaining the escalation, I emphasize mainly the role of the internal balance of power, dominated during 1979–80 by old thinking and traditional conceptions of security.

ALTERNATIVE EXPLANATIONS

In the West during the Cold War, arguments drawing on Marxist-Leninist ideology, stipulating that the state expands when opportunities arise, were often used to explain the Soviet intervention in Afghanistan. Harry Gelman,

---

[8] Studies of the American involvement in Vietnam tend to focus on a series of decisions that brought about the escalation. See for example, Larry Berman, *Planning a Tragedy: The Americanization of the War in Vietnam* (New York: Norton, 1982); Leslie H. Gelb and Richard K. Betts, *The Irony of Vietnam: The System Worked* (Washington, D.C.: Brookings, 1979). Raymond Garthoff notes that while the Soviet action in December 1979 is usually referred to as an "'invasion,' which in a political sense it was, the Soviet military intervention and occupation were largely unopposed." Garthoff, *Détente and Confrontation*, 1020.

for example, argued that an "attacking compulsion" that was "insatiable" characterized Soviet behavior in the Third World.[9] Soviets looked for "offensive opportunities" with the intent of filling the "nooks and crannies throughout the world which were previously dominated by Western influence."[10] Gelman wrote that "the Politburo thus expects its adversaries . . . to accept a . . . Soviet right to employ force in consolidating and extending Soviet domination over Afghanistan."[11] Anthony Arnold, another scholar using similar logic, argued that the invasion was the outcome of a "long-term pattern of Soviet aggressive intentions" that was "consistent and openly emergent as soon as conditions permitted."[12]

Explanations of foreign policy drawing primarily on the ideological nature of the state share methodological problems associated with other approaches that focus almost exclusively on motivation at the expense of process. These explanations are based on the assumption that an analyst can infer or postulate a belief system. The character of the belief system deduced by the analyst may be, however, overly influenced by an analyst's attitude about the subject; this calls into question the degree to which objective standards can operate and hypotheses can be falsified. As a result, events may appear predetermined because political contingencies are obscured. Specifically, in the case of the decision to intervene in Afghanistan, this approach masks the degree to which escalation was incremental and contingent upon events both in Afghanistan and the Soviet Union.

Explanations that interpret Soviet foreign policy primarily as a response to constraints and pressures from the international system can paint an equally deterministic picture, although less imbued with Cold War rhetoric. For example, the Soviet Union, like other states in similar situations, would have been expected to respond offensively when it perceived its interests threatened by either another great power or by regional instability. The dominant conclusion in both the 1985 and 1995 editions of Garthoff's *Détente and Confrontation* is that "the Soviet leaders did not see their decision to intervene militarily as an opportune option but as a serious imperative; not as an opportunity for expansion but as a reluctant necessity to hold on."[13] Moreover, the leadership seemed to believe that the United States was "coming closer

---

[9] Gelman, *The Brezhnev Politburo and the Decline of Détente*, 35–36. For another example of the argument, see Anthony Arnold, *Afghanistan: The Soviet Invasion in Perspective* (Stanford: Hoover Institution Press, 1985).

[10] Gelman, *The Brezhnev Politburo and the Decline of Détente*, 22.

[11] Ibid., 32.

[12] Arnold, *Afghanistan*, xviii. Arnold does allow, however, with considerable prescience, that "a new leader untainted by the decision to invade Afghanistan would be in a position to undertake dramatic ways of restoring momentum to Soviet society. . . . Withdrawing the occupation forces would be one such move" (136).

[13] Garthoff, *Détente and Confrontation*, first ed., 931; second ed., 1040. Another work using this approach is Bradsher, *Afghanistan and the Soviet Union*.

to completing a geostrategic encirclement of the Soviet Union" and that there was a possibility of American retaliatory action against Iran following the collapse of the Shah's government.[14] Garthoff argues that "the real Soviet fear" was that Afghanistan would turn to the West (like Egypt under Sadat), and thus, the Soviets would lose their "cumulative investment in Afghanistan— strategic, political, ideological and economic."[15]

The "black box" surrounding the decision making process in this approach has been, however, opened by the declassified documents on decisions such as the war in Afghanistan. Scholars now have a glimpse of a more complex picture of the decision making that led up to the intervention. While Garthoff kept much of the original argument in the second edition of the book, the evidence presented in the second edition, drawing on the archival material and the many articles published in the Russian press on the subject, paints a less deterministic portrait. For example, we know now that Andropov was hesitant to send tanks to Afghanistan; that eventually Andropov changed his mind on this and agreed with Defense Minister Ustinov, a civilian with no military experience, the main supporter of escalation; and that military leaders did not want the escalation.[16] The new evidence suggests that the difficult decisions taken by the leadership were driven by the fears and interests of the dominant political actors. The evidence suggests a contingent series of decision points that were mediated more by internal constraints than by external ones.

Imperial tendencies of overreach that are common among great powers, not just a belief system unique to the Soviet Union, certainly played a role in decisions about escalation. Similarly, Soviet responses to the international and regional systems affected decision making and the timing of the intervention. But to understand the incremental escalation in Afghanistan requires understanding the domestic political environment that conditioned how political actors responded to information about the situation in Afghanistan, leading them to opt for increased involvement. The focus on domestic factors allows one to differentiate between motivation and method in making a decision. It also highlights the contingent nature of such decisions.

Declassified Kremlin archival documents show that throughout 1979, the Soviet leadership had reluctantly and only partially met the requests for military support made by the PDPA leadership through the Soviet representa-

---

[14] The quotation is from Garthoff, *Détente and Confrontation*, first ed., 923; second ed., 1031. See also Bradsher, *Afghanistan and the Soviet Union*, 156–157, on the role of the international situation.

[15] Garthoff, *Détente and Confrontation*, first ed., 923; second ed., 1031.

[16] From Fond 89 as cited by Garthoff, *Détente and Confrontation*, 993, 1013. This information was confirmed in the author's interviews with Sergei Akhromeev (at the time Marshal Ogarkov's first deputy chief of staff, later chief of staff and main military advisor to Gorbachev), January 3, 1991, with Zagladin, and with Valentin Varennikov (former deputy chief of staff, head of main operations directorate, and later deputy minister of defense), July 12, 1993.

tives in Kabul. By October, after Hafizullah Amin had ousted and killed Nur Mohammad Taraki, the Soviet leadership felt deeply distrustful of the Afghan leadership. The decision to replace the Amin government with a government more responsive to Moscow came in December and was made by four Politburo members: Leonid Brezhnev, General Secretary of the CPSU; Dmitri Ustinov, Minister of Defense; Andrei Gromyko, Minster of Foreign Affairs; and Yuri Andropov, Director of the KGB.

These four decision makers were not in complete agreement over the escalation. The outcome ultimately was the result of the balance of power between these men. Ustinov was the main backer of the policy. Brezhnev, barely competent to make decisions after a stroke in the mid 1970s, and under the sway of Ustinov, went along. Gromyko followed Ustinov's and Brezhnev's lead as he always did in policy matters. Andropov was the dissenter, but eventually he acquiesced, and the Soviets continued their escalation.

Material released by the Ministry of Defense in 1989 and 1990 shows the war in Afghanistan in four phases. During the first phase, December 1979 through February 1980, the political leadership initially planned that troops, although used in the intervention, would not be involved in fighting but only in making the garrisons and instructing the Afghanis how to fight against the opposition. The decision to allow Soviet troops to engage in fighting in February 1980 marked the beginning of the second, largely offensive period which was to last until the mid-1980s.[17]

A few events in the early stages of the war are uncontested: Soviet troops intervened in Afghanistan, overthrew the government of Hafizullah Amin and installed Babrak Karmal as head of the PDPA. However, much of the rest of the story has been contested, including the Soviet government's claim that the Afghan leadership petitioned for Soviet military intervention; and the claim by the top Soviet military leadership that they advised against the intervention. The evidence presented below points to incremental decisions taken over many months in 1979 and the growing importance of certain institutional and ideological commitments as a result of these decisions. This story, like that of the withdrawal, is about the leadership's view of the world and where they fit in it. But it is also about competing interests among winners and losers. Here I present the winners, the old thinkers, who were later to lose.

INCREMENTAL ESCALATION

Judging by the Soviet reaction, the Soviet leadership appears not to have been involved in the coup of April 27, 1978, in which the government of President Mohammad Daoud was overthrown, and in his place "a revolutionary coun-

---

[17] "How the decision was taken," *Voenno-istoricheskii zhurnal*, 43–44.

cil" began to consolidate power. Nur Mohammad Taraki came to power as head of the PDPA and prime minister, while Hafizullah Amin was made minister of foreign affairs. "From April 27 to April 30 TASS called it a military coup d'état. This is hardly the term it would have used if it were merely concealing an Afghan communist takeover—that would have been called a popular revolution."[18]

The "people's revolution" developed through the spring and summer of 1978, as Taraki's and Amin's party consolidated power by purging members of the Parcham ("the Banner"), an opposing wing of the PDPA, and by attempting modernization in the countryside. But resistance spread as local tribes encountered attempts by the new government to centralize their tribal orders and "to overthrow their traditional social-religious-economic order." By the winter of 1978–79, resistance had spread through most of Afghanistan's 28 provinces. By March of 1979, the uprisings in the provinces had become extremely violent. In Herat, in the western part of the country, several dozen Russian advisors and their families were killed and their heads impaled.[19]

According to documents from the Politburo, the Central Committee, and Ministry of Defense, Amin and Taraki repeatedly requested military support from the Soviets beginning in mid March and early April 1979.[20] The amount of resistance to government policies was growing and the Afghan military could not contain it.[21] These requests were passed along to Moscow by Ambassador Alexander Puzanov and Boris Ivanov, the KGB chief in Kabul. A commission set up by General Valentin Varennikov in 1989 to investigate the

[18] Garthoff, *Détente and Confrontation*, second ed., 988. The Soviet leadership did not publicly address the situation in Afghanistan for many months. In a speech on September 22, 1978, Brezhnev declared that "a people's revolution" had taken place in Afghanistan, and that the West had accused Moscow of interfering. "The imperialists, who in effect do not recognize the rights of people to freely determine their fate at all . . . have rushed to put into circulation the hackneyed legends of the 'hand of Moscow'." Leonid Brezhnev, "Rech' na torzhestvennom zasedanii, posviashchennom vrucheniiu gorodu Baku ordena Lenina" (Speech in celebration of the meeting dedicating the delivery of the Order of Lenin to the city of Baku), *Kommunist* no. 14 (1978): 9.

[19] See Garthoff, *Détente and Confrontation*, second ed., 982 on splits between Parcham and the Khalq faction of the PDPA; for quotation, ibid., 990, on Herat, 989–991; see also Bradsher, *Afghanistan and the Soviet Union*, 100.

[20] See TsKhSD, Fond 89, Perechen' 25, Dokument 1, 15–16, "Zasedanie Politburo TsK KPSS 17 marta 1979 goda" (Meeting of the Politburo of the CC of the CPSU, March 17, 1979). For details of this meeting and the Soviet response, see Garthoff, *Détente and Confrontation*, second ed., 993. See also "How the decision was taken," *Voenno-istoricheskii zhurnal*, 41; and Oliynik, "The troops go into Afghanistan," *Krasnaya zvezda*.

[21] An American diplomat reported at this time (March 25, 1979) that the "Afghan government has no confidence in most of its army . . . and there have been cases of [Afghan] military units being bombed by the Air Force because they were believed to be untrustworthy." *Afghanistan*, Vol. I, 81.

war, reported that there was "no doubt" that in fact Taraki and Amin made these requests.[22]

Within the Politburo, the response was mixed: initially Gromyko urged a response and then he shifted his opinion to follow that of Andropov. The judgment in March 1979 seems to have been that, in the words of Gromyko, "this is their internal affair, a revolutionary internal conflict."[23] The Soviets responded not with the tanks that the Afghan government requested but by increasing the number of Soviet advisors. Soon after the uprising in Herat, Puzanov and Ivanov advised the leadership in Moscow to send Soviet military personnel to Bagram, the military airport outside of Kabul, "under the guise of technical specialists." Should the situation get increasingly complicated, the troops could help with the evacuation of Soviet personnel.[24]

In early April, Army General Aleksei Epishev, chief of the political administration in the Soviet armed forces, brought a delegation of six generals to Afghanistan to assess what kind of military support was needed for the Afghan army and air force.[25] By the middle of the month, Lev Gorelov, the chief Soviet military advisor in Kabul, reported to Moscow that Taraki requested 15–20 attack helicopters with Soviet teams. These helicopters would be used, in case of "extraordinary events," against revolts and terrorists along the border and in the central part of the country. The transport of the helicopters would be a covert operation.[26]

By late spring of 1979, as the requests from the Afghan leadership mounted and resistance continued, the political leadership in Moscow had grown increasingly concerned about the anti-government actions in Afghanistan. Amin and Taraki did not appear to be containing the situation, but rather fanning the flames of revolt with their programs of centralization and with purges against political foes in Parcham. In an effort to change the tide of events, Vasily Safronchuk, an experienced diplomat, was sent to Kabul as the unoffi-

---

[22] "How the decision was taken," *Voenno-istoricheskii zhurnal*, 41. See also General Lieutenant Gorelov, the chief military advisor in Kabul; Oliynik, "The troops go into Afghanistan," *Krasnaya zvezda*. Gorelov reports that eighteen requests were made because of the resistance, reportedly from Taraki and Amin themselves, and were transmitted by the ambassador, the KGB (Ivanov), and Gorelov to Moscow.

[23] TsKhSD, Fond 89, Perechen' 25, 16; see also Garthoff, *Détente and Confrontation*, second ed., 993.

[24] Muratov, "Afganistan," *Komsomolskaya pravda*, 3.

[25] Garthoff, *Détente and Confrontation*, second ed., 996. Epishev made a similar visit to Czechoslovakia in 1968 before the invasion. Olivier Roy, *The Lessons of the Soviet/Afghan War*, Adelphi Paper No. 259 (London: International Institute for Strategic Studies [IISS], Summer 1991), 17, suggests that the invasion in Czechoslovakia was the model for Afghanistan: quickly seize the capital and replace the government. Possibly because of this inference, Soviet leaders miscalculated both international reaction and domestic political resistance.

[26] Oliynik, "The troops go into Afghanistan," *Krasnaya zvezda*.

cial advisor to the Afghan Foreign Ministry.[27] Safronchuk's specific mission in Kabul was to attempt a change in tactics ("broaden the political base of the regime"), or alternatively, to bring about a change in the government.[28] In any case, Safronchuk relieved Puzanov, the ambassador, of advisory duties to the Afghan government.[29]

Requests by the Kabul government for military support from the Soviets increased markedly over the summer. The Ministry of Defense documents record requests teams of helicopters, teams of anti-aircraft gunners, units for defending specific government buildings, paratroopers, and even units of the Soviet militia. Soviet advisors on the ground in Kabul were at this time, according to the documents, talking about the necessity of sending troops. By July 7, 1979, the 600-man battalion of the Soviet 105th Guards Airborne Division was deployed at Bagram as "technical specialists." This division had been alerted in March following the grisly uprising in Herat and the suggestions of deployment by Puzanov and Ivanov of troops to Bagram.[30]

Shortly after the deployment to Bagram, according to these documents, the KGB station chief, Ivanov, reported that Taraki raised again the idea that the Soviets should covertly deploy in Kabul several military groups. Presumably as a response to Taraki's request, and because the government was reportedly getting ready for further confrontations with the mujahideen, Puzanov, Ivanov, and Gorelov urged the immediate preparedness of Afghan

[27] *Afghanistan*, Vol. II, 84–85. The American chargé d'affaires in Kabul, Bruce Amstutz, described Safronchuk as "intelligent," "extraordinarily open," "a man you can reason with." Ibid., Vol. I, 129. For a discussion that significantly downplays the role of Safronchuk, see Garthoff, *Détente and Confrontation*, second ed., 997.

[28] See Vasily Safronchuk, "Afghanistan in the Amin Period," *International Affairs* (Moscow), February 1991, 79–96. By the middle of July, leaflets spread at night were suggesting that Amin was a CIA agent. Safronchuk may have been involved in a campaign to discredit the Afghan leader. Garthoff, *Détente and Confrontation*, second ed., 997.

[29] The GDR ambassador to Afghanistan, Hermann Schwiesau, who served as a main U.S. source of information on Soviet policy in Afghanistan before his removal in August 1979, noted in a meeting with Amstutz that it was improper for the Soviet ambassador to be advising the Afghan government. If, for some reason, the advisor had to be expelled from the country, it would be less of an embarrassment for the Soviet Union to have the third ranking officer at the embassy leave than the first. *Afghanistan*, Vol. I, 181 (Amstutz, July 18, 1979). (As it turned out, the ambassador was expelled in November 1979.)

[30] See Oliynik, "The troops go into Afghanistan," *Krasnaya zvezda*, November 18, 1989; Muratov, "Afganistan," *Komsomolskaya pravda*; and Garthoff, *Détente and Confrontation*, second ed., 1002. The deployment at Bagram reminded American observers in Kabul of the U.S. government's experience in Vietnam of gradual escalation and commitment: "Soviet personnel were brought to Bagram to train Afghans to use their new air weapons. Soviet maintenance personnel were also required. Because of the threat of nearby insurgency activity, Soviet forces had to be brought in to protect the training and maintenance areas. This then led to a Soviet assumption of responsibility for the perimeter defense of the base." *Afghanistan*, Vol. II, 53 (Bruce Flatin, September 4, 1979).

helicopter teams. These teams, it was suggested, could perform reconnaissance operations along the border with Iran in addition to functions associated with the revolts.[31]

At this time, Boris Ponomarev, director of the International Department of the Central Committee, the branch of the Party that most closely monitored Soviet–Third World relations, reported to Moscow on his visit to Kabul. Again, Taraki and Amin had requested that the Soviets send two divisions of troops. The rationale for the request was still that the revolts were getting out of control, and that Soviet military support could play a decisive role in supporting the PDPA and reestablishing order. Ponomarev's reply was, "the Soviet Union cannot enter into that."[32] Throughout July, anti-government demonstrations continued and the Soviet team in Kabul passed on the PDPA's requests for more support.[33]

August brought more revolts and more requests for military assistance, but no initial response from the Soviets. Puzanov, Ivanov, and Gorelov urged Moscow to send a special brigade to Kabul in August or September. This request was made August 1 and repeated August 12 following revolts in the provinces on August 5 and 11 and an uprising in Kabul itself.[34] Gorelov's August 12 assessment included Amin's insistence that Soviet military support would not be considered interference; "that we [Afghans] are a sovereign and independent government and we decide all questions independently." The units would be needed "until spring" and would only be used in "critical moments."[35] Amin's assurances suggest that he was responding to concerns voiced by either the Soviet team in Kabul or the Soviet leadership in Moscow.

During this time the Soviet leadership responded to the situation in Afghanistan by forming a special Politburo Commission on Afghanistan and sending a delegation of senior military officials to assess the situation. The commission included Politburo members Gromyko, Andropov, Ustinov, and Nikolai Ogarkov, in addition to Georgi Kornienko, first deputy minister of foreign affairs and Gromyko's deputy. In the first meeting, Gorelov and Ivanov, who had flown up from Kabul, presented their reading of the situation in

---

[31] Muratov, "Afganistan," *Komsomolskaya pravda*. The requests came on July 11 and 12.

[32] Oliynik, "The troops go into Afghanistan," *Krasnaya zvezda*; Muratov, "Afganistan," *Komsomolskaya pravda*. The reply is dated July 19. These requests were repeated by Amin on November 17 and 20.

[33] Muratov, "Afganistan," *Komsomolskaya pravda*. On July 20 there was rioting. On July 21 Puzanov relayed a message to Moscow to send 8–10 helicopter teams. On July 24 KGB Lieutenant General Boris Ivanov reported that Amin was talking about deploying three Soviet army sub-units in Kabul.

[34] Muratov, "Afganistan," *Komsomolskaya pravda*; Oliynik, "The troops go into Afghanistan," *Krasnaya zvezda*.

[35] Oliynik, "The troops go into Afghanistan," *Krasnaya zvezda*. For a report that puts the request in late September, see David Gai and Vladimir Snegirev, *Znamya* 4 (April 1991), cited in Garthoff, *Détente and Confrontation*, second ed., 1009.

Afghanistan.[36] The issue of direct Soviet intervention was not raised at that time, although Gorelov later claimed to have argued that it was "inadvisable to strengthen . . . the military presence in Afghanistan." The Afghan army of approximately 90,000 men, could handle the resistance, he argued. Gorelov claimed that Ivanov then reported a contrasting assessment which urged the introduction of combat troops.[37]

The senior military delegation was led by Deputy Defense Minister and chief of the Soviet ground forces, General Ivan Pavlovsky, and included a delegation of sixty-three, including twelve generals and six colonels, for a two-month stay in Kabul in August and September. The mission involved co-ordination between the Soviet military advisors and the Afghan General Staff in addition to assessing the potential for getting control over the resistance. On the eve of the departure, Pavlovsky recounts that he called Ustinov in Sochi where the minister was vacationing and asked, "are we going into Afghanistan?" Ustinov is said to have replied at that time, "not under any circumstances."[38]

The way in which the Soviets understood and responded to the events in Afghanistan of September and October 1979 played a critical role in the decision to escalate participation. In early September, Taraki stopped in Moscow on his way back from Havana. Taraki requested more Soviet assistance in defending the revolution. He argued that Amin was playing a greater role in controlling much of domestic and foreign policy. Based on information from Kabul, the Soviet leadership was aware that conflicts between Amin and Taraki were growing. According to Safronchuk, Amin was showing signs of turning against Taraki. At that time, Brezhnev reportedly warned Taraki of Amin's "intrigues against the PDPA leaders."[39]

What happened upon Taraki's return to Kabul remains somewhat unclear. On September 14, there was a show-down between Taraki's and Amin's guards. Safronchuk writes that Taraki called Amin in for a visit with Ambassador Puzanov and a military advisor identified as "General E." Amin balked at the invitation and insisted that he be accompanied by his own guards to the meeting. When he arrived at the Revolutionary Council building, Taraki's and Amin's guards began to shoot at one another, killing several people. Taraki was taken prisoner and later shot. Safronchuk claims that Amin called him in

---

[36] Oliynik, "The troops go into Afghanistan," *Krasnaya zvezda*; see also Garthoff, *Détente and Confrontation*, second ed., 1009.

[37] Oliynik, "The troops go into Afghanistan," *Krasnaya zvezda*. See also Roy, *The Lessons of the Soviet-Afghan War*, 74–75, for a similar account.

[38] Pavlovsky notified Moscow shortly after arriving in Kabul that Amin had requested more troops to be used in different areas for fighting against the "counter-revolutionaries." Oliynik, "The troops go into Afghanistan," *Krasnaya zvezda*.

[39] Safronchuk, "Afghanistan in the Amin Period," 85. On the trip, see Garthoff, *Détente and Confrontation*, second ed., 1004; Belyaev and Gromyko, "So we got into Afghanistan."

and informed him that Taraki had resigned "for reasons of health." Amin then succeeded Taraki as head of the party and the government.[40]

Who set up the gun-battle and why is uncertain. Some accounts written by Russians suggest that Amin laid a trap for Taraki.[41] Garthoff argues that the Soviets laid a trap for Amin and it backfired; someone leaked the information to Amin that he was to be assassinated.[42] Garthoff, however, does not mention the fact that Ambassador Puzanov was to be present at the meeting; according to Safronchuk, the ambassador was in the room with Taraki.[43] While the evidence is inconclusive, if an assassination had been planned with Soviet assistance, it seems unlikely that the Soviet ambassador would have been present as a witness.[44]

On the other hand, it is clear that the Soviet leadership was not particularly supportive of Amin. In addition, when Taraki—the man that the Soviet leadership had backed—was killed, their options for influencing the situation in Kabul and elsewhere in Afghanistan were affected. It is plausible that Soviet leaders believed that if Amin had been taken out of power at that point, Taraki could have reversed some of Amin's policies and widened the support for the government; the insurgency would have subsided, making the Soviet escalation unnecessary. As it was, the Soviet leadership was presented with a fait accompli.

The Soviet leadership responded with equivocation to the Amin coup, according to Ministry of Defense documents. In a coded cable from Moscow to Kabul, the Soviet representatives in Kabul were ordered not to align with forces against Amin but also not to participate in Amin's repressive measures against his opponents. The advisors in Kabul and the leadership were aware, according to these documents, that Amin was erratic and autocratic.[45] The Soviet leadership eventually decided that Amin had to be eliminated.

According to the documents and analyses by Soviet experts, Amin's coup in September, whether a deliberate plan or the result of a foiled attempt to

[40] Safronchuk, "Afghanistan in the Amin Period," 87; Igor Belyaev suggests that Pavlovsky was demoted upon his return with this delegation in October due to the murder of Taraki; Belyaev and Gromyko, "So we got into Afghanistan." See also Cynthia Roberts, "*Glasnost*' in Soviet Foreign Policy: Setting the Record Straight?" *Report on the USSR* 1 (December 15, 1989):6.

[41] Safronchuk, "Afghanistan in the Amin Period," 86.

[42] Garthoff, *Détente and Confrontation*, second ed., 1005.

[43] Safronchuk, "Afghanistan in the Amin Period," 86.

[44] According to the American chargé, neither the GDR chargé, Klaus Maser, nor the Polish ambassador, Edward Baradziej, "thought the Soviets had a direct hand in the removal of Taraki. In fact, the Pole was sure that Moscow was embarrassed by it since only a few days before Brezhnev had given a bearhug to Taraki in Moscow." *Afghanistan*, Vol. II, 79–80 (Bruce Amstutz, September 19, 1979).

[45] Muratov, "Afganistan," *Komsomolskaya pravda*. See also Belyaev and Gromyko, "So we got into Afghanistan" on Amin. According to the American diplomats in Kabul, Amin had the reputation of being the "Afghan Stalin." *Afghanistan*, Vol. II, 75 (Amstutz, September 17, 1979).

depose him, greatly disturbed the Soviet leadership. Anatoly Gromyko, son of the former foreign minister, said in an interview, "I should just like to observe that Brezhnev was simply shaken by the murder of Taraki, who not long before had been his guest." This event more than any other "compelled" the leadership to reevaluate the situation in Afghanistan.[46] Specifically, the Soviets had been attempting to bring about a political change in the government by widening the base of support.[47] Amin presented them with a situation that, coupled with his hard-line policies, was likely to increase insurgency.

The documents show that the pattern from the spring and summer continued through October: Amin requested assistance and the Soviet advisors in Kabul urged Moscow to respond favorably to these requests, but Moscow hedged.[48] Meanwhile, relations between the Amin government and the Soviet advisors in Kabul took a dramatic and unpredictable turn. Safronchuk reported that on October 8, Shah Wali, the Afghan foreign minister, called a meeting of all the ambassadors from socialist countries. There, Wali announced that since the spring of 1979, Soviet Ambassador Puzanov had been in collusion with Taraki against Amin. Wali accused the Soviets and Taraki of organizing the shoot-out in September. Wali claimed that Puzanov had worked closely with military officers from the PDPA who were said to be hiding out in the Soviet embassy in Kabul. He then announced that Taraki was dead.[49]

Despite Wali's accusations, Soviet advisors remained in Afghanistan throughout the fall. Amin appeared, however, increasingly unpredictable in several ways as he assumed sole command of the PDPA. According to Safronchuk, Amin planned to redesign the Afghan state structure to parallel the Soviet republic system. Afghanistan would have been made up of republics based on nationality, like the Soviet Union. The prospect of having an Afghan Tajikistan or Uzbekistan sharing a border with Soviet Tajikistan and

[46] Belyaev and Gromyko, "So we got into Afghanistan." See also Oliynik, "The troops go into Afghanistan," *Krasnaya zvezda*; and "How the decision was taken," *Voenno-istoricheskii zhurnal*, 42. Anatoly Gromyko reiterated this statement in an interview with the author, July 13, 1993.

[47] According to the American Embassy, Soviet attempts to widen the political base of support were "publicize[d] all over town" by Safronchuk and the GDR ambassador, Schwiesau. *Afghanistan*, Vol. II, 124 (James Taylor, October 25, 1979). Garthoff, *Détente and Confrontation,* second ed., 1034, writes that the Soviets wanted to promote a more moderate leadership with a broader constituency while at the same time advising the Afghan military.

[48] Muratov, "Afganistan," *Komsomolskaya pravda.*

[49] Safronchuk, "Afghanistan in the Amin Period," 89–91. Safronchuk notes that the Chinese and Yugoslav ambassadors were also present at the meeting, which caused potential embarrassment for the Soviets. Usually the Chinese and Yugoslav delegations were kept separate from the Soviets. As a result of these accusations, Puzanov left Kabul November 19 and was replaced by Fikryat Tabeev, first secretary of the Tatar region and Central Committee member, on November 28. Tabeev's assignment followed a common Soviet pattern of sending regional party secretaries as ambassadors to Third World countries.

Uzbekistan was unacceptable to the Soviet leadership because of the potential for cross-border national identity based on ethnicity.[50]

Garthoff writes that, between September and November the Soviets responded to events with "a complete strategic reappraisal" of the situation. Amin was seen as a "burden" and "unreliable."[51] The unreliability of Amin recalled to Central Committee members that of Sadat; Amin might break away and go with the Americans.[52] While Amin was asking the Soviets for support and putting together Five-Year Plans for which the Soviets were to provide 66 percent of the funds, he was also making contact with the U.S. and Pakistani embassies in Kabul in an attempt to normalize relations. Although the Soviet leadership did not know it at the time, U.S. embassy personnel did not trust Amin.[53] The Iranian revolution, however, had deprived the United States of a strategic listening post from which to monitor the Soviet Union. Evidence suggests that the Soviet leadership feared a U.S. retaliation for the taking of American hostages in the form of an attack against Iran or by cultivating the Afghan government.[54] Moreover, the Soviets suspected that arms were being shipped into Afghanistan by the Chinese, Iranians, Pakistanis, and Saudi Arabians, and indeed, after the ousting of Amin, these suspicions were correct. There is no evidence, however, that the United States was sending aid before January 1980.[55]

From late November through December, Soviet military participation continued to increase incrementally, day by day and week by week. Gorelov's replacement, Colonel General Sultan Magometov, recorded a December 3 meeting with Amin in which Amin requested that militia units be sent to

[50] Safronchuk, "Afghanistan in the Amin Period," 92.

[51] Garthoff, *Détente and Confrontation*, second ed., 1026.

[52] Ibid., 1027.

[53] Safronchuk, "Afghanistan in the Amin Period," 91, 93. *Afghanistan*, Vol. II, 59 (September 9, James Taylor); ibid., 75 (September 17, Amstutz); Garthoff, *Détente and Confrontation*, second ed., 1027.

[54] "How the decision was taken," *Voenno-istoricheskii zhurnal*, 41; and Oliynik, "The troops go into Afghanistan," *Krasnaya zvezda*. An account of CIA involvement in Afghanistan does point to attempts in the mid-1980s by William Casey, then director of the CIA, to use the war to destabilize the southern tier of the Soviet Union and fire up nationalist and anti-communist sentiment. Steve Coll, "Anatomy of a Victory: CIA's Covert Afghan War," *Washington Post*, July 19 and 20, 1992.

[55] From various accounts, it seems that the United States was not providing direct assistance to the resistance before the Soviet escalation in December 1979. Pakistan and Saudi Arabia and possibly China seem to have provided assistance throughout 1979. *Afghanistan*, Vol. II, 148–152. In any case, as Garthoff, *Détente and Confrontation*, second ed., 1029–1031, points out, the Soviets may have believed that foreign assistance was quite substantial and felt threatened by it. Yuri Gankovsky, widely regarded as the senior Russian expert on Afghanistan, has said that Pakistan began sending aid to Afghanistan immediately following the April 1978 coup. See interview with Yuri Gankovsky conducted by V. Skosyrev, "A Lesson Worth Learning," *Izvestiia*, May 4, 1989, 5.

Kabul.[56] While this request was not met directly, two additional battalions of the 105th Guards Airborne Division were soon flown into Bagram air base, bringing the number of Soviet troops to 2500. They then went north along the Salang highway to secure the Soviet-built Salang tunnel, a key strategic point for traffic flowing from the Soviet border to Kabul.[57]

The significant decision "to intervene," according to Politburo notes and Ministry of Defense documents and Central Committee materials, was taken December 12, although Ustinov had given oral commands on December 10 indicating an escalation.[58] The decision seems to have been made only with a rump group of the Politburo commission responsible for Afghanistan: Andropov, Ustinov, and Gromyko, with Brezhnev's wobbly, small signature at the very bottom of the handwritten proclamation.[59] While the Soviets had been sending troops and material throughout 1979, the commitment intensified with this decision, as the Soviets determined to bring about a change in government, to get rid of Amin and bring in Babrak Karmal. To coordinate this action, an "operations group" was formed on December 13 directed by Sergei Akhromeev. The next day the group started to organize the Turkmenistan Military District (TMD). Troops went to readiness following oral directives from Ustinov, in the largest post–World War II mobilization in Turkmenistan and Central Asia.[60]

On December 24, Ustinov met with the commanders of the 40th Army to

[56] Oliynik, "The troops go into Afghanistan." See Garthoff, *Détente and Confrontation*, second ed. 1012, 1013, for a list of changes in Soviet personnel in Kabul related to the escalation.

[57] Garthoff, *Détente and Confrontation*, first edition, 911. For a discussion of the physical accessibility of Afghanistan for the Soviets, see Mahnaz Z. Ispahani, *Roads and Rivals: The Political Uses of Access in the Borderlands of Asia* (Ithaca: Cornell University Press, 1989), 130. By early December 5, motorized rifle divisions had been called up. The 103rd and 104th Airborne divisions were also alerted and tactical air units moved into Soviet Central Asia. Many of the reservists called up were from the same Central Asian ethnic groups as the Afghans they were fighting. By January, these reservists had been replaced by Slavs.

[58] "How the decision was taken," *Voenno-istoricheskii zhurnal*, 42. TsKhSD, Fond 89, Perechen' 14, Dokument 31, "K polozheniiu v 'A'" (On the situation in "A"), Protocol 176/125, December 12, 1979. This document is hand-written. For a full account see Garthoff, *Détente and Confrontation*, second ed., 1016–1017.

[59] The Soviet Ambassador to Afghanistan, Fikryat Tabeev, later reported to the Committee on International Affairs that in December 1979, he "was ordered to report nothing to Moscow, to send no assessments of the situation in Afghanistan and to make no proposals until he received special instructions." See Georgii Arbatov, *The System* (New York: Random House, 1992), 197–198.

[60] "How the decision was taken," *Voenno-istoricheskii zhurnal*, 42. See also Arbatov, *The System*, 197, for an account of Akhromeev's testimony to the Committee on International Affairs. Akhromeev claimed that Ustinov had come to him, Marshal Ogarkov, and General Varennikov on December 13 and ordered preparations for a December 28 operation. In the three weeks that followed, through December 31, the operations group issued over thirty directives. See also Oliynik, "The troops go into Afghanistan," *Krasnaya zvezda*. Muratov, "Afganistan," *Komsomolskaya pravda*, details the readiness of various motorized and tank divisions.

discuss the directive on the intervention. The border crossing took place at 15:00 on December 25. The rest of the 105th Airborne was brought to Bagram as artillery, anti-artillery, and aviation units were brought to full readiness. By December 27, the Kabul telephone and television system has been taken over and the Soviet troops had secured key administrative buildings.[61] Only then was a full Politburo meeting held regarding the escalation and a list of messages prepared for Soviet embassies around the world. On December 28, Radio Kabul announced that Babrak Karmal was President of the Revolutionary Council and the general secretary of the People's Democratic Party of Afghanistan.[62]

THE DECISION MAKING PROCESS

The PDPA leadership of Taraki and Amin repeatedly requested Soviet military assistance. Although the Soviet leadership at first responded to these requests in the negative, they eventually complied. Why? What role did information and advice play in the decision to escalate in December 1979? In short, who supported an escalation and why? Who opposed it and why?

The decision making process was exceedingly centralized: few experts, advisors, or officials were consulted.[63] Gromyko's aide, Georgi Kornienko, says that Gromyko suddenly stopped discussing events in Afghanistan sometime in October 1979 (presumably after the death of Taraki).[64] Mikhail Gorbachev's main foreign policy aide Anatoly Chernyaev, in discussing the reasons for escalation, pointed to the style of decision making: "It was the manifestation of a totally arbitrary ... [and] irresponsible approach to policy-making that at that time was typical of the Soviet leadership."[65]

Chernyaev's comment underscores what is true in any decision making group: the act of tapping some sources and not others is in itself political. Whose voice is heard and why? To explore options with the military and the

[61] "How the decision was taken," *Voenno-istoricheskii zhurnal*, 42–43; Muratov, "Afganistan," *Komsomolskaya pravda;* Garthoff, *Détente and Confrontation,* second ed., 1017–1018.

[62] On the Politburo meeting, see TsKhSD, Fond 89, Perechen' 14, Dokument 33, "O nashikh shagakh v sviazi s razvitiem obstanovki vokrug Afganistana" (On our steps in connection with the development of the situation around Afghanistan), December 27, 1979, Protocol 177/151. By the middle of January, 1980, the 40th Army was fully mobilized with seven divisions. Troop strength was increased in the first part of 1980 with another division and two more regiments.

[63] For a discussion on who was left out of the decision, see Garthoff, *Détente and Confrontation,* first ed., 933. Arbatov, Bogdanov, and Kornienko were all in the hospital with heart attacks around this time. In *Pravda,* October 24, 1989, Shevardnadze disclosed that he and Gorbachev were walking together on a beach at the time they found out about the invasion.

[64] Remarks by Alexandr Bessmertnykh, former Soviet foreign minister, in Fred I. Greenstein and William C. Wohlforth, eds., *Retrospective on the End of the Cold War,* Monograph Series No. 6 (Center of International Studies, Princeton University, 1994), 31.

[65] Ibid., 34.

KGB but not regional experts testifies to the fact that the decision to escalate was ultimately based on factors independent of the regional situation in Afghanistan. Advice from regional experts was not considered salient, and experts were not provided access to the leadership.

Four men—Ustinov, Andropov, Gromyko and Brezhnev—made the decision to escalate Soviet involvement in Afghanistan. At least three of them understood the potentially adverse effects of this action but decided that escalation was necessary.[66] As indicated by his shaky signature on the decree of December 12, 1979, and from the testimony of others, Brezhnev was only marginally functional at the time. Georgii Arbatov reported to war correspondent Arytom Borovik that "toward the end of the 1970s Brezhnev was incapable of making any political decisions on his own and couldn't even sustain an intelligent conversation for more than twenty or thirty minutes."[67]

The balance of power among these four men played a crucial role in determining the timing and the nature of the escalation. The dynamic was characterized in part by the fact that Brezhnev was sick and yet was still the general secretary. Beyond this, or perhaps because of it, was what one observer called a "gang mentality: to stick together, to be tough, to show that you are a true believer, that you are indeed a communist, you are a Leninist, you do everything to guard the system."[68] Leading the gang in this instance, according to many observers, was Ustinov. It is widely argued that Ustinov enjoyed great power, even occasionally with respect to the general secretary.[69] Gromyko, known as "'Comrade Yes' to his superiors," went along with Ustinov. Persuaded by the reasoning or by his power within the military-industrial complex, the ailing Brezhnev and his follower, Gromyko, fell in behind Ustinov.[70] There is some speculation that Andropov was initially against the decision to escalate.[71] If he did dissent, he was the only one to do so, and eventually fell in with the decision.

---

[66] Author's interviews with Akhromeev; and with Fikryat Tabeev (Soviet ambassador to Kabul 1980–86, member of the Supreme Soviet committee investigating the war), December 4, 1990. "How the decision was taken," *Voenno-istoricheskii zhurnal*, 42; Belyaev and Gromyko, "So we got into Afghanistan." The Supreme Soviet's Committee on International Affairs also concluded that these four men made the decision. Arbatov, *The System*, 198.

[67] Artyom Borovik, *The Hidden War* (New York: Atlantic, 1990), 6.

[68] Comments by Sergei Tarasenko, former Soviet foreign ministry official, in Greenstein and Wohlforth, *Retrospective on the End of the Cold War*, 32.

[69] Author's interview with Georgii Arbatov (director, Institute for the Study of USA and Canada), January 4, 1991; Arbatov, *The System*, 198–199; author's interview with Karen Brutents (former first deputy director, CCID), December 7, 1990; author's interview with Zagladin.

[70] Bessmertnykh argues that this dynamic was also true with regard to Gromyko's relationship with Ustinov and Andropov: Gromyko "was very cautious with those two men, and I don't know an instance when Gromyko would oppose any joint view that Ustinov and Andropov had." Greenstein and Wohlforth, *Retrospective on the End of the Cold War*, 32.

[71] KGB Major General Oleg Kalugin has said of August 1979 that: "I remember that when possible Soviet military intervention with the aim of helping Afghanistan was being discussed,

Conflicting assessments of how to respond to the situation in Afghanistan flourished. Nowhere was this conflict more significant than inside the military leadership. In addition, there were disagreements within institutions; for example, between representatives of the KGB in Kabul and their colleagues in Moscow. However, the category of policy experts was largely uninvolved in the decision to intervene.

At the highest level of the General Staff, there were disagreements over escalation in Afghanistan. For example, Akhromeev claimed "in general, before the introduction of troops, the leadership of the Ministry of Defense of the USSR was against the invasion in Afghanistan," including himself, Marshal Ogarkov, and General Valentin Varennikov. According to Akhromeev, the military simply carried out what, ultimately, had been a political decision.[72]

Akhromeev's reasons for opposing the intervention were both military and political. "To [the military leadership] it was clear that a military way to solving the problem in Afghanistan was impossible—the strength introduced was not sufficient, the quantity was little." In addition, Akhromeev argued that many in the military understood that the international consequences of the intervention included the worsening of relations with the United States.[73]

Valentin Varennikov, then deputy chief of the General Staff and head of Operations of the Main Directorate, also confirmed the military leadership's opposition to escalation. In an interview with Artyom Borovik, Varennikov stated that "the General Staff raised objections to the idea of the invasion of our troops in Afghanistan up until the moment it was no longer a decision." But he also warned against revisionist history of the intervention; he argued that the main goal of the General Staff was "the stabilization of the situation." While the General Staff was not arguing for military intervention, there was the sense that something had to be done to help the PDPA stay in power. The military leadership advocated a political solution and the political leadership advocated a military solution.[74]

Bruce Porter has noted that any protestations made by the top military

---

the then head of the Soviet intelligence Kryuchkov said: 'Andropov is against our military involvement.'" Despite Andropov's objections, "he couldn't say no to Brezhnev and his friend Ustinov." Natalya Gevorkyan interview with Kalugin, *Moscow News* 25 (1990): 13. On Andropov, see Diego Cordovez and Selig S. Harrison, *Out of Afghanistan: The Inside Story of the Soviet Withdrawal* (New York: Oxford University Press, 1995), 45.

[72] Author's interview with Akhromeev. Indeed the report in "How the decision was taken," *Voennoistoricheskii zhurnal*, 42, claims that "military specialists did not participate in making the decision to intervene in the DRA [Democratic Republic of Afghanistan]."

[73] Author's interview with Akhromeev.

[74] Borovik interview with Varennikov; author's interview with Varennikov, July 12, 1993. It is plausible that the senior military leadership advised against escalation and that escalation occurred anyway. Richard K. Betts, *Soldiers, Statesmen, and Cold War Crises* (New York: Columbia University, 1991), argues that military leaders are generally more cautious about intervention than their civilian counterparts.

leadership did not affect promotion rates.[75] Akhromeev was made chief of the General Staff in 1984, and Varennikov, who assisted Sokolov in planning the invasion but claims that he objected to it, eventually became deputy minister of defense.[76] Moreover, within the military leadership there were known conflicts that pitted Ustinov, allied with the political leadership, against the military. For example, Ustinov and Ogarkov were reportedly at odds over the nature of the military budget. Ustinov, a civilian who had been brought in as defense minister in 1976 as a political ally to Brezhnev, supported the political leadership's recommendations for lower military budgets against Ogarkov's advice.[77]

Much evidence corroborates Akhromeev's and Varennikov's claims. For example, although Georgii Arbatov, director of the USA/Canada Institute, was engaged in a feud with his former friend Akhromeev, he confirmed that Akhromeev told the leadership that he opposed the intervention.[78] In addition, Vadim Zagladin, then deputy head of the International Department of the Central Committee, stated that except for Ustinov, the military leadership, including Ogarkov, Varennikov, and Akhromeev, was against the war. Zagladin argued that not only was the military leadership's advice ignored, but that "the majority of the leadership learned about it from the newspaper. The decision was taken by four people at the very top: Brezhnev, Ustinov, Gromyko, Andropov."[79]

Among the lower echelons of the military establishment, intervention was also seen as inadvisable. For example, General Pavlovsky, who had been sent to Kabul to assess the situation in the fall of 1979, claimed that in November 1979 he advised Ustinov not to increase the Soviet presence in Afghanistan. In response, Ustinov reportedly stressed the need to respond to PDPA infighting with a show of Soviet force.[80] According to at least two accounts, so many people in the General Staff had advised against escalation that many did not believe it would happen. When Ustinov informed a small circle of the

[75] Bruce D. Porter, "The Military Abroad: Internal Consequences of External Expansionism," in Timothy J. Colton and Thane Gustafson, eds., *Soldiers and the State: Civil-Military Relations from Brezhnev to Gorbachev* (Princeton: Princeton University Press, 1990), 307–316.

[76] Author's interview with Varennikov.

[77] See Dale R. Herspring, *The Soviet High Command 1967–1989* (Princeton: Princeton University Press, 1990), 121, 157–168.

[78] Author's interview with Arbatov.

[79] Author's interview with Zagladin. See also Chernyaev's lengthy comments corroborating Akhromeev's and Varennikov's objections which, Chernyaev claims, were set down on paper. Ustinov's response according to Chernyaev was: "Well, is it that now generals will be defining policy in the Soviet Union?' He [Ustinov] said, 'Your task is to develop specific operations and to implement what you are told.'" Greenstein and Wohlforth, *Retrospective on the End of the Cold War*, 35.

[80] Oliynik, "The troops go into Afghanistan," *Krasnaya zvezda*; Belyaev and Gromyko, "So we got into Afghanistan."

General Staff that the escalation was proceeding and raised the combat readiness of two motorized infantry divisions from the Turkmenistan Military District, many were surprised.[81]

If much of the top military leadership was against the intervention, how and why did the civilian leadership make the decision to intervene? The answer lies in the balance of power within the top political leadership as well as the balance of power *vis à vis* the military leadership. Brezhnev was in very poor health, marginally in control, and some argue, incompetent. Gromyko, a sycophant who generally followed the instructions of his bosses faithfully, was also reportedly cowed by Ustinov.[82] The minister of defense presumably had the backing of the military-industrial complex, if not the military. When the decision was taken, the military leadership, a fairly unpoliticized force in the early 1980s, went along with the decision.[83]

For much of 1979, the KGB, like the military leadership, was split in its response to PDPA requests. But in this case, the division was mainly between the KGB station head in Kabul, Boris Ivanov, who urged a positive response to the requests for increasing the Soviet presence, and KGB head Yuri Andropov, who initially opposed military force. The KGB in Kabul was reporting that Amin had such bad relations with the Islamic leadership in the country that he would be overthrown and an anti-Communist government would come into power. The KGB in Moscow opposed escalation because of the potential damage to relations with the West.[84] Perhaps ultimately as a compromise, Babrak Karmal, the KGB's closest connection in the Afghan leadership, was chosen by the Soviets as head of the PDPA.[85]

In a 1982 interview, former KGB major Vladimir Kuzichkin discussed the KGB's role in the invasion. He said that Brezhnev ignored KGB Moscow ad-

---

[81] See in Oliynik, "The troops go into Afghanistan," *Krasnaya zvezda*, comments by General Lieutenant V. Bogdanov, deputy chief of the Military Science Directorate of the General Staff. See also veterans roundtable discussion with several generals in Pashev and Kazako, "Veterans and Perestroika," 2. There, Marshal V. G. Kulikov states that "at about 24:00, Ustinov came and announced: we are crossing the border tonight. And that was all."

[82] Arbatov, *The System*, 199.

[83] Author's interviews with Arbatov and Brutents. This lack of politicization may be contrasted with the relative increase in politicization of the military in the late 1980s and the 1990s. For example, officers served in the parliament while retaining their commissions. Following the collapse of the Soviet Union, and the increasingly worsening situation in the armed forces, particularly the war in Chechnya, officers became a political force with which to be reckoned. Arbatov suggests that the late Soviet and post-Soviet politicization is at least partly a result of a break in the tacit agreement between the civilian and military leadership to refrain from denouncing one another publicly.

[84] Christopher Andrew and Oleg Gordievsky, *KGB: The Inside Story* (New York: Harper-Collins, 1990), 573–574.

[85] On the Karmal-KGB connection, see ibid., 573; Vladimir Kuzichkin interview by Frank Melville, "Coups and Killings in Kabul," *Time*, November 22, 1982, 33–34; and Arbatov, *The System*, 199.

vice on the difficulty of backing a socialist government in Afghanistan and focused more on KGB Kabul's warnings of potential Muslim revolution if the Soviets did not boost the PDPA. Kuzichkin also claims that once the decision to escalate was made, many in the General Staff wanted a troop commitment of 80,000 and to seal off the border with Pakistan.[86]

Although by December 1979 Andropov approved the escalation, he had several possible reasons for earlier opposition to a military solution in Afghanistan. He was a strong supporter of détente and recognized—where many did not—that Soviet policies in the Third World undermined East-West relations rather than increasing Soviet security and status. This view was closer to that of the new thinkers than to Ustinov's or Gromyko's.[87] While not a new thinker himself, Andropov did differ from his peers in important ways. He was more politically independent from Brezhnev than other Politburo members. His political patronage had come through the KGB and not through regional party elites; his debts were not to the party bosses in Moscow and the other major cities.[88] In addition, military solutions to foreign policy problems tended to be disadvantageous institutionally to the KGB: funds were diverted away from the KGB and the image of the Soviet Union as an aggressor was only heightened.[89]

While senior military and KGB officers advised against the escalation but were ignored, Soviet experts on Afghanistan were systematically excluded from participating in the decision making process. As a result, scholars such as Yuri Gankovsky, the senior Russian scholar on Afghanistan at the Institute of Oriental Studies (IVAN), are particularly bitter about the war and the policy making process that led to escalation. "There are great Afghan scholars and they never came to them. . . . The incompetents were giving advice."[90] Aleksei Kiva, deputy editor of *Aziia i Afrika segodnia*, and resident at the same institute, stated that "there were no consultations with people who knew Afghanistan well. Those at IVAN were shocked when the intervention oc-

[86] Melville, "Coups and Killings in Kabul." General Mahmut Gareyev, then chief of the Central Operations Department of the General Staff, writes that the military command wanted thirty to forty divisions instead of seven. "The Afghan Problem: Three Years without Soviet Troops," *International Affairs* (Moscow), March 1992, 17.

[87] Andropov's patronage of new thinkers proved particularly important in their later ability to capture certain institutional bases, such as the Central Committee. This patronage grew out of his association in the early 1960s with a number of bright independent young thinkers who formed the core of the reformist movement within the CPSU. The men who worked with Andropov included Georgii Arbatov, Alexander Bovin, and Georgii Shakhnazarov among others. Archie Brown, "Power and Policy in a Time of Leadership Transition, 1982–1988," in Archie Brown, ed., *Political Leadership in the Soviet Union* (Bloomington: Indiana University Press, 1989), 169.

[88] Amy W. Knight, *The KGB* (Boston: Unwin Hyman, 1990), 85–86, 294.

[89] Ibid., 295–296.

[90] Author's interview, November 5, 1990. See also Gankovsky interview, "A Lesson Worth Learning," 5.

curred."[91] The policy process surrounding the escalation contrasts starkly with that of the withdrawal, both in terms of the type and the number of people consulted and the nature of the discourse on the issue.[92]

As several Western scholars have documented, Soviet Third World specialists in the 1970s had reevaluated Soviet policy and were moving away from Marxist determinism toward emphasizing the role of indigenous tradition and culture in discussions of political and economic development.[93] Debates, however muffled, had begun between traditional and non-traditional thinkers.[94] The debates in many ways centered around an issue underlying Soviet decision making in Afghanistan: was it accurate to characterize resistance in Afghanistan exclusively in terms of external aggression (i.e., driven by "imperialists") or were indigenous elements responsible for much of the conflict? Not unlike American policy makers in Vietnam, how one answered this question determined one's policy prescription; the Soviet reputation for resolve, and traditional notions of imperial duty were salient and reinforcing if the opposition was considered to be driven by external forces.

The decision makers, without the input of regional experts, publicly and privately stated that resistance was driven by external force.[95] Soon after the intervention and throughout the early 1980s, aggressive images of U.S. imperialism were a core part of the leadership's justification of the intervention. The events in Afghanistan were presented as the result of an undeclared war waged by external imperialist forces on the southern border of the Soviet Union, thus necessitating a defensive escalation of involvement.[96]

In Brezhnev's speeches throughout 1980, the imagery and the word order were often identical to his first speech following the Karmal coup: the people of Afghanistan "had collided with external aggression, with rude interference from outside in their own internal affairs."[97] Brezhnev declared that

[91] Author's interview, November 28, 1990. IVAN is the Institute for Oriental Studies of the Soviet (later Russian) Academy of Sciences.

[92] Akhromeev (author's interview) made a point of contrasting the "differences in the taking of the decision to intervene and withdraw."

[93] See for example, Elizabeth K. Valkenier, *The Soviet Union and the Third World: An Economic Bind* (New York: Praeger, 1983); and Jerry F. Hough, *The Struggle for the Third World: Soviet Debates and American Options* (Washington, D.C.: Brookings, 1986).

[94] Valkenier, *The Soviet Union and the Third World*, 53, 148–149.

[95] See, for example, Politburo notes from March 17 and 18, 1979, cited in TsKhSD, Fond 89, Perechen' 25, Dokument 1, Listy 1.

[96] The analysis by Arbatov, *The System*, 196, of Soviet–Third World relations in the 1970s and early 1980s rests on the notion that important factions in the leadership wanted to take part in "the anti-imperialist struggle." He implies that the leadership believed, on some level, their own rhetoric. See also *Pravda* record of meeting with Ustinov, February 14, 1980, 2, in which he claims that the United States was using events in Afghanistan to establish military bases along the southern border of the Soviet Union.

[97] L.I. Brezhnev, "Otvety na voprosy korrespondenta gazeti 'Pravda'" (Answers to the *Pravda* correspondent's questions), *Kommunist* 2 (1980), 14.

Afghanistan was in danger of "losing its independence," and this loss posed a threat to the Soviet Union due to "the imperialist military beachhead on the southern border of our country." Brezhnev compared the United States to a wild animal: failure "to assist" the Afghan people, he claimed, "would mean throwing Afghanistan to the claws of imperialism."[98] In the years 1980–82, up to Brezhnev's death, the portrayal of events in Afghanistan remained consistent, although not often evoked: of nearly forty speeches examined between January 1980 and October 1982, he spoke about Afghanistan on less than half a dozen occasions.[99] Brezhnev's explanation of events in Afghanistan was echoed in most political commentators' articles.

This unitary response belies, however, a slightly more diverse—if not particularly vocal—body of opinion that existed in Moscow following the escalation. The best-known response was a letter of protest sent to the Central Committee in January 1980 by the Institute of the Economics of the World Socialist System (as it was then called), run by Oleg Bogomolov.[100] Compared to documents published in the late 1980s, the document is a rather mild critique of Soviet Third World policy in the spirit if not yet the words of new thinking; it argued that the Soviet Union had been wasting resources and reputation by competing with the West in the Third World, and Afghanistan was essentially the latest example of that trend. It contained, however, no categorical condemnation of the war.[101] Bogomolov said there was no reaction to the letter; he suggested that whoever received it at the Central Committee may just have filed it without showing it around.[102]

[98] Ibid., 13. See also L. I. Brezhnev, "Rech' na vstreche s izbirateliami" (Speech on meeting with the voters), *Kommunist* no. 4 (1980): 3–10; and L. I. Brezhnev, "Rech' na torzhestvennom zasedanii v Alma-Ate, posviashchennom 60-letiiu Kazakhskoi CCP i Kommunisticheskoi Partii Kazakhstana" (Speech in celebration of the meeting in Alma-Ata, consecrating sixty years of the Kazakh SSR and the Communist Party of Kazakhstan), *Kommunist* no. 13 (1980): 10–17.

[99] Sarah E. Mendelson, "Change and Continuity in Soviet Explanations of Resistance in Afghanistan: The Hand Uncovers The Wound," paper delivered at RAND Corporation Conference, "Prospects for Change in the Soviet Union," April 1988.

[100] Soon after the decision to withdraw troops had been announced, Bogomolov came forward and claimed that his institute had objected to the invasion. His comments and excerpts from the letter were printed in "Who Was Mistaken," *Literaturnaya gazeta* March 16, 1988, 10. See also O. Bogomolov, "Afghanistan as seen in 1980," *Moscow News* no. 30 (July 30–August 6, 1988).

[101] The "letter" is actually a report authored by V. Dashichev entitled "Nekotorie soobrazheniia o vneshnepoliticheskikh itogakh 70-kh godov" (Some thoughts about foreign policy results of the 1970s). The 32-page document is dated January 20, 1980. My thanks to Gavin Helf for helping me obtain the document from Bogomolov's Institute. According to Bogomolov, this was a "collective document prepared by the institute." "My task was to simply present it as the opinion of the institute and not the opinion of a specific person." Author's interview, January 2, 1991.

[102] Author's interview with Bogomolov. According to Bogomolov, the procedure for sending a letter to the leadership was to pass it to people in the Central Committee secretariat, and they would decide to whom it should be forwarded.

A veiled but notable condemnation of the war came from Georgii Arbatov's son, Alexei Arbatov, in an article entitled "The Dead End of a Policy of Strength," an exegesis on the lessons of the U.S. war in Vietnam.[103] "The lessons of the Vietnam war demonstrated the fruitlessness of a policy of strength." The U.S. war showed the problems of gradual escalation and, with each step, the increasing difficulty of withdrawal. "In retrospect the events show clearly that the damage would have been much less to American prestige . . . if the U.S. had gotten out of Vietnam sooner." Arbatov concludes: "Those who forget the lessons of history are doomed to repeat their mistakes."[104] There was no mention of Afghanistan, but the implicit analogy was a bold step for a young scholar in the early 1980s.

CONCLUSION

The introduction of Soviet troops into the Third World caused outrage in the West, hastening the end of an already unraveling détente. What compelled the Soviet leadership to escalate their involvement in Afghanistan? What was the process by which the leadership decided to send in combat troops? An analysis of the decision to intervene, as in the decision to withdraw Soviet troops, requires determining how the relative pressures of the international system, the regional situation, and domestic political bargaining contributed to the motivation, the timing, and the process of the decision.

In this chapter, I have argued that domestic political bargaining emerges as the most salient variable in explaining the decision to escalate. Although international and regional factors contributed to the decision, they were ultimately mediated by the internal balance of power, and specifically, by the role of old thinkers in the decision making process. Soviet escalation in Afghanistan was the result of a domestic political balance of power that favored traditional notions of empire and commitments to client states. Traditional conceptions of imperial duty were used to mobilize and justify the use of force in Afghanistan: failure to respond to the PDPA would have jeopardized the Soviet reputation for resolve. The most striking features of the decision making process included the centralized nature of the process and the fact that traditional Soviet conceptions of security prevailed.

The level of Soviet military involvement grew steadily through 1979. Month by month, the Soviets got more involved, more entrenched, and more invested in the survival of the PDPA. This involvement can be measured in

[103] Alexei Arbatov, "V tupike politiki sily" (The dead end of a policy of strength), *Voprosii istorii* no. 9 (1981): 104–118. Arbatov is a foreign policy expert currently at IMEMO, and a Duma deputy from the reformist Yabloko party.
[104] Ibid., 118.

TABLE 3.1
Number of Soviet Military Advisors in Afghanistan,
April 1978–Summer 1979

April 1978	350 Soviet military advisors
June 1978	650 Soviet military advisors
May 1979	3000 Soviet military advisors
Summer 1979	3500 military advisors
	4200 combat troops

Source: Based on U.S. Embassy intelligence in Kabul; cables published as *Afghanistan* (Tehran: Moslem Students Followers Imam, 1981), Vols. I and II.

many different ways: First, the level of Soviet military and technical advisers grew steadily, as shown in Table 3.1. Second, Soviets worked in all main Afghan ministries and in key positions in the Afghan defense and security apparatus.[105] Third, U.S. intelligence reported that Soviet pilots were flying combat missions throughout 1979 in the MI-24 helicopter gunships that the Soviets had provided the Afghan military. In short, Soviet advisors became increasingly involved in the repression of factions that opposed the Afghan government.[106]

In 1979, the world and indeed their country itself had looked very different to the leadership of the Soviet Union than it did in 1989 when the last Soviet troops came home. During what was later called the "period of stagnation," the economy had chugged along, the military had appeared invincible, and the party was still in control. The dominant traditional ideas of foreign policy that the leadership consistently evoked centered around the "liberation of humanity" that followed in many senses from the Soviet experience in World War II. The war in Afghanistan was initially seen by many as part of that general mission of liberation.

Despite the fact that the Soviet military got bogged down in Afghanistan, observers and participants argue that the projections for the involvement were very limited. Eduard Shevardnadze, who worked in support of the withdrawal, said that "the people who made the decision about intervening with armed force did not plan to stay in Afghanistan for any length of time, or to create the sixteenth or the seventeenth Soviet republic. They were driven, like past generations, by the concept of revolutionary solidarity and interna-

[105] *Afghanistan*, Vol. I, 136.
[106] Ibid., Vol. II, 52. On the domestic battles in the United States surrrounding the deployment of the Stingers, see Cordovez and Harrison, *Out of Afghanistan*, 194–198.

tionalism."[107] Nor did the military engage in preparations for long-term counter-insurgency warfare.[108]

What went wrong? The decision makers continued to increase Soviet military participation incrementally. In the first two months of 1980, Soviet troops had not been involved in offensive maneuvers and were mainly building and guarding garrisons. After February 1980, however, the Soviets began another stage of escalation involving offensive fighting. No single decision got the Soviets into the war; it was rather a series of decisions, taken in a context driven by traditional notions of security, that made each progressive step of escalation appear necessary and reasonable.

[107] Adam Michnik interview with Shevardnadze, in *Gazeta Wyborcza*, October 27–29, 1989, 4–5; in FBIS-SOV, October 31, 1989, 24.

[108] Roy, *The Lessons of the Soviet-Afghan War*, 17

CHAPTER FOUR.

The Groundwork for Change, 1982–1984:
Old Thinkers Rule but New Thinkers Are Mobilized

THE CENTRALIZED decision making process and the traditional conceptions of national security that led to the Soviet intervention in Afghanistan were not unique to that case. Soviet decision making in the late 1970s and early 1980s regarding all policy issues, foreign and domestic, was highly centralized and driven by old thinking. It was also corrupt. Under Brezhnev, the leadership attempted to satisfy different constituencies' competing demands. As Thane Gustafson noted, "to the Party apparatus, [Brezhnev] offered privileges and stability; to the military-industrial elite, growing budgets and professional autonomy; to the non-Russian politicians, affirmative action and a blind eye to corruption; and to the population at large, vast economic subsidies."[1] This arrangement and its attending organizational culture was challenged by Andropov shortly after Brezhnev's death in 1982.

While Andropov was not himself a new thinker, he created important permissive conditions for the institutionalization of new thinking. He encouraged the mobilization of an expert community galvanized by a belief in the need for reform. Specifically, he instructed Mikhail Gorbachev, then secretary of agriculture, and a few progressives in the party apparatus to tap into networks of critical thinkers that had existed for years.[2] Gorbachev and the reformers made a conscious effort to bring together specialists from different fields to work on pressing economic, political and social problems. The experts provided detailed and accurate information on a variety of problems that various members of the leadership recognized and acknowledged. In the 1980s, the more members of the leadership challenged the status quo—the further they got from traditional party directives—the more they relied on experts to both guide and legitimize policy change.[3]

---

[1] Thane Gustafson, *Crisis amid Plenty: The Politics of Soviet Energy under Brezhnev and Gorbachev* (Princeton: Princeton University Press, 1989), 14.

[2] For a discussion of the history of these networks, see Archie Brown, "Power and Policy in a Time of Leadership Transition, 1982–1988," in Archie Brown, ed., *Political Leadership in the Soviet Union* (Bloomington: Indiana University Press, 1989), 186; Hedrick Smith, *The New Russians* (New York: Random House, 1990), 5–16, 68–78; Elizabeth Kridl Valkenier, "New Soviet Thinking about the Third World," *World Policy Journal* 4, no. 4 (Fall 1987): 654.

[3] This pattern changed in 1990 as reform spun out of the leadership's control with increasing demands for independence from various republics and calls for marketization in the Congress of People's Deputies. See Anatoly Chernyaev, *Shest' let s Gorbachevym: po dnevnikovym*

The growth and institutionalization of a dominant expert community, in addition to personnel changes, were important variables in shifting the internal balance of power in favor of reformists. They permitted the creation in the Soviet Union of a political environment hospitable to new thinking, *perestroika*, and *glasnost*, a condition that enabled the withdrawal from Afghanistan.[4] Later, when the internal balance of power had shifted, the expert community's access to the leadership and to various resources outside traditional Soviet institutions affected the selection of certain ideas put on the policy agenda and made changes such as the withdrawal from Afghanistan possible. But before specialists commanded resources and the leadership changed the policy agenda, experts had to be mobilized: they had to be called upon to question what had been long-held assumptions about the national interest in both domestic and foreign policy. In this chapter, I discuss the initial organization of this specialist network in the years 1982 through 1984 and the network's contact with reformist members of the political leadership.

Two conditions necessary for explaining change in Soviet foreign policy were present during this period: experts had access to critical thinkers from the Party elite and the experts' ideas had salience—in fact, they resonated—to these insiders. But a third, critical variable was not yet present: new thinkers had not yet shifted the internal balance of power allowing ideas that challenged the status quo to get onto the political agenda.[5] During this period, old thinking policies, including the war in Afghanistan, continued.

I look at both the international and domestic political context in which the network was mobilized, focusing mainly on the years 1983 and 1984. I argue that the international system was highly indeterminate in bringing about reform; the mobilization of the expert community and reform in general went on despite and not because of events in the international system. In the domestic context, I focus on the leadership style of Andropov, important aspects of which Gorbachev later adopted. Specifically, I discuss in detail the expert community that Gorbachev began to assemble under Andropov's tutelage, including the different echelons within the community and the varying degrees of access to the leadership that defined each echelon.

---

zapisiam (My six years with Gorbachev: notes from a diary) (Moscow: Progress "Kultura," 1993).

[4] On how intellectuals and specialists helped change the Soviet political environment, see Brown, "Power and Policy in a Time of Leadership Transition," 190; Valkenier, "New Soviet Thinking about the Third World," 654; Allen Lynch, *The Soviet Study of International Relations* (Cambridge: Cambridge University Press, 1989), xxxvi.

[5] The third condition, the ability of the expert communities and reformers to command resources, is detailed in Chapter 5. In the Soviet case, this condition was dependent on the Gorbachev coalition's degree of political authority and did not occur until after 1986. On cases where ideas that fit are more likely to be implemented, see Kathryn Sikkink, *Ideas and Institutions: Developmentalism in Brazil and Argentina* (Ithaca: Cornell University Press, 1991); and Judith Goldstein, *Ideas, Interests and American Trade Policy* (Ithaca: Cornell University Press, 1993).

THE INTERNATIONAL CONTEXT

While the international system did not play a determining role in the move toward accommodationist foreign policy in the 1980s or the withdrawal from Afghanistan, it did affect the domestic political environment in which decisions were made. The stalemate in Afghanistan reinforced Cold War thinking about the United States that Soviet hardliners used to maintain the status quo, making the job of the reformers more difficult. The Americans consistently increased aid to the mujahideen, and U.S. foreign policy in the early 1980s was confrontational toward the Soviet Union. In addition, transnational governmental and non-governmental contact between political and intellectual elites may have influenced and bolstered new thinking, but seems to have been largely limited to arms control.[6]

The War in Afghanistan and Regional Players

The decisions to escalate made by four men in the Politburo in December 1979 rather quickly led to a stalemate in Afghanistan. Soviets troops were, from the beginning, poorly prepared, ill-equipped, and not suitably trained to fight counter-insurgency warfare. Their overly centralized command structure limited the mobility and independent decision-making ability of units.[7] The troops suffered from inaccurate estimations made by the Soviet leadership as to the ability of the Afghan army to subdue the resistance on its own and as to the ability and motivation with which the mujahideen fought.[8]

The period of 1980 through 1982 was characterized by the use of "classic large-scale armored warfare." The Soviets borrowed tactics from the European Central Front (entirely different terrain) designed to counter NATO forces (completely different opponents). In 1982, the Soviet military changed tactics and, through 1985, fought with more mobile offensive maneuvers. The pattern of the offensives involved aerial and artillery bombardment fol-

---

[6] On transnational influences in Soviet arms control policy during the 1980s, see Matthew Evangelista, "The Paradox of State Strength: Transnational Relations, Domestic Structures, and Security Policy in Russia and the Soviet Union," *International Organization* 49, no. 1 (Winter 1995): 1–38.

[7] Olivier Roy, *The Lessons of the Soviet-Afghan War*, Adelphi Paper no. 259 (London: International Institute for Strategic Studies [IISS], Summer 1991), 51–52. Roy argues that, overall, the military leadership made relatively few changes in command, tactics and weaponry throughout the war.

[8] Valentin Varennikov claimed that the General Staff in 1979 had anticipated such problems and had "categorically opposed the intervention" because they recognized that they did not know important aspects of the indigenous situation including "the tradition, the ethnic groups, the nationalities, the tribal relations, the Islamic religion." Author's interview, July 12, 1993.

lowed by motorized forces in columns pursuing targets. The worst Soviet casualties from the war came during this period, in 1984, with 2060 dead (up from 1057 in 1983). After this poor showing, the Soviets stopped the large offensives.[9]

U.S. Governmental and Non-Governmental Action, 1980–1984

Perhaps the most important response of actors in the international system to the war was to set up supply lines to the mujahideen which Soviet troops never succeeded in cutting.[10] Another significant response was to attempt to mediate the war by negotiating the withdrawal of Soviet troops. Riaz Khan, a member of the Pakistani negotiating team, enjoyed a front row seat at all the rounds of indirect talks on Afghanistan, beginning in June 1982 and continuing on through April 1988. He wrote an account of Pakistan's efforts to terminate the war in Afghanistan and to maneuver between the superpowers and the regional powers of South Asia.[11] He describes complex and often futile attempts to cut bargains with Kabul, Moscow, Washington, and Islamabad on issues such as the withdrawal of Soviet troops, guarantees of foreign non-interference, the return of refugees, and a design for an interim government after the withdrawal had been accomplished. These attempts were difficult precisely because, as even he—a negotiator—admits, the locus for the withdrawal was Soviet domestic politics and not the international context.[12]

A dual strategy for dealing with the war in Afghanistan that Riaz Khan helped formulate was adopted by Pakistan and funded by Washington. On the diplomatic front, Pakistan's foreign office applied pressure for a negotiated settlement. On the military front, President Zia ul-Haq and Pakistan's Inter-Services Intelligence Directorate (ISI) coordinated aid sent by Washington to the mujahideen; the funds in the early 1980s ranged from $280 million to $470 million by 1986.[13] The goal of this strategy was to pressure the Soviets into withdrawal and to strengthen an Islamic-based alliance between Pakistan and the mujahideen against the Soviets and India.

---

[9] Roy, *The Lessons of the Soviet-Afghan War*, 18–19.

[10] Ibid., 20. The supplies included weapons from the United States, Egypt, Saudi Arabia, and Iran. As the war went on, the quality of the weapons improved. By 1984, the mujahideen were receiving AK-47s, heavy machine guns, and rockets. The role of heat-seeking anti-aircraft "Stinger" missiles sent in 1986 is discussed in Chapter 5.

[11] Riaz M. Khan, *Untying the Afghan Knot: Negotiating Soviet Withdrawal* (Durham, N.C.: Duke University Press, 1991). For another account, see Diego Cordovez and Selig S. Harrison, *Out of Afghanistan: The Inside Story of the Soviet Withdrawal* (New York: Oxford University Press, 1995).

[12] Ibid., 92–165. Khan provides an extensive discussion of negotiation details and the positions held by different countries from 1982 to 1988.

[13] Khan, *Untying the Afghan Knot*, 88.

U.S. policy toward Afghanistan involved the largest covert operation since World War II. Initial operations began in 1980 under President Jimmy Carter and were aimed primarily at harassing the Soviets and not forcing a withdrawal. Through the CIA, the United States channeled funds, weapons, and support to the ISI, which carried out the day-to-day operations. After January 1981, U.S. involvement escalated and CIA director William Casey himself handled the policy.[14]

In 1984, U.S. intelligence reported that the Soviets had changed tactics and were using more mobile helicopter assaults. U.S. intelligence argued that "Soviet hard-liners were pushing a plan to attempt to win the Afghan war within two years." In October of that year, Casey went to Islamabad to help plan strategy. His response to the intelligence report on the change in tactics was to suggest taking the war into Soviet territory. "Casey wanted to ship subversive propaganda through Afghanistan to the Soviet Union's predominantly Muslim southern republics." In March 1985, as Gorbachev came to power in Moscow, the United States escalated covert action with National Security Council Directive 166: U.S. policy goals shifted from harassment to defeat of the Soviets.[15] Soviet decision makers were not unaware of the general tenor of U.S. policy toward Afghanistan. In a November 1986 Politburo meeting, Gromyko reported to Gorbachev that the United States was not interested in an end to the war but in seeing it "drag on."[16]

Beyond the war in Afghanistan, U.S. policy toward the Soviet Union was notably aggressive. In March 1983, President Ronald Reagan delivered both his "evil empire" speech, in which the Soviet Union was characterized as "the focus of evil in the modern world," and his speech introducing the Strategic Defense Initiative (SDI).[17] It is the SDI initiative that many American observers claim forced the Soviet political leadership to reassess their ability to compete militarily, and to shift to a policy of accommodation.[18] However, ev-

---

[14] Steve Coll details some of the CIA's actions in two articles based on interviews with Pakistani intelligence officers and senior Western officials. See Steve Coll, "Anatomy of a Victory: CIA's Covert Afghan War," *Washington Post*, July 19 and 20, 1992. For a comprehensive picture, see the declassified U.S. government documents gathered by the National Security Archive, *Afghanistan: The Making of U.S. Policy, 1973–1990* (Alexandria, Va.: Chadwyck-Healey, 1990).

[15] Coll, "Anatomy of a Victory," July 19, 1992.

[16] "Zasedanie Politburo TzK KPSS" (Session of the Politburo CC CPSU marked "Top Secret"), Fond 89, November 13, 1986, 26. Valentin Varennikov (author's interview) also expressed this opinion, stating that the U.S. position made ending the war more difficult, not easier. "They [the Americans] said, 'We also want to be involved in the process,' but they did nothing. On the contrary, the opposition began to receive more and more means for conducting military activities."

[17] Don Oberdorfer, *The Turn* (New York: Poseidon, 1991), 22–25.

[18] See, for example, comments by Paul Nitze and George Shultz in Fred I. Greenstein and William C. Wohlforth, eds., *Retrospective on the End of the Cold War*, Monograph Series No. 6 (Center of International Studies, Princeton University, 1994), 13.

idence drawn from Soviet decision makers and observers suggests that SDI was, at a maximum, harmful for the reformers, and at a minimum, irrelevant to changes in policy. Georgii Arbatov, director of the Institute of USA and Canada (ISKAN), responding to George Bush's statement at the 1992 Republican National Convention that the arms build-up under Reagan brought about the end of the Cold War, argued that "It put pressure on the Soviet military. The Reagan policy helped sustain the perception by our hardliners of a besieged country."[19] Alexander Bessmertnykh, former Soviet foreign minister, has commented that the importance of SDI in an explanation for reform should be replaced by an appreciation of the role of the economy in change in policy:

> When Gorbachev came into power in Moscow, the economic statistics already indicated that the economy was doing not so good. So when you [American participants] were talking about SDI and arms control, the economic element . . . in my view, [was] the number one preoccupation of Gorbachev.[20]

Anatoly Basistov, a senior ballistic missile defense expert at the Institute of Scientific Research who knew many in the military leadership, recounts that he was given a copy of Reagan's speech the day after it was delivered and asked by the General Staff to assess the probability of deploying an anti-ballistic missile defense system such as SDI. He claims that he and all the specialists that he knew found it "ridiculous." Rather than being intimidated, they dismissed it as improbable.[21] While these comments in and of themselves do not disprove a causal role of SDI in the reform process, they—along with Soviet reactions to other U.S. policies—form a consistent body of evidence that SDI and other U.S. foreign policy initiatives were indeterminate in the shift to new thinking.

Some western scholars argue that transnational relations encompassing non-governmental actors played a role in the shift to reform. For example, Matthew Evangelista argues that contact between members of the Soviet and American arms control elite influenced Soviet policy on SDI and nuclear testing. Organized conferences such as the Dartmouth meetings and the Pugwash movement brought members of the Soviet elite, reformist or not, face-

---

[19] Georgii Arbatov, UPI interview, August 30, 1992. Arbatov had made the same comment in author's interview, January 4, 1991.

[20] Greenstein and Wohlforth, *Retrospective on the End of the Cold War*, 17.

[21] Author's interview with Anatoly Basistov, Stanford University, December 7, 1992. Christopher Andrew and Oleg Gordievsky, *KGB: The Inside Story* (New York: Harper and Collins, 1990), 590–591, claim that SDI was understood as impractical by the KGB. Evidence suggests that Soviet responses to SDI were mixed. See Mary C. Fitzgerald, *Soviet Views on SDI*, Carl Beck Papers No. 601, Center for Russian and East European Studies, University of Pittsburgh, May 1987, 39–40, cited in Evangelista, "The Paradox of State Strength," 16.

to-face with alternative points of view.[22] Other observers argue, however, that these meetings were tools of Soviet propaganda.[23]

That these meetings were allowed to occur meant that they had approval from the Soviet leadership. Evangelista makes the argument that Gorbachev used state strength to permit Soviet experts' access to critical discussions on the risks of nuclear war. (These meetings had of course been occurring since 1957, long before Gorbachev came to power.) Whatever the reason for the willingness of previous Soviet leaders or Gorbachev to allow Soviet scientific participation, such transnational contacts were rare and highly controlled. Contact may or may not have made a difference in arms control, but given the general opacity of the Soviet state, these contacts were not widespread in other issue-areas. Any influence that they did have on policies seemed to have been significantly mediated by domestic politics.

THE DOMESTIC CONTEXT

Reform in the Soviet Union, I argue, stemmed from how decision makers responded to conditions inside the Soviet Union and not the international environment. Change in foreign policy derived from the success of leadership strategies involving reformist ideas and experts, coalition building, and personnel changes in altering the internal balance of power. Before power shifted, however, the challengers to the status quo had to make known to the elite the real social, political, and economic conditions inside the country. Andropov sponsored such an effort and, however improbable, this former KGB director became an important patron of reform in the Soviet Union.

Andropov's constituency and therefore his political allegiances were different. Chernenko, Brezhnev's aide, inherited the party bureaucrats, while Andropov was connected to the technocrats, the experts in the institutions, and the KGB.[24] Because of this different legacy, Andropov was politically ca-

---

[22] For a discussion of these conferences, see Evangelista, "The Paradox of State Strength," 12–13. For a Russian account, see Georgii Arbatov, *The System* (New York: Random House, 1992), 310–311. For an argument on transnational influence on arms control during an earlier period, see Emanuel Adler, "The Emergence of Cooperation: National Epistemic Communities and the International Evolution of the Ideas of Nuclear Arms Control," in Peter M. Haas, ed., "Knowledge, Power and International Policy Coordination," a special issue of *International Organization* 46, no. 1 (Winter 1992): 101–145.

[23] See comments by Frank J. Gaffney, Jr., former Reagan administration official, director of the Washington-based Center for Security Policy, in Richard W. Stevenson, "Peace Prize Goes to A-Bomb Scientist Who Turned Critic," *New York Times*, October 14, 1995.

[24] Dusko Doder and Louise Branson, *Gorbachev: Heretic in the Kremlin* (New York: Viking, 1990), 42. See also Amy W. Knight, *The KGB* (Boston: Unwin Hyman, 1990), 90, on Chernenko's inheriting Brezhnev's base.

pable of instituting an anti-corruption campaign that directly threatened the interests of party bureaucrats.[25]

Andropov mixed old and new thinking. Given his career, he cannot be considered a "liberal."[26] He had been the Soviet ambassador to Hungary during the invasion in 1956.[27] As head of the KGB, he had increased measures against dissidents. Yet in a significant way he was a sponsor of new thinking.[28] This occurred perhaps by accident beginning with his return from Hungary in 1957, when he ran the department at the Central Committee responsible for relations with socialist countries. There, for ten years, he gathered around him people who would later become influential members of the Gorbachev coalition.[29] According to Arbatov, Andropov fostered the idea of working with the intelligentsia; he felt that it was not wise to treat all scientists and writers as potential spies.[30]

During Andropov's brief rule, from October 1982 to February 1984, there was a break with some, but not all, of Brezhnev's policies. The former head of the KGB waged an anti-corruption campaign that directly threatened Brezhnev's cronies. Andropov's domestic agenda, however, never encompassed the type of economic or political change initiated under Gorbachev. In foreign policy issues as well, while Andropov distanced himself slightly from Brezhnev, he did not adopt policies that approached the "new thinking" under Gorbachev.[31] U.S.-Soviet relations continued to be extremely tense, deadlocked over numerous issues, including Afghanistan. On policy toward the Third World, Andropov called for less interference in the internal affairs of other countries. Andropov "disavowed radical activism by emphasizing limited Soviet support to revolution, although he did not question Soviet internationalist duty to aid national liberation and progressive forces."[32]

---

[25] Knight, *The KGB*, 91.

[26] On his career, see Amy W. Knight, "Andropov: Myths and Realities," *Survey* 28, no. 1 (Spring 1984): 22–44.

[27] Georgii Arbatov, "Iz nedavnego proshlogo" (From the recent past), *Znamya* no. 10 (October 1990): 211, 214, claims that Andropov developed a "Hungarian complex" which manifested itself in extreme caution; he understood the need for serious reform but was very cautious in implementing it.

[28] See also Natalya Gevorkyan's interview with KGB Major General Oleg Kalugin on sponsorship, *Moscow News* no. 25 (1990): 13.

[29] These included Arbatov, Alexander Bovin, Fedor Burlatsky, Oleg Bogomolov, and Georgii Shakhnazarov. See Archie Brown, "The Foreign Policy Making Process," in Curtis Keeble, ed., *The Soviet State: Domestic Roots of Soviet Foreign Policy* (London: Gower, 1985), 198.

[30] Arbatov, "From the recent past," 212.

[31] Knight, *The KGB*, 295–296, argues that Andropov was, however, one of the first decision makers to question Soviet policy toward the Third World, East-West relations, and the economic burdens incurred by foreign policy.

[32] Celeste A. Wallander, "Third-World Conflict in Soviet Military Thought: Does the 'New Thinking' Grow Prematurely Grey?" *World Politics* 42, no. 1 (1989): 36.

Andropov, Chernenko, and the War in Afghanistan

Leadership speeches, declassified Kremlin documents, and interviews offer a complex account of how Andropov responded to and thought of the war in Afghanistan. On the one hand, the dominant public image of "the hand of imperialism" continued to characterize the official Soviet version of the war. This image was accompanied by boilerplate comments on the progress of Afghanistan's development as a socialist country and on the success of the Soviet and Afghan troops in repelling U.S. "imperialists." On the other hand, much evidence suggests that Andropov was aware a military solution to the war was not possible, but that he was politically unable to initiate a withdrawal.

In approximately 19 speeches by Andropov from November 1982 through January 1984, Afghanistan was mentioned explicitly once and implicitly once.[33] In April 1983, in an interview with *Der Spiegel*, Afghanistan was referred to as "the Afghan problem," an oblique reference to the stalemate. But, as if to say that there was nothing substantially new or different about the situation in that country, he then directed the reader to the words of Brezhnev, and repeated the ubiquitous phrase "external interference" to explain the nature of the resistance.[34]

In an article in the *Washington Post*, based on declassified Kremlin documents, Moscow correspondent Michael Dobbs has claimed that Andropov "had no intention of conceding defeat" in Afghanistan, although it was clear to him by 1982 that a quick victory was not possible. Dobbs quotes Andropov as saying at a meeting on March 10, 1983, that "miracles do not happen. We may sometimes get angry at the Afghan [government], and accuse them of inconsistency and delay. But let us remember our own struggle with the *Basmachi*."[35] He essentially rejected the political solution or compromise that was being suggested by Gromyko.

Dobbs is correct that Andropov supported the war publicly, and he may have done so in front of certain colleagues. The story is more nuanced, however. That the withdrawal from Afghanistan did not occur during this period

---

[33] Sarah E. Mendelson, "Change and Continuity in Soviet Explanations of Resistance in Afghanistan: The Hand Uncovers the Wound," paper delivered at RAND Corporation Conference, "Prospects for Change in the Soviet Union," April 1988.

[34] Y. Andropov, "Otvety Zhurnali *Shpigel*" (Answers to the journal *Der Spiegel*), *Kommunist* no. 7 (1983): 15–16.

[35] Michael Dobbs, "Withdrawing from Afghanistan: Start of Empire's Unraveling," *Washington Post*, November 16, 1992. This quotation may be found in "Zasedanie Politburo TsK KPSS" (Session of the Politburo CC CPSU), March 10, 1983, 13. The *Basmachi* (roughly, "raiders") were Turkestani insurgents who fought in the 1920s against Soviet attempts to control Central Asia. Martha B. Olcott, "The Basmachi or Freemen's Revolt in Turkestan 1918–1924," *Soviet Studies* 33, no. 3 (July 1981): 352–369.

should not be taken as evidence that the war was viewed favorably by all. According to officials and experts in Moscow, some members of the political leadership, among them Andropov and Gorbachev, and many in the specialist network believed long before February 1988 that the situation in Afghanistan could not be solved by military means.[36] Evidence suggests that Andropov himself was especially influential in the evolution of this attitude; a critical policy review of the war in Afghanistan began at the highest level during his chairmanship.[37]

Both Sergei Akhromeev and Georgii Arbatov claim that Andropov, while not a new thinker, came to the conclusion in 1983 that a military solution to the war in Afghanistan was not possible. Both men, who knew Andropov well, argue that for political as well as personal reasons, he could not initiate the withdrawal. They claimed that at that time, Andropov had neither the physical strength nor the time; once he embarked on the anti-corruption campaign, he had little energy for anything else.[38]

[36] Author's interviews with Sergei Akhromeev (former chief of the Soviet armed forces), January 3, 1991; Fikryat Tabeev (Soviet ambassador to Afghanistan, 1980–86; former deputy chairman of committee on international affairs, Supreme Soviet, USSR), December 4, 1990; Arbatov; Vadim Zagladin (former director, Information Department, Central Committee [CCID]), December 12, 1990. Arbatov told Gorbachev that he was against the war and claims that Alexander Yakovlev and Evgeni Primakov also did so. Vitali Korotich, former editor of *Ogonëk*, says he "knows" that Yakovlev was very much against the war and that they talked about it many times. Author's interview with Korotich, December 14, 1990 and January 9, 1991. On December 27, 1991, Alexander Yakovlev publicly discussed Gorbachev's early opposition to the war and both men's attempts to get the withdrawal on the political agenda. See the television interview on December 27, 1991; Central Television, First Channel; Foreign Broadcast Information Service-Soviet Union (FBIS), December 31, 1991, 3–5. Doder and Branson, *Gorbachev*, 46, claim that on Gorbachev's trip to Canada in May 1983, in an off-the-record comment, Gorbachev told his host Eugene Whelan, then the Canadian agricultural minister, that the invasion of Afghanistan had been a mistake.

[37] In May 1989, Arbatov also told Janice Gross Stein about this policy review. For a general discussion, see Stein, "Cognitive Psychology and Political Learning: Gorbachev as an Uncommitted Thinker and Motivated Learner," in Richard Ned Lebow and Thomas Risse-Kappen, eds., *International Relations Theory and the Transformation of the International System* (New York: Columbia University Press, 1995).

[38] Author's interviews with Akhromeev and Arbatov. Akhromeev claimed that "when [Andropov] became general secretary, he was extremely sick, and he had neither the strength nor the time to decide the Afghan problem. I know this very well. He wanted to do this but he couldn't. Life did not leave him time for it." (Author's interview.) Zagladin makes similar remarks in Cordovez and Harrison, *Out of Afghanistan*, 96. Georgii Arbatov (author's interview) said that "even Andropov understood that withdrawal was necessary. Of course it was difficult that he himself participated in the decision making, but he was a smart person." Arbatov conceded that although "Marshal Akhromeev is not my great friend, we talked then about the war, and he said then that there was no military solution but only a political one. Akhromeev said this even to the leadership. The question was how to do it [withdraw]. And such people, like myself, attempted to ease the decision by looking for contacts with Afghan's neighbors, with the opposition."

According to Fikryat Tabeev, the Soviet ambassador to Afghanistan (1980–86), Andropov understood that withdrawal was necessary but would be difficult. "Andropov was not against the withdrawal. It was simply not possible to do it [snaps fingers]: bring in troops and then without warning . . . withdraw troops."[39] Oleg Bogomolov, director of the Institute of International Economic and Political Research, also states that the "process" of withdrawal began under Andropov.

> He already understood that it was necessary to reconsider this policy. . . . But he understood that it was very complicated. It touche[d] the interests of the ruling elite and to come to this quickly in a definitive way was impossible; it demanded a defined time-period. And that which he began, Gorbachev continued.[40]

The political environment had to be transformed in order for a withdrawal to take place.

Diego Cordovez, the UN representative to the talks on Afghanistan in Geneva, stated that in a meeting with Andropov on March 28, 1983, the Soviet leader made it clear to him that he understood the need to withdraw troops. "He ended [the meeting] by holding up his hand and pulling down his fingers, one by one, as he listed the reasons why the Soviet Union felt a solution had to be found soon to the Afghan problem." These reasons apparently included external as well as internal issues.[41] According to Riaz Khan, the Pakistanis in Geneva detected, around this time, some of the first rumblings of the long, withdrawing roar that later transformed Soviet foreign policy. Pakistani negotiators were briefly optimistic in the spring of 1983 because of what seemed to be a slightly accommodationist shift, however subtle, in the Soviet approach to the war.[42]

Andropov did not want or need to withdraw necessarily for the same reasons as Gorbachev. Andropov may have felt that the war had to end for strategic reasons unconnected to domestic policy: that fighting a war on the southern flank was a waste of resources when major battles with the main opponent were more likely to come on the Central Front in Europe. These reasons did not include a changed conception of the international system but involved

---

[39] Author's interview with Tabeev.

[40] Author's interview with Bogomolov, January 2, 1991. In a similar vein, Nodari Simoniia claims: "At the time, many people said to me that when the decision was taken about Afghanistan, [Andropov] had in the beginning great doubt. . . . [But] it was impossible to vote against it. You must understand that he may not have agreed but there was nothing he could do." Author's interview with Nodari Simoniia, deputy director of IMEMO, October 18, December 21, 1990.

[41] Selig Harrison, "Inside the Afghan Talks," *Foreign Policy* 72 (Fall 1988): 42.

[42] Khan, *Untying the Afghan Knot*, 106–107. Michel Tatu reports that as early as mid-December 1982, the Soviet press printed for the first time a relatively positive discussion of the negotiations going on in Geneva. *Pravda*, December 16, 1982, cited in Michel Tatu, "U.S.-Soviet Relations: A Turning Point," *Foreign Affairs* 61, no. 3 (May/June 1983): 603.

specific judgments about the war itself. Andropov's desire to end the war appears to have been, at least, not inconsistent with later motivations for withdrawal.

There is almost no information available about the attitudes of Andropov's successor, Chernenko, toward the war in Afghanistan. In thirty-five speeches, he never explicitly referred to Afghanistan.[43] However, given his close proximity to Brezhnev on most policy issues, it is possible to guess that he was in general agreement about the need for Soviet troops to fight in Afghanistan.

Chernenko had written about Afghanistan while Brezhnev was general secretary. In September, 1980, he claimed that:

> The events in Afghanistan were perceived and used in the United States as a pretext for departure from the policy of détente. . . . Now it is obvious to all that exactly the outside aggression against the revolutionary Afghanistan perpetuated by counter-revolutionary bands, which were organized and are armed and encouraged by American special services joined with the Peking militarists, made Soviet assistance necessary in defending the Afghan people's gains. In fact Washington, with the assistance of Peking, provoked the "Afghan crisis" in order to finally gain a free hand in the policy of anti-détente.[44]

Chernenko's description of the war was identical to that of Brezhnev, with resistance classified as the product of the hand of imperialism.

Several years later, in September of 1984, while addressing members of the Portuguese Communist Party, Chernenko compared the foreign policy of the United States with that of Nazi Germany. In one sentence, he referred to the "aggressive acts of the USA," while in the next, to the fact that "our people have not forgotten how, in June 1941, Fascist Germany . . . attack[ed] our country." The point of these comments was apparently that caution and vigilance with regard to the United States was necessary in order to avoid what had happened with Germany.[45]

These statements are consistent with the "old thinking" tone of Chernenko's interregnum of February 1984 through March 1985, and are characteristic of the reaction by Soviet hard liners to U.S. policy. Stagnation, however, had reached such proportions that momentum for reform was increasing.[46] Despite the ostensible reinforcement of the status quo under Chernenko, the efforts by Gorbachev and others at gathering and mobilizing groups of critical experts and generating reformist ideas continued.

[43] Mendelson, "Change and Continuity in Soviet Explanations of Resistance in Afghanistan."

[44] Konstantin Chernenko, "Trust and Cooperation among Peoples—A Guarantee of Peace and Security," *International Affairs* (Moscow) no. 9 (1980): 7.

[45] Konstantin Chernenko, "Khorosho znat' i ponimat' drug druga" (It's good to know and understand one another), *Kommunist* no. 14 (1984): 12–13.

[46] Arbatov, "From the recent past," 221.

The Andropov-Gorbachev Connection

Much has been written about Andropov's mentoring relationship to Gorbachev.[47] Two interrelated aspects of this relationship played a critical role in Gorbachev's political success in the mid 1980s and affected political, economic, and social reform in the Soviet Union. First, Gorbachev received important promotions in the party organization with Andropov's help. Second, these promotions brought Gorbachev into contact with reformist thinkers. The combination of these aspects helped Gorbachev situate himself politically so that, in the years 1982 through 1985, he was able to gather together like-minded experts and politicians to reconsider, in essence, the state of the union. This positioning helped Gorbachev become general secretary and later to wage political battles against old thinkers.

In Gorbachev's early career as first secretary of the Stavropol city party committee, he did not have much contact with the political leadership in Moscow. But in 1970, as first secretary of the provincial committee, he became a member of the Central Committee (CC) and began traveling to Moscow a few times a year for CC meetings. More important perhaps, because of his region's hot springs and other natural amenities he played host to members of the leadership on vacation.[48]

In 1978, he became secretary of agriculture, a position that allowed him to move to Moscow. In addition to this job, under Andropov's leadership in 1982, Gorbachev became the senior personnel secretary of the CC, an extremely important position that enabled him to select regional party secretaries.[49] The ability to influence these appointments meant that he could sponsor local politicians who were likely to share his outlook. In return, these first secretaries, who had some power and autonomy in their respective regions, could potentially help a government headed by Gorbachev to carry out reforms.[50]

Gorbachev inherited several policies and practices from Andropov, the most important of which was seeking critical appraisals from a broad range of specialists not wedded to traditional Party dogmas. As secretary of agriculture, Gorbachev followed the example set by Andropov when he was a sec-

[47] See Mikhail Gorbachev, *Memoirs* (New York: Doubleday, 1996), 95–96; Doder and Branson, *Gorbachev*, 35–39; Smith, *The New Russians*, 62–78; Jerry F. Hough, *Russia and the West: Gorbachev and the Politics of Reform* (New York: Touchstone, 1988), 39–42.

[48] Doder and Branson, *Gorbachev*, 37–39.

[49] Hough, *Russia and the West,* 151; Doder and Branson, *Gorbachev*, 30, 52; Gavin Helf, "Gorbachev and the New Soviet Prefects: Soviet Regional Politics 1982–1988 in Historical Perspective," in *Analyzing the Gorbachev Era: Working Papers of the Students of the Berkeley-Stanford Program in Soviet Studies* (Berkeley and Stanford, Calif.: University of California and Stanford University, 1989), 10–12.

[50] Boris Yeltsin, appointed regional party secretary of Sverdlovsk at the end of Brezhnev's career, benefited from this type of sponsorship. See Boris Yeltsin, *Against the Grain* (New York: Summit, 1990).

retary in the CC of surrounding himself with bright, critical thinkers. He worked with and promoted many of the CC advisory group that had been associated with Andropov in the early 1960s.[51] This group had been, one participant observed, "very unusual" precisely because it had been composed of "young party intellectuals, perhaps the first ever in the Central Committee."[52] Gorbachev contacted these people and, in a sense, revived the group.

Gorbachev went beyond Andropov in his consultative activities; he also tapped into groups of experts that had been around for years and whose ideas and writings were often so controversial that the experts had been restricted in their professional mobility. Most important, Gorbachev was in contact with the directors and the top scholars of the major economic institutes. In fact, Gorbachev's vision of reform emerged during this period as a result of his study of local conditions and not of foreign policy.[53]

POWER AND KNOWLEDGE IN THE SOVIET UNION

The history of power and knowledge in the Soviet Union was characterized by experts' dependence on the political leadership for sponsorship, professionalization, and influence. Competing and often contradictory forces—science, ideology and the state—existed together uneasily. To understand the changes in leadership-expert relations in the mid-1980s, one must have a sense of this history and its various stages.[54]

[51] See Brown, "The Foreign Policy Making Process."

[52] Fedor Burlatsky interview cited in Stephen F. Cohen and Katrina vanden Heuvel, *Voices of Glasnost: Interviews with Gorbachev's Reformers* (New York: W. W. Norton, 1989), 176. Arbatov, "From the recent past," 208, indicates that this was a formative experience in his own relationship with Andropov. When Andropov became chairman of the KGB, he continued to call Arbatov, sometimes two or three times a month. When Andropov went back to the Central Committee in May 1982, they met often.

[53] Gorbachev was also familiar with domestic issues as party chief in Stavropol. Author's interviews with Zagladin; Valeri Sidorov (former aide to Alexander Yakovlev and Evgeni Primakov), November 15, 1990; Arbatov; and Elizaveta Dyuk, assistant to Tatyana Zaslavskaya, National Center of Public Opinion, November 27, 1990. Doder and Branson, *Gorbachev*, 46, claim that Gorbachev began to learn about foreign affairs only in preparation for his June 1983 visit to Canada. According to Akhromeev (author's interview), Gorbachev had no real relationship with the military prior to 1985. He had not served in the military, and while he had some limited contact with them while working in Stavropol, the contact was not instrumental in forming his "worldview" (*mirovozzrenie*). "He had his party and economics work. He was busy with other things," Akhromeev explained.

[54] Indeed, to understand the relation of experts to policy making in post-Soviet Russia, one needs to know this history; "the Academy" struggled to emerge as an independent force generating criticism, which was a precondition for the development of a civil society. See Oksana Antonenko, "New Russian Analytical Centers and Their Role in Political Decisionmaking," Strengthening Democratic Institutions Project, Kennedy School of Government, February 1996.

Professionalization—the establishment of institutes, funding of research, and publication of journals—occurred in the 1960s for those branches of social science encouraged by the leadership.[55] For example, the Academy of Sciences (ANSSSR), an organization with strong ties to the Party and in control of many resources, considered economics a science worth study, while sociology was tainted with "bourgeois" characteristics.[56] Political science as a subject existed only in terms of Marxist-Leninist political theory.[57]

A large literature traces specialists' roles in policy making from the 1950s through the 1970s; within this literature there are debates.[58] Some scholars looking at the 1960s argue that specialists had minimal influence on policy agendas.[59] Looking at the same period, other scholars argue that specialists played some role in policy making but largely as mobilizers of policies already determined by the political leadership.[60]

A third and larger group of scholars considers a slightly different period, the late 1960s to mid-1970s. During that period, specialists experienced some degree of influence; ultimately, the leadership could ignore or overrule the

[55] My discussion is restricted to experts in the social sciences—the types of experts who mainly made up the expert community mobilized by Gorbachev and his cohort—and not experts from the hard sciences. In fields like nuclear physics, scientists had enjoyed a high level of professionalization beginning in the years following World War II. See Andrei Sakharov, *Memoirs* (New York: Knopf, 1990); and David Holloway, *Stalin and the Bomb: The Soviet Union and Atomic Energy, 1939–1956* (New Haven: Yale University Press, 1994).

[56] Sociology was not considered a "legitimate" social science until Gorbachev's promotion of Tatyana Zaslavskaya to head the National Center of Public Opinion in 1988. Zaslavskaya interview in Cohen and vanden Heuvel, *Voices of Glasnost*, 115–139. In post-Soviet Russia, in an effort to help develop formerly neglected social science fields, particularly sociology and political science, Western foundations such as MacArthur and Ford have disbursed millions of dollars in the newly independent states to sponsor social science research.

[57] See Archie Brown, "Political Science in the Soviet Union: A New Stage of Development?" *Soviet Studies* 36, no. 3 (July 1984): 317–344. Institutes studying foreign countries were set up in the 1950s and 1960s. See Oded Eran, *Mezhdunarodniki: An Assessment of Professional Expertise in the Making of Soviet Foreign Policy* (Tel Aviv: Turtledove, 1979); Elizabeth K. Valkenier, *The Soviet Union and the Third World: An Economic Bind* (New York: Praeger, 1983), 41–46. The Institute of World Economics and International Relations (IMEMO) was founded in 1956; it replaced the Institute of World Economy that had been shut down after World War II by Stalin. The Institute of the Economics of the World Socialist System was founded in 1960. The Latin American Institute was reorganized in 1961. The African Institute started in 1962. The Oriental Institute (IVAN) began in 1966; the USA and Canada Institute (ISKAN) in 1967. Institutes studying the Third World, like IVAN, tended to command smaller resources and were generally not as plush as institutes such as ISKAN that studied capitalist countries.

[58] The following discussion draws on Peter Solomon's analysis in *Soviet Criminologists and Criminal Policy: Specialists in Policy Making* (New York: Columbia University Press, 1978), 1–8.

[59] See, for example, Robert Conquest, *Power and Policy in the USSR: A Study in Soviet Dynastics* (New York: St. Martin's Press, 1961).

[60] See, for example, Zbigniew Brzezinski and Samuel P. Huntington, *Political Power: USA/USSR* (New York: Viking Press, 1964).

advice of the specialist. Experts could not force issues onto the political agenda without the consent of the leadership.[61]

The period 1982 to 1985 is an important time of transition in the relationship between power and knowledge in the Soviet Union. The relationship retained some constraints from earlier stages: for example, experts needed sponsorship in order to affect the political agenda. But the nature of the consulting was different: the needs and interests of the reformist thinkers in the leadership and certain experts converged around issues much more than in earlier periods. The issues were so controversial—from slightly reformist to radically reformist—that the necessity of mutual support was very high. The support flowed two ways: from the leadership, the specialists got attention and, ultimately, resources with which to affect the political climate. From the specialists, the leadership got legitimation and guidance, no longer perfunctory matters as policies moved further away from traditional party directives.[62]

The change in the relationship between knowledge and power was highly threatening to conservative members of the political elite. A scandal involving the Institute of World Economics and International Relations (IMEMO) in 1982 just before Brezhnev's death suggests that some people in the Central Committee felt that the institutes were already too influential in the policy process and had given bad—accommodationist—advice on détente. Critics of IMEMO argued that détente formally collapsed (after the intervention in Afghanistan, which hardliners argued had been a necessary response to pleas from a client state), because the Americans had never wanted it to work in the first place. The Soviet government had pursued détente, the hardliners implied, because institutes such as IMEMO had urged the government to go along with it. Some young scholars at IMEMO were accused of being

---

[61] See for example, Franklyn Griffiths, "A Tendency Analysis of Soviet Policy-Making," in H. G. Skilling and Franklyn Griffiths, eds., *Interest Groups in Soviet Politics* (Princeton: Princeton University Press, 1971). Valkenier, *The Soviet Union and the Third World*, 56–62, found that divergence of opinion among Third World experts existed on a number of issues and that the opinions eventually—in some cases a decade later—affected the political environment. She argues that experts were used in more pragmatic and less ideological ways, and as examples cites the following: Georgii Mirsky, head of the "Less Developed Countries" department at IMEMO in 1976, was not optimistic about prospects of socialism. Karen Brutents at CCID was also gloomy about the situation in the Third World from the point of view of Soviet foreign policy. Viktor Kremenyuk, deputy director of ISKAN, stated that "since the 1970s the institutes (ISKAN, IMEMO, IVAN) have all been involved in foreign policy but in a marginal way." The institutes were involved in sending reports (*zapiski*) that were "very polite and restrained" and consulting for the Central Committee. Author's interview with Kremenyuk, November 1, 1990. Zagladin (author's interview) corroborates Kremenyuk's statement. He claims that "there was always contact" after the 1970s between the leadership and the specialists but that it did not take on political significance until the early 1980s.

[62] Brown, "Political Science in the Soviet Union," 338, argues that the role of specialists "illustrates how great [was] the oversimplification involved in viewing the USSR as an extreme monolith in which policy and doctrine flow[ed] only in one direction—from the top downwards."

anti-communist, and a special commission was set up to review the work of the institute.[63]

Specialists were indeed more and more voicing opinions on policy issues, but the attacks were misguided: increasingly powerful members of the political leadership were the important forces behind accommodationism. Experts were relied upon more heavily and provided "liberal" advice because certain members of the leadership had begun to question the status quo. The more the reformists in the leadership questioned, the more critical the advice to altering the internal balance of power became.[64]

In the years before Gorbachev became general secretary, reform-minded members of the Central Committee, with Andropov's blessing and Chernenko's benign neglect, cultivated reformist analyses and a consultative approach to policy making. According to Vadim Zagladin, a former advisor to Gorbachev who worked for many years in the Central Committee, Gorbachev had extensive contact with specialists prior to 1985. Specifically, Andropov commissioned a series of reports on domestic and foreign policy issues and put Gorbachev in charge of them.

> Already in 1983 there was a decision to conduct a careful analysis of the domestic situation of the country. . . . Then it was done by a commission that studied the situation inside the country and foreign policy and there were about 100 reports put together, consultations with specialists. . . . Gorbachev led this work. Many people worked on it. This decision was taken under Andropov. They worked . . . nothing changed under Chernenko, and by 1985 there was an enormous packet of findings.[65]

Gorbachev himself indicated that in the early 1980s, he, with the help of Nikolay Ryzhkov, then the head of the economic department of the Central Committee (appointed by Andropov), solicited approximately 110 reports from intellectuals on the need for change in the Soviet Union. Speaking to a group of scientists and cultural figures in January 1989, Gorbachev acknowledged that while all of *perestroika* had not been formulated prior to March

---

[63] According to the editor of IMEMO's journal, German Diligensky, "certain people" in Brezhnev's cohort disapproved of consultations with IMEMO, and made life difficult for the scholars at IMEMO, arresting some on trumped-up charges. Author's interview, December 19, 1990. See also Jeffrey T. Checkel, *Ideas and International Political Change: Soviet-Russian Behavior and the End of the Cold War* (New Haven: Yale University Press, 1997).

[64] See also Gustafson, *Crisis amid Plenty*, 17, on this issue.

[65] Zagladin (author's interview) stated that all the heads of scientific organizations and the research institutes, including Arbatov, Aganbegyan, Zaslavskaya, Primakov, and later Yakovlev, were consulted. Arbatov (author's interview) stated that in foreign policy, "for those who knew Gorbachev, these relations began much earlier" than 1985. Doder and Branson, *Gorbachev*, 57, describe Gorbachev as "acting as a loyal deputy" at the same time that he gathered these critical position papers, highlighting the contingency with which events unfolded; Gorbachev's reformist activities could have backfired before he ever came to power.

1985, the April 1985 plenum where he first spoke as general secretary about the need for reform, "could only have taken place on the basis of vast preliminary work of previous years." Gorbachev explained what he meant by the term "preliminary work":

> *Gorbachev:* Indeed, I personally, among others, had had occasion to meet many of you more than once to discuss these matters (of reform) well before the April (1985) Central Committee plenum. (He turns to Ryzhkov.) How many documents were worked out on the basis of these discussions, Nikolay Ivanovich?
>
> *Ryzhkov:* 110.
>
> *Gorbachev:* Nikolay Ivanovich Ryzhkov and I have 110 identical documents. All of them belong to a period when the April plenum was still a long way off. They are the conclusions of the academicians, writers, prominent specialists, and public figures. The results of the discussions and their analysis formed the basis of the decisions of the April (1985) plenum and the first steps thereafter.

These reports, authored by heads and deputy heads of scientific organizations and institutes, writers, and intellectuals, covered domestic as well as foreign policy issues. Some of the reports addressed the war in Afghanistan, mostly, according to Zagladin, in a critical manner.[66]

The Expert Community

The people with whom Gorbachev had contact in the expert community included domestic policy specialists, with backgrounds in economics, sociology, and regional politics, and foreign policy specialists with a globalist perspective. Most worked in the scientific institutes, although there were a few writers, both journalists and novelists. Several had had contact with the Central Committee over the years and many had worked under Andropov there or

[66] *Pravda*, January 7, 1989 in FBIS-SOV, January 9, 1989, 53. Zagladin (author's interview) states that "the Afghan theme was then without doubt touched upon." Apparently, it was suggested that the Soviet Union move away from a military course in Afghanistan to a political one. The proposals were sometimes collaborative and involved members of the younger generation who are now extremely active in running post-Soviet Russia. For example, Pyotr Aven, minister of foreign economic relations in the fall of 1992, along with Yegor Gaidar, later acting prime minister and head of the political party Democratic Russia's Choice, were both students of Stanislav Shatalin, a reformist economist most famous for his "500-day proposal," which involved shifting the Soviet economy away from command administrative measures towards market forces (which Gorbachev rejected). Aven comments that in 1983 and 1984, Shatalin asked them "to write the first complex proposal on economic reform." Steven Erlanger, writing about this link, notes also that "in the course of that project they met counterparts from Leningrad" such as Anatoly Chubais, later deputy prime minister in charge of privatization and currently minister of finance, and Sergei Glaziev, later head of the political party PRES and now working in the Federation Council. Steven Erlanger, "Reform School," *New York Times Magazine*, November 29, 1992, 74.

knew him or Gorbachev through regional party organizations. Most of these people had known one another for years.[67]

Among the most prominent members of this group (those who formed the top echelon) were economists and sociologists such as Abel Aganbegyan, later dean of the Academy of National Economics; Tatyana Zaslavskaya, later director of the National Center of Public Opinion; Leonid Abalkin, later Deputy Prime Minister; Stanislav Shatalin, former member of the Presidential Council; Nikolay Petrakov, former economics advisor to the president. The top echelon's foreign policy specialists included Alexander Yakovlev, later Gorbachev's closest advisor and member of the Presidential Council and Politburo; Georgii Arbatov, the long-time director of the Institute of USA and Canada; Evgeny Primakov, later a member of the Presidential Council; and editors of newspapers and magazines such as Vitali Korotich, later *Ogonëk* editor; and Yegor Yakovlev, later editor of *Moscow News*.[68]

The other echelons of the community consisted of specialists in the scientific institutions and writers at newspapers and journals who had expressed discontent with policies in their writing, openly or cryptically.[69] The work of the lower echelon was known to the top echelon and their ideas were thus transmitted to the leadership.[70]

Conceptually, this group of domestic and foreign policy scholars formed a tacit alliance with Gorbachev, both supporting and being supported by him. Those scholars studying domestic politics shared certain ideas about the economy and the society, and agreed on ways to deal with the harsh realities lurking behind the glowing five-year reports that Gosplan inevitably churned out. One foreign policy implication of these scholars' analyses of the economy called for enhanced cooperation with the West. Scholars studying foreign policy shared ideas about the nature of the international system, and about how Soviet foreign policy should be conducted.[71] The domestic political implication of reformist perspectives was a more open society and a different relationship between the government, the Party, and the people.

[67] Author's interviews with Korotich and Arbatov.

[68] Author's interview with Arbatov. Zagladin (author's interview) confirmed that most of the people listed in the text as key members of the expert community had written reports for Gorbachev between 1983 and 1985 on many topics concerning domestic and foreign policy.

[69] A good example is the article by Alexei G. Arbatov, "V tupike politiki sily" (The dead end of a policy of strength), *Voprosii istorii* no. 9 (1981): 104–118.

[70] One of the easiest places for this transmission of ideas to take place was at IMEMO, where Yakovlev and Primakov were both directors in the mid to late 1980s. As directors of the institute they were aware of critical thinking on, for example, Soviet Third World policy expressed by scholars such as Georgii Mirsky and Nodari Simoniia. Author's interview with Simoniia. See also Checkel, *Ideas and International Political Change*.

[71] Kremenyuk (author's interview) noted that scholars in Novosibirsk, a mainly domestic policy think-tank, and at ISKAN, "have been aware of one another for a long time—that serious change should be introduced. Both had liberal platforms, in domestic policy and external policy."

Institutionally, most of these policy experts came from the Soviet Academy of Sciences (ANSSSR). Until 1988, the economic institutes and the foreign policy institutes were under the same branch at the ANSSSR. In the 1980s, this institutional grouping meant that there were many opportunities to share ideas at regular conferences. Viktor Kremenyuk has stated that these connections meant that there was frequent contact between economists such as Aganbegyan and Shatalin, and foreign policy thinkers such as Arbatov and Primakov.[72]

In addition, scholars and party functionaries studying different issues had regular contact with one another through conferences and written reports (*zapiski*). Gorbachev, in his post as agricultural secretary of the Central Committee, had had contact with the heads of all major economic institutes, including Aganbegyan's center in Novosibirsk and IMEMO in Moscow, where Yakovlev and Primakov were later directors. Intellectuals and writers also prepared the party plenum and congress reports. By the mid-1980s, reformist thinkers had largely replaced hardliners in this work.[73]

Critics of both domestic and foreign policy inhabited the institutions and universities of the Soviet Union. The professional and intellectual connections binding these groups of people were an important locus of *perestroika*. At the most fundamental level, both groups existed within the same political environment and the same administrative command system. That process of policy making had resulted in enormous problems in both the domestic and foreign policy spheres.

The web of connections was quite intricate and had developed, in some cases, over the course of two decades. For example, Aganbegyan knew Arbatov and had been coming to Moscow for regular meetings at the USA/Canada Institute (ISKAN) and other institutes since 1975.[74] Arbatov knew Yakovlev well from their service together under Andropov in the early 1960s and also in their respective capacities as director of ISKAN and ambassador to Canada. Yakovlev knew Korotich and it was through him that Korotich met Gorbachev.[75] At other echelons of the community there were connections as well. For example, researchers at ISKAN, IMEMO, and the Oriental Institute (IVAN) knew the work of Shatalin, Abalkin, and Aganbegyan.

The locus of *perestroika* and the general challenge to the status quo in the Soviet Union, emerged primarily from the domestic policy sphere. This phenomenon is explained by the fact that Gorbachev's dossier was until 1985 dominated by regional political matters, agriculture, and economics. These were the issue-areas with which he was familiar. Alexander Yakovlev explains

[72] Author's interview with Kremenyuk.
[73] Author's interviews with Sidorov and Arbatov.
[74] Author's interview with Viktor Sheynis, December 24, 1990.
[75] Author's interviews with Kremenyuk; Korotich; Arbatov.

that domestic reform began earlier than foreign policy reform because the basic ideas already existed "in all strata of society."[76]

Internal Problems and Reform

Among the domestic policy specialists, a special place may be assigned to the experts from Novosibirsk: Abel Aganbegyan, head of the Institute of Economics and Industrial Organization, and Tatyana Zaslavskaya, head of its sociology section.[77] Aganbegyan has claimed: "if perestroika is a 'revolution from above,' it is also to some extent a 'revolution from Siberia'."[78] There is truth to the statement; his institute, far from Moscow, was pioneering in its economic and sociology research.

Aganbegyan disseminated the statistics and other information collected by scholars at the institute in two main ways. He published a journal, *Eko*, that reported information on the state of the union forbidden in the open press.[79] Along with Zaslavskaya, he also sent many *zapiski* to Premier Aleksey Kosygin from 1976 through 1978 discussing such phenomena as rural migration and the rampant corruption on collectivized farms.[80] Kosygin, around this time, had publicly spoken out about agricultural difficulties, contradicting Brezhnev's explanations for failures in the economy.[81] Perhaps it seemed reasonable to channel the institute's findings to Kosygin. In any case, Aganbegyan felt it was his "duty" (*dolg*) to do so. Kosygin was, however, displeased with the material, and Aganbegyan's freedom to meet with foreign colleagues began to be limited; ultimately, he was prevented from going abroad to either socialist or capitalist states.[82]

Zaslavskaya had her own problems as a result of the research. She had done much work in the countryside in the late 1960s and believed that the Soviet Union was in danger of losing its rural agricultural population unless living conditions improved; conditions approached those of "slavery—in the full

---

[76] As cited in Cohen and vanden Heuvel, *Voices of Glasnost*, 41. Chernyaev's diaries chronicle Gorbachev's evolution from domestic reformer to someone who reconceptualizes national security. Chernyaev, *My six years with Gorbachev.*

[77] Cohen and vanden Heuvel, *Voices of Glasnost*, 115–117.

[78] Abel Aganbegyan, ed., *Perestroika Annual II* (London: Brassey's, 1989), 141.

[79] Although the journal itself went through censors, there were periods in the early 1970s when even very negative information, such as the statistics on rural migration to the cities (about 50 percent) could be published. At other times, for example, during the period 1976 through 1980, the censor grew stricter and all demographic information was "out of bounds." Author's interview with Dyuk.

[80] "Aganbegyan and Zaslavskaya are not the kind of people who could let this sort of information just lie around as long as they knew about it." Author's interview with Dyuk.

[81] See George W. Breslauer, *Khrushchev and Brezhnev as Leaders: Building Authority in Soviet Politics* (London: George Allen and Unwin, 1982), 226–229.

[82] Author's interview with Dyuk; Cohen and vanden Heuvel, *Voices of Glasnost*, 117.

sense of the word." Her work on agricultural economics and sociology was based on extensive research and first-hand encounters with the rural poverty. She had, however, great difficulty getting her books published.[83]

By 1982, however, the circumstances under which Aganbegyan, Zaslavskaya, and other critics of Soviet economics and agriculture worked began to change. Gorbachev, as agricultural secretary, enlisted Zaslavskaya and others in his program of reform of various agricultural organizations that distributed farm equipment and supplies.[84]

After Gorbachev and Zaslavskaya met, Aganbegyan began to send *zapiski* directly to Gorbachev. Gorbachev, in his capacity as a deputy to Andropov, asked Aganbegyan to bring together the best economists to work on pressing political and economic issues.[85] In April 1983, economists and sociologists from Novosibirsk invited reformist analysts from all over the Soviet Union to discuss "the social mechanism underlying our system." This focus involved discussing "economic processes as social processes."[86]

Despite problems with the censor, approximately 100 copies of the reports from the conference were printed, two of which ended up in the hands of a *Washington Post* correspondent. In it, Zaslavskaya presented a general critique of the command administrative system underscoring the incompatibility of centralization with technical innovation. She discussed severe problems with a labor force that experienced no incentives and whose creativity was discouraged, issues that became central tenets of Gorbachev's reform effort.[87] As a result of publicity in the West, Zaslavskaya was brought before the KGB and was prevented from leaving the country.[88] But from that time on, the re-

---

[83] Author's interview with Dyuk.

[84] Author's interview with Dyuk; Cohen and vanden Heuvel, *Voices of Glasnost*, 118. Examples of such organizations included *SelKhozKhimika* and *SelKhozTekhnika*. These organizations typically required that a *kolkhoz* buy equipment they did not need in order to receive the equipment they did need. They might make a *kolkhoz* in Siberia that wanted a tractor also buy a cotton harvesting machine, even though cotton was not grown in the region. Gorbachev proposed attaching these distribution centers to the *kolkhoz* so that the money could be reinvested.

[85] Author's interview with Dyuk; Doder and Branson, *Gorbachev*, 81–82, 93–96. See Brown, "Power and Policy in a Time of Leadership Transition," 186, on relations between Zaslavskaya, Aganbegyan, and Gorbachev in the early 1980s.

[86] Cohen and vanden Heuvel, *Voices of Glasnost*, 121; author's interview with Dyuk. This was a topic that, according to Dyuk, "people only talked about in their kitchens."

[87] According to Dyuk, when the censor read the report, he said it would never be published anywhere, ever. Aganbegyan took out some material from the report on, for example, corruption in the government *apparat* and, as director of the institute, he got it past the censor and published it. A copy was reprinted as the "Novosibirsk report" in the British journal, *Survey*, Spring 1984, 88–108. Thane Gustafson and Dawn Mann, "Gorbachev's First Year: Building Power and Authority," *Problems of Communism*, May–June 1986, 15, summarizes the report.

[88] According to Dyuk, Gorbachev was helpful during this very rough period; he felt the report should not have ended up in the West but that it was worse that nothing had been done about the problems she addressed. Partly because of this support, Zaslavskaya developed loyalty to Gorbachev. Dyuk claimed that "much of the reason for Zaslavskaya moving to Moscow [in 1988] had to do with her wanting to help Gorbachev."

formers became known to one another and they decided to form "an all-union scientific collective." This group of people, as they laid what Zaslavskaya called the "groundwork" for reform, made it increasingly difficult for the leadership to ignore the social, political, and economic ills that plagued the Soviet system. They lent important support for reform to people working within party organizations.[89]

External Problems and Reform

Gorbachev inherited a conception of foreign policy from Andropov, shared by many specialists, that informed his understanding of force used abroad: a state's reputation was connected to domestic efficiency, not merely to strategic resolve.[90] Reform of domestic policy was of primary importance, but conceptually and institutionally, it was linked to foreign policy.

The link was perhaps best represented by the top echelon of specialists who advised Gorbachev in the 1983–85 period, which included foreign policy generalists and other specialists. Alexander Yakovlev was one of the most prominent and exceptional; he was both an expert on international relations and, eventually, an insider in the party organization once Gorbachev had consolidated power.

In May 1983, Gorbachev was sent by Andropov to Canada for a ten-day trip where Yakovlev, then Soviet ambassador to Canada, was his guide. The purpose of the trip may have been for Gorbachev to take the political temperature of Yakovlev or vice versa.[91] Whatever the purpose, following intense discussions between Gorbachev and Yakovlev, Andropov ended Yakovlev's "exile" and brought him back to Moscow as head of IMEMO.[92] This move enabled Yakovlev to have close and frequent contact with Gorbachev.

Georgii Arbatov claims that prior to Brezhnev's death, Gorbachev was not particularly interested in foreign policy. He argues that when Andropov became general secretary, Andropov began to groom Gorbachev as his successor, and Gorbachev's contact with foreign policy specialists increased dramatically. Arbatov briefed Gorbachev before his 1983 Canada trip. Arbatov "thought that he needed to know about Canada in connection with agriculture, but he said, 'No, I know all that. I am interested in questions of general

---

[89] Author's interview with Dyuk; Cohen and vanden Heuvel, *Voices of Glasnost*, 122. During this time, the institute began sending material to progressive members of the party leadership in an effort to penetrate and bolster the liberal factions within the party.

[90] See Doder and Branson, *Gorbachev*, 112, on the Gorbachev-Andropov link on foreign policy. On state reputation, see Jonathan Mercer, *Reputation and International Politics* (Ithaca: Cornell University Press, 1996).

[91] See, for example, Hough, *Russia and the West*, 225.

[92] He had worked with Andropov at the Central Committee in the early 1960s; Brown, "The Foreign Policy Making Process." He had also been a party official in the same Yaroslavl party organization out of which Andropov had come in the 1930s. Hough, *Russia and the West*, 224.

foreign policy.' And, thus, we began to have regular relations although they were not formal."[93]

Reformists at lower levels of the expert community who inhabited the main foreign policy institutes in Moscow did not have contact with Gorbachev at this time. They did, however, have contact with the directors of the major institutes: Arbatov, Yakovlev, and Primakov. These directors would prove to be important links for ideas between the specialists and the leadership. As one expert noted,

> Under *perestroika* there [was] a chain. [The leadership] created more of a possibility to influence policy. It created a situation that when there [was] a good fresh idea, it [could] go pretty nearly to the top, straight to Gorbachev. . . . An example [was] Yakovlev. He knew all the people to ask about certain issues. Primakov, he knew us all. He [could] find a person quickly who [had] information that they need[ed].[94]

Among the researchers, there were many debates on Soviet foreign policy in general and, specifically, toward the Third World. A policy debate that directly affected Soviet policy toward Afghanistan involved stressing indigenous economic and social conditions in relations with Third World countries rather than the bipolar, ideological context.[95] Nodari Simoniia, then a researcher at IVAN, typified the experts at this echelon. Simoniia argued that national liberation movements had failed in much of the Third World because of an indigenous underdeveloped economic base. The capitalist step of development could not be skipped if socialism were to be achieved; "socialist oriented" countries lagged far behind those Third World states that had chosen the capitalist path of development.[96]

During the war in Afghanistan, although never explicitly mentioning it, Simoniia discussed the importance of local conditions in assessing revolutionary potential, a point that critics of the war brought up explicitly only after the announcement to withdraw had been made.[97] Gradually, in contrast to years

[93] According to Arbatov (author's interview), at least once a year, starting in 1978, Arbatov met Gorbachev, along with other members of the Central Committee, to prepare Brezhnev's speech and materials for the approaching party plenum. Gorbachev's relations with Oleg Bogomolov and Yakovlev also increased.

[94] Author's interview with Simoniia.

[95] See, for example, Nodari Simoniia, *Strana vostoka: puti razvitiia* (Moscow: Nauka, 1975). See Valkenier, *The Soviet Union and the Third World*, 86–87; Elizabeth K. Valkenier, "Revolutionary Change in the Third World: Recent Soviet Reassessments," *World Politics* 38, no. 3 (April 1986): 415–434, esp. 428, 432–433; Jerry F. Hough, *The Struggle for the Third World: Soviet Debates and American Options* (Washington, D.C.: Brookings, 1976), 63, 84, 253. Scholars at ISKAN also warned that the Third World was a hotbed for bipolar fighting and urged Soviet policy to move away from supporting revolutionary movements. Hough, *The Struggle for the Third World*, 253.

[96] See Hough, *The Struggle for the Third World*, 84.

[97] On Simoniia, see Valkenier, "Revolutionary Change in the Third World," 428. On local conditions in Afghanistan after the announcement of withdrawal had been made, see Artyom

of being ignored and sometimes verbally attacked by the International Department of the Central Committee, specialists like Simoniia were listened to by advisors to the leadership.[98]

The general tone and direction of the specialists' criticisms—urging policy away from ideology toward pragmatism—was important and long-lasting. These scholars did not cause changes in Soviet–Third World policy or the shift to accommodationism. But they helped change the intellectual and political climate in which policy decisions were made.[99] This change in climate only became dramatic once the specialists gained some access, whether direct or indirect, to members of the leadership favoring reform; the ideas espoused by specialists in the 1970s and early 1980s were used by the leadership to legitimize and guide controversial policy decisions of the mid and late 1980s. Without access to or salience for the leadership, the ideas would have existed only on the pages of journals and in the halls of institutes.

CONCLUSION

Many of Gorbachev's ideas about domestic reform were articulated before he became General Secretary, in spite of the Brezhnevian political climate under Chernenko. In December 1984, Gorbachev outlined his agenda at an All-Union Scientific and Practical Conference.[100] Among those in attendance were such members of the old guard as Boris Ponomarev, head of the International Department of the Central Committee, and Grigori Romanov, party

Borovik's interview with Major General Kim Tsagalov, "Afghanistan: Preliminary Results," *Ogonëk* no. 30 (July 1988): 25–27.

[98] Simoniia had a long-standing fight with Rostislav Ulianovsky, the department head of CCID in the 1970s and early 1980s, over the importance of local conditions. See T. H. Rigby, "The Afghan Conflict and Soviet Domestic Politics," in Amin Saikal and William Maley, eds., *The Soviet Withdrawal from Afghanistan* (Cambridge: Cambridge University Press, 1989), 74.

[99] "Many of the more moderate and less ideologically confrontational concepts—such as global interdependence, the complex multisectoral nature of third-world societies, and the rules of conduct that constrain the superpowers from projecting their interests unilaterally—were formulated by academic experts before they appeared in official speeches or proposals." Valkenier, "Revolutionary Change in the Third World," 433.

[100] Mikhail Gorbachev, "Sovershenstvovanie razvitogo sotsiolizma i ideologicheskaya rabota partii v svete resheniy iyunskogo (1983) plenuma TsK KPSS" (The perfection of developed socialism and the ideological work of the party in light of the decisions of June [1983] Plenum of the CC of the CPSU), in M. S. Gorbachev, *Izbrannye rechi i stat'i* (Selected speeches and articles), Vol. 2 (Moskva: Izdatel'stvo "Politicheskaya literatura," 1986), 75–108. See also Rudolfo Brancoli, "Mikhail Gorbachev's Secret Report," *La Republica*, March 27, 1985, in FBIS-SOV, March 28, 1985, 1–4. Branson and Doder, *Gorbachev*, 58, write that this speech contrasted starkly with Chernenko's pronouncements. Brown, "Power and Policy in a Time of Leadership Transition," 186, notes that with this speech, "many of Gorbachev's reformist ideas and some of the key concepts of the Gorbachev era were given an early airing."

chief from Leningrad. The meeting was reported in *Pravda* at the time, but Gorbachev's 43 page speech was cut down to two innocuous pages.[101]

Gorbachev argued that in order to enter the next century with a strong and efficient economy, the Soviet Union needed to work on the "reorganization of economic management." A gap had emerged in "production forces and relations," resulting in the stratification of society. A "redistribution of income" would be necessary, as well as a move toward "better socialist ownership." The "improvement" in economic relations would affect the political realm as well. "There is no other way forward," Gorbachev reasoned.[102]

In many ways, the ideas expressed in the 1984 speech were quintessential Gorbachev. At the 27th Party Congress in February 1986, Gorbachev would reiterate the themes of the speech: "comrades, the acceleration of the country's socioeconomic development holds the key to all our problems in the near and more distant future—economic and social, political and ideological, internal and external ones."[103] Yet, as Archie Brown has noted, the December 1984 speech was much more radical than anything Gorbachev would say or do in his first year and a half as leader of the country. Brown explained this contrast as a result of the difference between Gorbachev as a party secretary and Gorbachev as the general secretary of the party. When he spoke as a party secretary, he could express reformist ideas much more readily than when he spoke as the general secretary.[104] However, Brown argued, it was a "clear invitation to social scientists to get on with the elaboration of ideas for economic reform."[105]

Gorbachev was not able to implement any of the ideas he articulated in December 1984—or indeed, many of those articulated in the 110 policy reports he gathered from domestic and foreign policy experts—until he and his cohort had successfully shifted the internal balance of power in their favor. That would take further mobilization of experts, further personnel changes, and coalition-building strategies.

Neither ideas nor experts alone changed policy. But they did influence the political climate and helped the leadership shift the internal balance of power in favor of reformers. Gorbachev responded to experts' concerns and ideas because the problems resonated with him; in his capacity as secretary of agri-

---

[101] For Gorbachev's speech as it appeared in *Pravda*, see "The Improvement of Developed Socialism and Ideological Work in the Light of the CPSU Central Committee June 1983 Plenum Decisions," *Pravda*, December 11, 1984, in FBIS-SOV, December 11, 1984. According to author's interview with Valeri Sidorov, Konstantin Chernenko and Richard Kosolopov, the editor of the ideological journal of the Communist Party, *Kommunist*, organized an angry retort to Gorbachev. See K. Chernenko, "Na uraven' trebovanii razvitogo sotzialisma" (On the demands of developed socialism), *Kommunist* no. 18 (1984): 3–21.

[102] Brancoli, "Mikhail Gorbachev's Secret Report."

[103] *Pravda*, February 26, 1986, in FBIS-SOV Supplement, February 26, 1986.

[104] On the contrast, see Brown, "Power and Policy in a Time of Leadership Transition," 188.

[105] Ibid., 187.

culture, he had become familiar with the actual state of the economy and not just boilerplate reports. The analyses of the specialists confirmed what he and a few other members of the leadership already knew or suspected: real reform of domestic and foreign policy was necessary. Specialists were involved early on, after 1983, in evaluating the situation in the Soviet Union and they thus affected the climate of ideas in which reform occurred. The top echelon of the expert community had, for the most part, direct access to the leadership, and their access provided indirect access to the members of the lower echelons, the many reformist specialists inhabiting research institutes all over the Soviet Union. In this sense, the experts legitimized and guided policy options.

The international system reinforced rather than challenged traditional conceptions of security, including the tendency to see relations in the Third World through a bipolar prism. U.S. policy during this time tended to confirm old thinking about the nature of the opponent, making the job of reformers more difficult. At the non-governmental level, contact with Western political and intellectual elites through conferences and seminars may have helped new thinkers in the Soviet Union formulate ideas or confirm hypotheses. Their influence on the overall shift in policy—domestic and foreign—was mediated by the leadership.

In summary, Gorbachev began mobilizing an expert community in the early 1980s. The advice and reports of the specialist advisers helped lay the ground work for *perestroika* so that by March 1985 many of the basic ideas for reform were already formulated, including withdrawal from Afghanistan. But an important necessary and sufficient condition had not yet been realized. In Chapter 5, I examine the strategies used by Gorbachev and his cohort for shifting the internal balance of power and thus enabling the placement of reformist ideas on the political agenda.

CHAPTER FIVE

Changing the Political Agenda, 1985–1989: New Thinkers Gain Control of Political Resources

IN THE EARLY 1980s, Gorbachev and other like-minded members of the Soviet leadership tapped into the reformist ideas proposed by various domestic and foreign policy specialists. By the mid-1980s, reformers in the leadership used these ideas to influence the development of traditional and nontraditional institutions. The restructuring and evolution of old and new institutions—*perestroika*, in its essence—proved an important central strategy in shifting the internal balance of power in favor of new thinkers. Mikhail Gorbachev and his cohort implemented personnel changes in the central institutions of power such as the Politburo and the Central Committee. But just as important, they cultivated support for reform outside these institutions by empowering influential members of expert communities and by encouraging a more independent press.[1] This development of alternative blocs of support was instrumental in shifting power from the Party to the government and, to a certain extent, to society.[2]

The personnel changes in these institutions and the support of experts, formerly marginalized by the party structure but newly empowered under Gorbachev, are central to this story. With national platforms, the experts used the resources to disseminate new thinking. In turn, this dissemination affected the political climate in which policy agendas were set, and most important, legitimized and publicized the linkage of domestic reform with accommodation abroad.

Chapter 4 detailed how, although for years many in the leadership had believed that problems in Afghanistan could not be solved by military means, they were unable politically to implement the withdrawal. To get withdrawal on the agenda—and indeed, any policy that directly challenged the status quo, any idea that did not fit with old thinking—they had to make it politi-

---

[1] While all the members of the dominant expert community identified in Chapter 4 had party affiliation—a prerequisite for, among other things, admission to the best universities in the country—they were, for the most part, not from the party apparatus. They were also not dissidents. Moreover, *glasnost* was never meant by the leadership to be understood as license for a totally free and independent press, but one that instrumentally supported reform.

[2] My argument is similar to that of Thane Gustafson, *Crisis amid Plenty: The Politics of Soviet Energy under Brezhnev and Gorbachev* (Princeton: Princeton University Press, 1989), 293, where he claims that it was "Gorbachev's aim to remove the Party from the job of day-to-day economic management and to strengthen the authority of the government."

cally viable. In this chapter, I trace how the Gorbachev cohort accomplished this, and I argue that the story is characteristic of many political battles that took place over reform in the Soviet Union.

The Soviet war in Afghanistan and other foreign policy issues were not the dominant struggle of the 1980s for policy makers in Moscow; the dominant struggle concerned reform at home. Consequently, the need for withdrawal was not derived exclusively or even mainly from events in Afghanistan or in the international system but as a result of events in the Soviet Union. The withdrawal grew out of "new thinking," the foreign policy platform of the domestic reform program known as *perestroika*, and was conceived as part of the overall transformation of foreign policy.[3] "*Perestroika* demanded other relations with the outside world."[4]

In the early period of Gorbachev's leadership, from March 1985 to November 1986, major policy changes in either domestic or foreign policy had been politically problematic to initiate.[5] During this period, instead, the Gorbachev coalition had brought about major changes in the composition of political institutions and empowered an expert community. Gorbachev continued Andropov's anti-corruption campaign, coupling it with an unsuccessful anti-alcohol campaign, but there is little sign of the more radical political and economic reforms that would emerge later. Foreign policy at this time consisted of a slight warming of the Cold War, with summits and fireside chats, but without concrete manifestations of change such as arms control or cease-fire treaties.

Substantive changes did not come until 1987 and 1988, after Gorbachev's political base and alternative sources of power and legitimacy had been established. After gaining control of political resources in late 1986 and early 1987, the leadership expressed what was by then a decision in principle to withdraw from Afghanistan, and implemented policies aimed at getting the Soviet Union out of the war.[6] By February 1988, the reformers prevailed and the withdrawal was announced. But from March 1985 through February 1989 when the withdrawal was completed, Gorbachev and his cohort (principally Alexander Yakovlev and Eduard Shevardnadze) continuously faced internal

[3] This linkage explains in part why foreign policy generalists and not Afghan specialists advised the leadership on the war. Author's interview with Yuri Gankovsky (Afghan specialist, IVAN), Moscow, November 5, 1990.

[4] Author's interview with Vadim Zagladin (former director, Information Department, Central Committee [CCID]), December 12, 1990.

[5] Hough argues that no radical policies could be launched before Gorbachev consolidated his power. See Jerry F. Hough, "Gorbachev Consolidating Power," *Problems of Communism* 36, no. 4 (July–August 1987): 21–43. For a contrasting opinion, see Patrick Cockburn, *Getting Russia Wrong: The End of Kremlinology* (London: Verso, 1989).

[6] At this time, Soviet losses in Afghanistan were decreasing despite the use of Stinger missiles by the mujahideen. V. Izgarshev, "Afganskaia bol'," *Pravda*, August 17, 1989, 6. The intention to withdraw preceded the introduction of these weapons into the war.

battles over the withdrawal. The resistance by many in the upper echelons of the foreign policy elite demonstrates that even with the shift in the internal balance of power, the withdrawal was extremely controversial; if Gorbachev and the reformers had not gained control of political resources, withdrawal would have been impossible.

In the period 1985 through 1989, the burden for reformists was to make challenges to the status quo appear reasonable and necessary. Even when leaders realize that they are in bad situations, they may encounter difficulty extracting themselves. The Soviet leaders eventually succeeded in extracting themselves by linking the need to get out of Afghanistan with domestic economic problems; reform at home became a sufficient condition for accommodation abroad. The programs of *glasnost, perestroika,* and new thinking put together by the leadership and the expert community in Moscow could not fully develop as long as the Soviets had troops in Afghanistan. Gorbachev reported to the 28th Party Congress in July 1990:

> When drawing up a program for *perestroika,* we understood that it could not be carried out unless the external conditions surrounding the life of our country were changed fundamentally. And to accomplish that we were going to have to change our approach and offer a new foreign policy to the world.[7]

The termination of the war was one of several policies that directly challenged the old thinking that inhabited such institutions as the press, the military, the foreign ministry, and the military-industrial complex. For example, until 1988, *glasnost* or openness in the press largely concerned domestic issues. Foreign policy and the war in Afghanistan were not subject to robust criticism in the popular press until after the announcement of withdrawal in February 1988.[8] With the implementation of policies such as the withdrawal, Gorbachev and his cohort were able to institutionalize new conceptions of security based on cooperation with the West.

The influence of the international system on the Soviet withdrawal from

---

[7] *Vestnik,* August 1990, 15.

[8] On coverage of the war in the Soviet popular print press in 1980–87, see Sarah E. Mendelson, "Change and Continuity in Soviet Explanations of Resistance in Afghanistan: The Hand Uncovers the Wound," paper presented at the RAND Corporation, April 1988. The Soviet press was not monolithic in its approach to the war. On the one hand, articles criticizing aspects of the war did appear in the military press prior to the announcement of withdrawal. See Bruce D. Porter, "The Military Abroad: Internal Consequences of External Expansion," in Timothy J. Colton and Thane Gustafson, eds., *Soldiers and the State: Civil-Military Relations from Brezhnev to Gorbachev* (Princeton: Princeton University Press, 1990). On the other hand, in the scholarly journals there was no discussion of the war in direct, critical terms until after the withdrawal had been completed. Television coverage of the war changed substantially in 1987 (more correspondents, more stories), but unlike the print press, it was never as critical and was always more closely monitored. See Laura Roselle Helvey, "Political Communication and Policy Legitimacy: Leadership, TV and Withdrawal from War" (Ph.D dissertation, Stanford University, 1993); and Victor Yasmann, "Glasnost' and Soviet Television in 1987," *Radio Liberty Research Bulletin* 5 (RL 31/88), 1988.

Afghanistan, as in earlier periods, played a largely indeterminate role; decision makers could have responded in a variety of ways to events. This chapter details the domestic political context from 1985 through 1989 in which challenges to the status quo, such as the withdrawal, were mounted. Personnel changes occurred in traditional institutions including the Politburo, the Central Committee, and the organs used in foreign policy decision making such as the International Department and the Foreign Ministry. Specialists and journalists sympathetic to reform used the resources provided to them by the leadership to help shift the balance of power. Throughout this discussion, I focus on the internal battles that occurred in the process of putting withdrawal from Afghanistan on the policy agenda. Both the personnel changes and the empowerment of the expert community changed the internal balance of power in favor of the reformers, making the withdrawal viable.

THE INTERNATIONAL CONTEXT

Many scholars argue that Soviet foreign policy changed in the 1980s as a result of lessons learned about the international system.[9] Yet the events in the international system reinforced for many Soviet decision makers traditional conceptions of international relations and national security. The two superpowers continued to engage in balancing actions against one another through proxy warfare in the Third World. Specifically, the United States was running its largest covert operation since World War II, supporting the *jihad* against the Soviet-backed Afghan government.[10] Events in the international system, including events on the ground in Afghanistan and U.S. foreign policy, did not provide the type of stimulus sufficient for a shift toward accommodation in Soviet foreign policy. Rather, events appear to have encouraged hardliners to resist the changes advocated by Gorbachev and his cohort.

The War in Afghanistan and U.S. Policy

From 1984 through 1986, the Soviets waged the main offensives of the war.[11] During this time, the military continued to move away from the heavily armored large-scale offensives they had used in the early years of the war and

---

[9] See, for example, Daniel Deudney and G. John Ikenberry, "The International Sources of Soviet Change," *International Security* 16, no. 3 (Winter 1991/92): 74–118.

[10] Steve Coll, "Anatomy of a Victory: CIA's Covert Afghan War," *Washington Post*, July 19 and 20, 1992. Coll's articles were based in part on interviews with the Pakistani General, Mohammed Yousaf, who, says Coll, "supervised the covert war between 1983 and 1987."

[11] See Olivier Roy, *The Lessons of the Soviet-Afghan War*, Adelphi Paper no. 259 (London: International Institute for Strategic Studies, Summer 1991), 19. Roy had visited Afghanistan seven times since 1979 and in 1991 had spent ten weeks traveling there. See also Gilles Bertin,

increasingly adapted to the nature of counter-insurgency warfare by relying on airborne maneuvers and high-altitude bombing.[12] Yet even at the height of the war, in 1984 and 1985, the vast majority of troops were ground-based and therefore less mobile; of twelve divisions in Afghanistan, ten were motorized and only two were airborne.[13] More important, however, the Soviets ultimately failed in two critical maneuvers: they never successfully sealed the borders with Pakistan, and thus they never cut the supply lines to the mujahideen.[14]

Actors in the international system—led by the United States and Pakistan—continued to respond to the war primarily by diplomatic negotiation and by supplying weapons to the opposition. Riaz Khan, the Pakistani representative to the Geneva accord meetings, argues that negotiations were largely ineffectual in bringing about the withdrawal but provided the Soviets with a face-saving measure for a policy that had already been decided upon.[15]

While American money had been flowing into Pakistan since January 1980, the amounts increased dramatically in 1985, especially in March 1985, just as Gorbachev was coming to power in the Soviet Union.[16] The Reagan admin-

---

"Stingers Change the Face of the War in Afghanistan," *Jane's Defense Weekly* 8, no. 14 (October 10, 1987).

[12] Roy, *The Lessons of the Soviet-Afghan War*, 20; and Valerii Konovalov, "Afghanistan and Mountain Warfare Training," *Radio Liberty Research Bulletin* (RL 118/88), 3.

[13] Porter, "The Military Abroad," 322. At this time, the Soviet military also used non-military tactics such as ethnic-based propaganda campaigns that emphasized how much better the lives of Uzbeks, Tajiks, and Turkmen were in the Soviet Union than in Afghanistan. Alexander Alexiev, "The War in Afghanistan: Soviet Strategies and the State of the Resistance," P-7038 (Santa Monica, Calif.: RAND, November 1984), 4–5.

[14] Roy, *The Lessons of the Soviet-Afghan War*, 20–22.

[15] Islamabad had intended this response of negotiation and supply to be complementary and coordinated, but from late 1986 through 1987, Pakistan's Prime Minister Junejo and President Zia fought over control of Pakistani policy on Afghanistan. Just as Pakistan's diplomatic maneuvers were falling out of step with the military operations, the Gorbachev coalition was winning its battle at home to place the issue of withdrawal on the political agenda. After years of negotiation, the Pakistani response to the announcement of the withdrawal in 1988 was divided. Zia declared that Pakistan would not sign the treaty as long as the Soviet-installed People's Democratic Party of Afghanistan (PDPA) was in power. He wanted the settlement to be conditional on the withdrawal of Soviet troops and the composition of an interim government. (Later developments in Afghanistan, where the PDPA collapsed and mujahideen forces continue to fight one another, prompted some observers to argue in the Pakistani press that Zia had been right to make the accord conditional on an interim government. See *The Dawn* [Karachi], May 19 and 23 1992.) Junejo, however, wanted to sign the settlement and solve the problem of a successor government later. U.S. pressure and fear of Soviet retribution eventually induced Zia to drop the interim government issue as a treaty-signing condition. The Pakistani government did win agreements to continue military assistance to the warring factions. See Riaz M. Khan, *Untying the Afghan Knot: Negotiating Soviet Withdrawal* (Durham, N.C.: Duke University Press, 1991).

[16] Figures of U.S. aid vary for the pre-1984 years: Roy, *The Lessons of the Soviet-Afghan War*, claims that it was $50 million a year. Don Oberdorfer, "Afghanistan: The Soviet Decision to Pull Out," *Washington Post*, April 17, 1988, claims that it was $30 million. The United States sent $120 million in 1984; $250 million in 1985; $470 million in 1986 and $630 million in 1987. See

istration decided to escalate U.S. covert action sharply; *Washington Post* correspondent Steve Coll writes that "the United States received highly specific, sensitive information about Kremlin politics and new Soviet war plans in Afghanistan." This intelligence revealed that Soviet hardliners in the Kremlin were pushing a policy of escalation in order to win the war within two years.[17]

According to one Western official, escalation of American involvement in 1985 "was directed at killing Russian military officers." The Americans reportedly had a great deal of intelligence on the habits of senior Soviet military personnel in Kabul, and the Pakistanis had requested rifles with scopes for assassinations. Eventually, CIA lawyers prevented the distribution of this information as a violation of the 1977 Presidential Directive against CIA involvement in assassinations.[18] But U.S. involvement escalated in other ways.

As Soviet tactics relied increasingly on air power, the United States began to supply the mujahideen with counter-measures: "Stinger" heat-seeking anti-aircraft missiles.[19] Stingers and their British equivalent, "Blowpipes," were first shipped in September 1986. Americans trained the Pakistanis to use the weapons and the Pakistanis then trained the mujahideen. The day-to-day control of the covert operations lay in the hands of the ISI.

Did the deployment of Stingers bring about the withdrawal of Soviet troops? Various sources suggest that Soviet responses were largely short-term and tactical in nature, and that when viewed against the overall political context in which the war took place, they were largely irrelevant in bringing about a withdrawal.[20]

The Soviets developed a few methods of rendering the Stingers less effective. Richard Burke, an American scientist who worked on countermeasures to Soviet SAMs, suggests that had this war gone on longer, then presumably

---

also Selig Harrison, "Inside the Afghan Talks," *Foreign Policy* no. 72 (Fall 1988): 50. The Americans were not the only ones supplying aid to the mujahideen; Saudi Arabia matched U.S. contributions and the United States bought many of the weapons it gave to the Afghans from the Chinese. It is estimated that by the mid-1980s, China was earning over $100 million a year in arms sales. See Coll, "Anatomy of a Victory."

[17] Coll, "Anatomy of a Victory." According to Coll's sources, the Soviets were planning to deploy one-third of their "*spetsnaz*" force—2000 highly trained paratroopers and many KGB officers. Scholars dispute the presence of *spetsnaz* forces in Afghanistan.

[18] Coll, "Anatomy of a Victory."

[19] In addition to Stingers, the United States supplied much equipment, including "extensive satellite reconnaissance data of Soviet targets on the Afghan battlefield, plans for military operations based on the satellite intelligence, intercepts of Soviet communications, secret communications networks for the rebels, [and] delayed timing devices" for explosives. Coll, "Anatomy of a Victory."

[20] For a similar interpretation, see "SAMs in Afghanistan: Assessing the Impact," *Janes' Defense Weekly* 8, no. 3 (July 25, 1987): "The initial results of the introduction of sophisticated SAMs to Afghanistan are a mixed bag at best. There was an increase in the number of Soviet-DRA [Democratic Republic of Afghanistan] losses. However, the missiles had no impact on the general course of the war."

TABLE 5.1

Surface-to-Air Missiles

Weapon	Period	Shipped to Pakistan	Received in Afghanistan
Blowpipes	September 1986	50	38
	July–August 1987	300	225
Stingers	October 1986–January 1987	200	150
	March–August 1987	600	450
Totals	September 1986–August 1987	1150	863

Source: Aaron Karp, "Blowpipes and Stingers in Afghanistan: One Year Later," *Armed Forces Journal,* September 1987, 38. The discrepancy between the numbers of weapons shipped from the United States and Britain and those received by the mujahideen is presumably accounted for by diversion of weapons by American, British, or Pakistani operatives.

the Americans would have developed ways to get around the Soviet counter-measures; "this [was] a cat-and-mouse game."[21] Soviet pilots altered their flight habits: pilots flew either below or above the Stinger's range. This brought its own hazards: when pilots flew very high, they traded safety for ac-curacy in bombing. When pilots flew very low, they increased their chances of crashing. The timing of maneuvers also changed from day to night, because the Stingers were not outfitted with night vision and could not be used in the dark.[22]

Other counter-measures included the use of "automatic decoy flare dis-pensers." As helicopters took off or flew through high-risk areas, they would eject flares at two-second intervals in an attempt to confuse the heat-seeking Stinger. Problems with the flares were quite significant however; they burned much hotter than engine fuel and a Stinger could be programmed to distin-guish one from the other, rendering this counter-measure useless.[23] A more sophisticated version of mixing "signatures," that is, the emissions that the Stinger encountered, included the use of "Hot Brick infra-red jammers." This jammer burned closer to the temperature of jet fuel (cooler than flares) and was invisible to the human eye. In addition, after 1987, Soviet helicopters were fitted with missile warning systems that enabled pilots to see the bear-

[21] Author's inteview with Richard Burke, Office of the Secretary of Defense, (Program, Analy-sis, and Evaluation), Department of Defense, Spring 1993.

[22] Ibid.; David Isby, "Soviet Surface-to Air Missile Countermeasures: Lessons from Afghanistan," *Jane's Soviet Intelligence Review* 1, no. 1 (January 1, 1989); Ian Kemp, "Abdul Haq: Soviet Mistakes in Afghanistan," *Jane's Defense Weekly* 9, no. 9 (March 5, 1988): 380; Mark Urban, "Soviet Operations in Afghanistan—Some Conclusions," *Jane's Soviet Intelligence Re-view* 2, no. 8 (August 1, 1990): 366; and Roy, *The Lessons of the Soviet-Afghan War,* 20–23.

[23] Other problems included the flares' aerodynamic qualities; if the flare separated too rapidly from the aircraft, the seeker in the Stinger could detect and reject the flare. Author's inteview with Burke.

ing and range of an incoming missile from the cockpit and to take evasive measures.[24]

Both critics and supporters of the Stingers' military effectiveness tend to agree that these missiles negatively affected the morale of the Soviet troops; one account notes that pilots sometimes crashed as a result of evasive actions against a real or imagined oncoming Stinger.[25] But assessments of the SAMs' tactical effectiveness are, at best, mixed. For example, one critic writes that "very few independent observers ever saw these weapons hitting anything and the kill rates exceeding 50 percent claimed by some analysts cannot be accepted."[26] This contrasts with the decidedly up-beat reports from the U.S. army that claim that in some cases Stingers had a 79 percent success rate.[27]

Even members of the mujahideen claim that the Stingers were not particularly effective at hitting their targets. Abdul Haq, the military commander of one of the mujahideen factions, questioned the impact of the missiles on the war. "How could we stop all the Soviet aircraft because we have twenty-five or thirty Stingers? No, it is impossible."[28] The United States claimed in late 1986 that the mujahideen had hit 90–100 enemy helicopters. Yet other sources claimed the Stingers hit only twenty-three aircraft. Generally, Western sources tended to claim a greater role for the Stingers than did reports from the mujahideen.[29]

Olivier Roy spent months in the battlegrounds of Afghanistan; he claims that the distribution of Stingers run by the ISI was driven, not surprisingly, by the ISI's own political purposes. The result was that Stingers did not always go to the most effective fighters and many were stockpiled, used against other mujahideen, or sold.[30] In any case, Stingers did not result in an increase in Soviet casualties. In fact, casualty rates decreased despite missile deployment.[31]

Beyond issues of accuracy and effectiveness, the argument that Stingers caused the withdrawal cannot be sustained chronologically. Many inside the leadership believed in the necessity of withdrawal long before the mujahideen received the Stingers; the issue of withdrawal began to appear on

[24] Isby, "Soviet SAM Countermeasures"; author's inteview with Burke.

[25] Isby, "Soviet SAM Countermeasures," 44. For positive or neutral accounts of the effect of the Stingers, see "Army Lauds Stinger Effectiveness in Afghan War," *Defense Daily* 164, no. 3 (July 6, 1989). For negative assessments, see Kemp, "Abdul Haq"; Urban, "Soviet Operations in Afghanistan." On the overall low morale and poor discipline of the Soviet military fighting in Afghanistan, see Alexander Alexiev, "Inside the Soviet Army in Afghanistan," R-3627-A (Santa Monica, Calif.: RAND, May 1988).

[26] Urban, "Soviet Operations in Afghanistan."

[27] See "Army Lauds Stinger Effectiveness."

[28] Kemp, "Abdul Haq."

[29] See "SAMs in Afghanistan." The political motivations for inflation or deflation of the success rate figures make accurate assessments problematic.

[30] Roy, *The Lessons of the Soviet-Afghan War*, 36.

[31] The highest casualties were sustained in 1984, two years before the deployment of Stingers, with 2343 dead. Casualties in 1985 were 1868; in 1986, 1333; in 1987, 1215; in 1988, 759; and in 1989, 53; *Pravda*, August 17, 1989. See also Urban, "Soviet Operations in Afghanistan."

the political agenda in late 1986 before the Stingers became militarily effective in the spring of 1987.[32] Additional evidence suggests that before Stingers arrived in Afghanistan, the Soviet negotiators became more conciliatory, suggesting that at least certain members of the political leadership considered withdrawal favorably.[33]

Finally, as policy makers and observers were quick to point out, the deployment of the Stingers could have prompted the Soviets to respond more aggressively rather than with accommodation. Marshal Sergei Akhromeev noted that Soviet foreign policy had changed despite U.S. foreign policy: "And we even did this [withdrawal] with Reagan—it was not easy to begin this with such a president, but in spite of this we took such a decision."[34]

Georgii Arbatov has been quite vocal and adamant about the role that U.S. policy played in changing Soviet policies. "*Perestroika* is without a doubt *not* the result of Reagan's politics and armament. This is a stupid idea. . . . This could only interfere. It could only make the military and the conservatives stronger."[35] Another high-level official close to Gorbachev has suggested that several reformers in the Kremlin believed that there were factions in the United States that wanted the Soviets to stay active in Afghanistan and that U.S. policy was designed with this goal in mind.[36]

All in all, the two primary responses of the international system to the war in Afghanistan—negotiation and arms supplies—did not play a central role in getting the Soviets to withdraw. The withdrawal was instead a result of the larger context of the process of domestic reform. It is there that one must look in order to understand how the dominant character of Soviet foreign policy turned from competition to accommodation.

THE DOMESTIC CONTEXT

The balance of power between the General Secretary, the Central Committee, and the Politburo had direct relevance for policy toward Afghanistan; it defined and limited political possibilities, thus shaping the political environ-

---

[32] On Stingers' effectiveness, see Roy, *The Lessons of the Soviet-Afghan War*, 23, 36.

[33] Harrison, "Inside the Afghan Talks," 32, argues that "serious negotiations" were going on more than a year before the Stingers allegedly brought the Soviets to the table. Khan, *Untying the Afghan Knot*, 148, claims that by 1986 there was "the belief that the Soviets were serious in seeking a settlement."

[34] Author's interview with Sergei Akhromeev, chief of the Soviet armed forces, 1984–88, and senior military advisor to Gorbachev, January 3, 1991.

[35] Author's interview with Georgii Arbatov, January 4, 1991. See also Georgii Arbatov, *The System* (New York: Random House, 1992).

[36] Author's interview with Valentin Varennikov, head of Soviet Ground Forces in Afghanistan, July 2, 1993.

ment. The configuration of this balance of power at the time of Gorbachev's ascension, however, is disputed among Western Sovietologists. For example, Thane Gustafson and Dawn Mann have argued that the general secretary's power was curtailed by the Politburo and other institutions with vested interests; an "oligarchic" struggle between institutions in Moscow determined policy outcomes.[37] The general secretary's power was greatly restricted as groups struggled to get their share of resources.

Jerry Hough offers a contrasting portrait: the general secretary in 1985 was the most powerful part of the system. Hough argues that the source of power lay in the ability to control the regional party apparatus. In using the "cadres weapon," the general secretary influenced the selection of the regional party secretaries, who, in turn, controlled the selection of the delegates to the Party Congresses. These delegates elected the Central Committee, which elected the Politburo, which in turn elected the general secretary.[38] Control over the selection of the cadres insured control over policy.

These contrasting descriptions of the balance of power in the Soviet leadership, however, are not necessarily mutually exclusive. The oligarchic scenario proposed by Gustafson and Mann describes the situation when Gorbachev came to power. In order to begin the process of change, Gorbachev had to maneuver politically and form alliances following this pattern. The Hough scenario of the cadres weapon and a stronger general secretary, however, would emerge following personnel changes in 1986, as Gorbachev gained control of both the Politburo and the Central Committee.

The oligarchic scenario is exemplified by the conservative political climate in the Politburo during the policy review of Afghanistan in April 1985.[39] On the one hand, except for Defense Minister Dmitrii Ustinov (no small exception), the military leadership, including Nikolai Ogarkov, Valentin Varennikov, and Sergei Akhromeev, had been against the war, and many senior military personnel were in favor of a withdrawal.[40] Akhromeev himself gave approval for publishing Artyom Borovik's controversial articles on the Soviet

---

[37] Thane Gustafson and Dawn Mann, "Gorbachev's First Year: Building Power and Authority," *Problems of Communism*, May–June 1986, 1–19. See also Gustafson, *Crisis amid Plenty*, 14; Harry Gelman, *The Brezhnev Politburo and the Decline of Détente* (Ithaca: Cornell University Press, 1984) and Jack Snyder, "The Gorbachev Revolution: A Waning of Soviet Expansionism?" *International Security* 12, no. 3 (Winter 1987/88): 93–131, for similar analyses.

[38] Hough, "Gorbachev Consolidating Power," 21.

[39] At the February 17, 1988, plenary session of the CPSU, Gorbachev spoke of this early policy review. *Pravda*, February 19, 1988, 1–3, in *Current Digest of the Soviet Press (CDSP)* 40, no. 7: 9.

[40] Author's interviews with Akhromeev and Zagladin; and with Vitalii Korotich (former editor of *Ogonëk*), December 14, 1990, and January 9, 1991. If military leaders actively opposed the war, they did so for different reasons than the specialist network, including their judgments about the difficulty of fighting a guerilla war.

Afghan war in *Ogonëk*, where for the first time, Soviet readers got a sense of the death and destruction taking place.[41] However, an immediate withdrawal or cessation of the war was politically impossible.[42]

Instead, what appears to have happened in 1985 was a decision to escalate involvement and to postpone any kind of serious reappraisal of the war. According to some sources, the military was given one year to achieve victory.[43] Borovik claims that at a Politburo meeting in April 1985, Gorbachev appointed Eduard Shevardnadze as the new head of the Central Committee's commission on Afghanistan, a job previously in Andrei Gromyko's portfolio.[44] Borovik claims that Gorbachev at that time agreed to an escalation in the fighting (although not as high as some in the military wanted) and insisted that casualties were to be kept low.[45]

Some members of the leadership wanted to withdraw. They recognized the situation as a quagmire, and yet they escalated involvement. Why? They did so because sizeable sectors of the party apparatus, the military, and the military industrial complex were not willing to consider a withdrawal seriously. The precise role of the military leadership in the decision to intervene and to withdraw is still a matter of debate. Alexander Yakovlev, in contrast to other reports, has called into question the military leadership's willingness to withdraw troops. He implies that despite what members of the military leadership have said, many, including Akhromeev and Varennikov, passively resisted the withdrawal. Yakovlev argued that their tactics through early 1989 were aimed at stopping the withdrawal.[46]

According to Viktor Kremenyuk, deputy director of ISKAN, "By the time Gorbachev came to power there was already a confrontation between two major communities," those who talked about the necessity of stopping the war and those who felt the Soviets could not withdraw without a victory. Kre-

[41] These articles could not have been researched and published without high-level military approval. Korotich (author's interview) also said that Varennikov was very helpful. Author's interviews with Artyom Borovik, October 29 and December 6, 1990.

[42] Author's interview with Akhromeev; and interview with Alexander Yakovlev on Central Television, First Channel, December 27, 1991 in FBIS-SOV, December 31, 1991, 3–5.

[43] Author's interviews with Borovik; Andrei Grachev, former Deputy Director, CCID, December 25, 1990; Korotich; and Viktor Kremenyuk, deputy director of ISKAN, November 1, 1990, all confirmed this. Arbatov and Akhromeev said they had no memory of this, and Zagladin had "no comment."

[44] Perhaps this appointment was a testing ground for Shevardnadze or an early attempt to shift some power away from Gromyko. Either way, by July 1985 Shevardnadze had replaced Gromyko as foreign minister.

[45] Borovik (author's interview) claims that the military argued that it needed 60,000 or 70,000 more troops in order to win the war. Oberdorfer, "Afghanistan," has also written about this plan for escalation. "There were credible reports from Kabul and elsewhere that [General M.] Zaitsev [who in July 1985 was appointed commander-in-chief of military operations in Afghanistan] had one year, in another version two years to start winning in Afghanistan."

[46] Central Television interview with Yakovlev.

menyuk claims, "Gorbachev was aware of this situation so he decided to give the military a chance to prove themselves."[47]

Arbatov's memoirs describe the tremendous influence of the military-industrial complex on the Soviet leadership, from the time of Brezhnev through to the ascension of Gorbachev. This institutional force was very strong when Gorbachev came to power; in order to get certain policies implemented, Gorbachev and his advisors had to engage in coalition building and compromise. But both Arbatov and Akhromeev point out that it was politically impossible for Gorbachev to initiate a withdrawal of troops right after coming to power, regardless of how he or his advisors felt about the use of military force in Afghanistan.[48]

First, Gorbachev and his cohort had to change the balance of power in order to get the withdrawal, as well as overall reform, on the agenda. To do this, they altered the conservative party apparatus as much as possible and went outside this apparatus as much as possible by consulting scholars and others not wedded to the conservative dogma of the Brezhnev years.[49] I describe this process next.

New Thinking and Old Institutions

As senior personnel secretary of the Party since 1982, Gorbachev had begun to change the party apparatus.[50] From 1982 through 1985, Gorbachev had been in an excellent position to place centrist or reform-minded regional party secretaries in the Central Committee.[51] Hough argues, however, that "until a new Central Committee was elected at the 27th Party Congress in March 1986, it was not prudent for [Gorbachev] to show his hand too clearly."[52]

The amount of change in the Central Committee should be compared to the lack of it at other Party Congresses: 38 percent of the Central Commit-

[47] Author's interview with Kremenyuk.

[48] Author's interviews with Arbatov and Akhromeev. See also Georgii Arbatov, "Iz nedavnego proshlogo" (From the recent past), *Znamya* nos. 9 and 10 (1990).

[49] See Alexander Rahr, "Leadership Changes at the Central Committee Plenum in February," *Radio Liberty Research Bulletin* no. 8 (RL 64/88), February 6, 1988, 1–2.

[50] Jerry F. Hough, *Russia and the West: Gorbachev and the Politics of Reform* (New York: Simon and Schuster, 1990), 151. For an extended discussion of personnel selection patterns from 1982–87, see Gavin Helf, "Gorbachev and the New Soviet Prefects: Soviet Regional Politics 1982–1988 in Historical Perspective," in *Analyzing the Gorbachev Era: Working Papers of the Students of the Berkeley-Stanford Program in Soviet Studies* (Berkeley and Stanford, Calif.: University of California at Berkeley and Stanford University, 1989), 10–12.

[51] Hough, "Gorbachev Consolidating Power," 28. Between March 1986 and December 1989, 67 percent of the regional party secretaries had been newly appointed. Hough, *Russia and the West*, 174.

[52] Hough, *Russia and the West*, 188.

tee was newly elected at the 27th Congress, while just 10 percent had been new at the 25th and 26th Party Congresses. By the end of the 27th Congress, the Central Committee had shrunk from 319 to 307 members, 125 of whom were new.[53] In addition to these changes, the secretaries responsible for numerous policies regarding ideology, foreign affairs, economics, agriculture, and industry were all new, and most were inclined towards reform of the administrative command system.[54]

The changes in the Central Committee were matched by equally sweeping personnel changes in the Politburo. Between March 1985 and March 1986, eight new men were added, all with ties to Gorbachev or to Andropov.[55] Of the original nine full members on the Politburo when Gorbachev came to power, three were dismissed and one was put in a ceremonial position. None of the remaining men were promoted.[56] By June 1987, one of the main architects of *perestroika* and a strong voice in the specialist network, Alexander Yakovlev, had become a full member of the Politburo.

The KGB had formed Andropov's base of patronage and although Gorbachev did not come out of this organization, he had its backing by late 1984. Gorbachev used his ties to Andropov to enlist the KGB's support in the early stages of reforming the party apparatus. The KGB provided the Politburo with reports that "as a whole were deliberately designed to support Gorbachev's arguments." By 1987, when the party apparatus had been substantially altered and domestic reform was on the agenda, Gorbachev then went to work reforming the KGB.[57]

There was comparatively little change in the military command in the early period.[58] There appear to be two reasons for this. First, many in the military leadership agreed with the need to restructure the economy; they felt that emphasis should be placed on high-technology weaponry and that directing resources away from the military to the civilian sector, if accompanied by the development of more sophisticated weaponry, would be helpful for stabilizing the external balance of power.[59] But many in Moscow attribute the mili-

---

[53] Ibid., 171.

[54] Hough, "Gorbachev Consolidating Power."

[55] See Gustafson and Mann, "Gorbachev's First Year"; Hough, "Gorbachev Consolidating Power," 27.

[56] Hough, *Russia and the West*, 171.

[57] Quoted in Christopher Andrew and Oleg Gordievsky, *KGB: The Inside Story* (New York: HarperCollins, 1990), 608; on Gorbachev and the KGB, see Amy W. Knight, *The KGB* (Boston: Unwin Hyman, 1990), 97–99.

[58] In July 1985, Gorbachev forced retirement of some senior officers. After the 27th Party Congress, in July 1986 Gorbachev replaced the commander in chief of ground forces, the chief of the navy, the chief of civil defense, and the chief of the main inspectorate of the armed forces. In early 1987, he brought Dmitri Yazov to Moscow as deputy minister of personnel from his post as commander of the far eastern theater. See Dusko Doder and Louise Branson, *Gorbachev: Heretic in the Kremlin* (New York, Viking, 1990), 206–207.

[59] Dale R. Herspring, *The Soviet High Command, 1967–1989* (Princeton: Princeton University Press), 250–251.

tary's lack of change to the internal balance of power. Until Mathias Rust landed his small Cessna aircraft on Red Square in May 1987, the military had been relatively "untouchable," but this obvious and gross breakdown of the country's defense system provided Gorbachev with the excuse he needed to change the top military leadership and bring in a defense minister that he could—at least in theory—control more easily.[60]

Before Gorbachev came to power, the International Department of the Central Committee (CCID) played a very important role in foreign policy making, providing the Politburo with much of the documentation that they needed to make policy.[61] In fact, the CCID and the "Communist and Workers' Parties of Socialist Counties" department were the main institutions, aside from the Politburo, that participated in forming policies toward socialist countries. (In the old days, the foreign ministry had essentially been locked out of much policy making; the Party rather than the government ran foreign policy.[62]) With Gorbachev's arrival as General Secretary, the CCID's role and outlook changed.

Personnel changes began in earnest in March 1986 at the 27th Party Congress when the head of the CCID since 1955, Boris Ponomarev, was replaced by Anatoly Dobrynin, the long-time ambassador to the United States. Deputy Director Rostislav Ulianovsky was replaced by Georgi Kornienko, a former deputy foreign minister and an arms control expert who had much experience with Americans. Vadim Medvedev was made head of the Socialist Countries department, and Alexander Yakovlev, former ambassador to Canada and former head of IMEMO, became the secretary supervising both departments.

These changes represented the strategy behind *perestroika*: 1) replace party ideologists with pragmatic, knowledgeable people; 2) tie foreign policy to economic—not ideological—conditions; and 3) shift power from party to governmental institutions. The CCID was staffed after 1986 by men and women from the foreign ministry, by Americanists or Europeanists whose knowledge came from working in academic institutes or in the foreign service. This new group was quite different in orientation from the party apparatchiks in the CCID who, since the 1950s, had dealt with relations toward the Third World and Eastern Europe. The overall portfolios of the CCID and foreign ministry (MID) were merged after Gorbachev came to

[60] Sergei Sokolov, who had been defense minister since late 1984 after Ustinov's death, was dismissed and Yazov was made defense minister. Doder and Bransonm *Gorbachev*, 235–238; author's interviews with Akhromeev; Arbatov; and Borovik. Yazov was one of those who later helped stage a putsch to oust Gorbachev in August 1991.

[61] The classic work on the CCID is Leonard Shapiro, "The International Department of the CPSU: Key to Soviet Policy," *International Journal* (Toronto) 32 (Winter 1976–77): 41–55. See also Archie Brown, "The Foreign Policy Making Process," in Curtis Keeble, ed., *The Soviet State: Domestic Roots of Soviet Foreign Policy* (London: Gower, 1985), 205.

[62] Author's interview with Igor Malashenko, former senior researcher, CCID, November 21, 1990.

power; MID began to deal more extensively with issues in the Third World, and CCID had more impact on policy toward the United States than ever before.[63]

Changes at MID began in July of 1985 with the appointment of Eduard Shevardnadze as foreign minister, a man with "not a stitch of foreign policy experience [who] had never even worked in Moscow."[64] Eventually, eight new deputy foreign ministers were named, along with new ambassadors to the countries with which the Soviet Union had the most extensive relations.[65]

Beyond the fact that MID was increasingly involved in de-ideologizing Soviet-Third World relations, its role in the process of policy making began to change. According to Vadim Zagladin, at a closed session in July 1986, Gorbachev "raised the question of the necessity of serious change of the methods of work."[66] Foreign policy making was changing because the balance of power was shifting away from the party apparatus. In the old days, the Politburo and the Central Committee had power over MID. In the era of new thinking, with Shevardnadze as a powerful and independent actor, not merely the yes-man for the general secretary that Gromyko had been, and with the redistribution of portfolios, MID had become a player in the policy making process.[67]

New Thinking and New Institutions

In addition to repopulating the Central Committee, the Politburo, the Foreign Ministry, and the various other institutions of power, Gorbachev cultivated a source of support outside these traditional institutions in the form of an expert community. This community had become mobilized in the period 1982–84, as I discussed in Chapter 4. After 1985, Gorbachev further empowered several members of the top echelon of this group by giving them access to national platforms inside and outside the party apparatus.[68] Every echelon of the expert community benefited as the style of foreign policy mak-

[63] Ibid.; Timothy J. Colton, *The Dilemma of Reform in the Soviet Union* (New York: Council on Foreign Relations, 1986), 178–179; George W. Breslauer, "All Gorbachev's Men," *National Interest*, Summer 1988, 95; Brown, "The Foreign Policy Making Process," 205. Zagladin (author's interview) noted that by the late 1980s, half of the people working in the CCID had doctorates of science.

[64] Colton, *The Dilemma of Reform in the Soviet Union*, 179.

[65] Hough, "Gorbachev Consolidating Power," 32–34.

[66] Author's interview with Zagladin.

[67] Author's interviews with Nodari Simoniia, deputy director, IMEMO, October 18, December 21, 1990; Malashenko; and Grachev.

[68] The most important placement was that of Alexander Yakovlev overseeing domestic ideological affairs and foreign relations in the Central Committee.

ing gradually became less centralized and consultations became increasingly frequent and routine.[69]

Participants in and observers of the policy making process repeatedly spoke of the qualitatively different relationship between experts and various parts of the decision making apparatus that developed after Gorbachev came to power. For example, Karen Brutents, the deputy head of the CCID, noted that "the peculiarity of Gorbachev is that he understands the role of scholars, of consultations." German Diligensky, editor of IMEMO's journal *MEiMO*, said of Gorbachev that, "as soon as he came to power, he began to surround himself with people of a completely different type than was around Brezhnev; not so much as functionaries as people he could sort out by their minds, their qualifications, etc." Andrei Grachev, then a deputy director of CCID, said that Gorbachev "value[d] a lot his ties with the intellectual circles."[70] In 1987, Nodari Simoniia argued that "it was necessary to involve scientific and specialist circles before taking this decision [to withdraw troops from Afghanistan]. This was not done sufficiently in 1979. Today, the government is trying to involve such specialists when deciding something important in a variety of fields including foreign policy."[71]

Viktor Kremenyuk, deputy director at ISKAN, explained how policy making had changed as well as the role of the expert in this process:

> Gorbachev did not have sufficient knowledge of foreign policy when he came to power. But he was unhappy with foreign policy at the time, and talked of the necessity to look forward. Unofficially he was unhappy and he was inviting people to give suggestions of what should be done. He knew Arbatov personally, he knew Yakovlev. . . . Gorbachev likes different proposals, while Brezhnev and even Andropov wanted to hear only their style, their points of view reiterated. . . . Since Gorbachev came to power, especially when preparing for a summit, ISKAN and others institutes wrote position papers. From September 1985 on there was really a general mobilization. What was new was that we were writing what we thought was necessary about U.S.-Soviet relations. We gained an increasingly loud voice.[72]

[69] Author's interview with Zagladin. See also the report on a conference on "Social Science and the Achievement of a Qualitatively New State of Soviet Society," attended by Yakovlev, Primakov, and Bogomolov; *Pravda*, April 18, 1987, cited in *CDSP* 39, no. 15: 3.

[70] Author's interviews with Karen Brutents, Deputy head, CCID, December 7, 1990; German Diligensky, December 19, 1990; Grachev. See also Vladimir Shlapentokh, *The Politics of Sociology in the Soviet Union* (Boulder: Westview), 231. Arbatov was quoted by Doder and Branson, *Gorbachev*, 75: "He likes to call in experts and grill them in detail on topics he feels uncertain about. He keeps you on your toes."

[71] Lawrence Lifshultz, "Afghanistan: A Voice from Moscow," *Monthly Review* 39, no. 4 (September 1987): 14.

[72] Author's interview with Kremenyuk. Zagladin (author's interview) corroborated this statement, noting that the leadership paid much more attention to *zapiski* after 1985. One specific result of the new approach was that a senior scholar at ISKAN provided a frank appraisal of

In short, Gorbachev's leadership style was, by all accounts, one that cultivated the advice of experts, providing them with resources in order to challenge the status quo. The experts gained prominence and a voice from the leadership, while the leadership gained legitimacy and support from the experts.

Another important new strategy for changing the internal balance of power involved the policy of *glasnost* or "openness" in the press. Use of the press *per se* was not new or different; the press had been used by the leadership to bolster policies since the time of Lenin.[73] What was new was the critical tone of reporting and the recognition that support—beyond that of the party apparatus, the political elite, or even an expert community—was needed to achieve reform. In addition, *glasnost* directly benefited the specialist network in support of reform at home and cooperation abroad; it permitted experts a public voice to address issues and thus affect the climate in which decision making occurred.[74]

Personnel changes in the editorial staffs of publications were the most direct means by which Gorbachev put *glasnost* into motion. But in sponsoring this new source of support, the reformists proceeded cautiously: unwilling to encroach first upon the ideological territory of such mainstream institutions as the party newspaper *Pravda* or the government newspaper *Izvestiia*, instead they brought new and daring editors in to run heretofore obscure publications. New editors turned these publications into extremely popular and important sources of information, challenging the role of "old think" publications in shaping the political environment. For example, after Vitali Korotich was brought in by Alexander Yakovlev to head *Ogonëk*, at that time a little known magazine, its circulation went from 260,000 to 4 million. The editors received thousands of letters every day versus the twenty that were received in the pre-*glasnost* days.[75]

Soviet-U.S. policy that, according to sources, proved important in redirecting Soviet policy toward the United States; it represented the kind of innovative thinking Gorbachev wanted.

[73] Gorbachev held meetings with members of the press and the expert community, often prior to major policy shifts, to discuss how certain issues should be covered or, in his words, "to synchronize watches." See, for example, Gorbachev's meeting with the press, February 13, 1987, three days before the "Peace Forum"; *Pravda*, February 14, 1987, in *CDSP* 39 no. 7: 6–8; and his meeting of May 7, 1988, on the media's role in preparation for the 19th All-Union Party Conference held in June 1988; *Pravda*, May 8 and 11, 1988, in *CDSP* 40, no. 19: 1–8. See also Vera Tolz, "Soviet Journalists Are Given New Instructions," *Radio Liberty Research Bulletin* no. 3 (RL 19/88), January 8, 1988, 3: "One of the Party's goals in 1987 . . . had been to stimulate the Soviet population—in particular, the intelligentsia—to take an active interest in reform and contribute their ideas. That is why the publication of many unprecedented materials in the cultural sphere was welcomed."

[74] See Central Television interview with Yakovlev; and Doder and Branson, *Gorbachev*, 143, on the use of *glasnost* to support *perestroika*.

[75] Other examples include the broadsheet *Argumentii and Fakti* which went from a circulation of 10,000 to 32.5 million, and which published shocking and previously undisclosed facts and scandals about the Party and the government. See John Newhouse, "Profiles Chronicling the Chaos," *The New Yorker*, December 31, 1990, 38–39.

Other new editors included Yegor Yakovlev at *Moscow News*, and Boris Pyadishev at the Ministry of Foreign Affairs journal, *International Affairs*. Otto Latsis was brought in to run *Kommunist* in 1987, and Yegor Gaidar, who would become a leading post-Soviet reformer and Russian prime minister, was made its economics editor. Gaidar claimed that his work on this journal both helped push reform and educated him about the need for reform: "The leading party journal was one of the places you could actually change the situation. . . . And there I had access to real information about the economy, and the real process of decision making."[76]

Glasnost affected the war most dramatically after the announcement to withdraw had been made in February 1988. But long before that, from March 1986, as Gorbachev instituted some of the most important changes in personnel in the party apparatus, he redefined the dominant image of the war: no longer the "hand of imperialism," it had become the "bleeding wound." While this metaphor was symbolic of new thinking in foreign policy and Gorbachev's sentiments about the war, its use also underscored the constraints that the internal balance of power placed even on the General Secretary: Gorbachev's ability to distinguish a regional conflict from an ideological one was not as yet accompanied by a public willingness to acknowledge mistakes made in the name of an "internationalist duty."[77] Regardless of the fact that he and his cohort wanted to withdraw from Afghanistan, he publicly assigned responsibility for this wound to "counter-revolution and imperialism" and not to Soviet involvement in the war.[78]

By replacing the Brezhnevian "hand of imperialism," with the new image of the bleeding wound, Gorbachev acknowledged that the situation inside Afghanistan had grown increasingly problematic.[79] Further, the criticism that a confrontational foreign policy sapped strength and health from society, suggested by the new metaphor, was consistent with the view that domestic priorities should include an accommodationist foreign policy. Yet Gorbachev stopped short of assigning any blame to Soviet military policy for conditions inside Afghanistan. No public acknowledgement of a mistake would come until three and a half years later, with Shevardnadze's remarkable discussion

---

[76] Steven Erlanger, "Reform School," *New York Times Magazine*, November 29, 1992, 74.

[77] Gorbachev had been discussing Afghanistan as a regional issue since the first Gorbachev-Reagan summit in Geneva. "It would be wrong and very dangerous to depict all these seats of contradictions [regional conflicts] as the product of rivalry between the East and the West." Gorbachev, "Press-konferentsiia v Sovetskoi press-tsentre v Zheneve" (Press conference in the Soviet Press Center in Geneva), *Kommunist* no. 17 (1985): 21.

[78] Mikhail Gorbachev, "Politicheskiy doklad tsentral'nogo komiteta KPSS XXVII s'ezda kommunisticheskoy partii Sovetskogo Soyuza" (Political report of the Central Committee CPSU XXVII Congress), *Kommunist* no. 4 (1986): 58–59.

[79] For the first appearance of the "hand of imperialism" image, which was the dominant image of the war until February 1986, see L. Brezhnev, "Otvety na voprosy korrespondenta gazety 'Pravda'" (Answers to the *Pravda* correspondent's questions), *Kommunist* no. 2 (1980): 13–16.

of Afghanistan as "immoral and illegal" in October of 1989.[80] According to Zagladin, this hesitancy was due to the political constraints on Gorbachev at the time; the "bleeding wound" was as far as Gorbachev could go given the internal power balance.[81]

Shevardnadze writes in his book, *The Future Belongs to Freedom*, that Gorbachev and the reformers in February 1986 could literally not get the withdrawal on the political agenda. Early drafts of the Congress's Political Report had mentioned the "need to withdraw our forces from Afghanistan." Later drafts were written without this statement. Shevardnadze asks, "Why had it disappeared? At whose insistence?" His implicit answer supports the argument that political conditions prohibited reformers from publicly addressing this controversial issue at that time.[82]

INTERNAL BATTLES AND EXTERNAL WARS

After a year as general secretary, Gorbachev and his cohort had brought significant change to most of the important institutions of power, and they had succeeded in supplying at least some resources to members of the expert community. With the internal balance of power shifting in their favor, the reformers began to take steps toward getting the withdrawal on the agenda.

Don Oberdorfer has written that "1985 was a year of testing and temporizing about Afghanistan, 1986 a year of showdown on the battlefield, and 1987 the year of decision to withdraw. By no later than July of [that] year, the die was cast." Oberdorfer argues the decision was made between April and July of 1987.[83] Interviews and declassified Kremlin archival material suggest that while his account is basically accurate, the issue was being debated seriously in policy circles by late 1986. The withdrawal did not arise from a sudden realization that the war was a bad policy, but was part of the larger struggle for reform.[84] The time at which withdrawal made it on to the agenda was a result of the domestic struggles involved in setting the political agenda.

One practical consideration for those working toward withdrawal involved

---

[80] Shevardnadze described the Soviet invasion of Afghanistan as a violation of "the norms of proper behavior." Shevardnadze's characterization of the Soviet's role in the war as "illegal and immoral was the harshest yet uttered by a top official." Bill Keller, "Moscow Says Afghan Role Was Illegal, Immoral," *New York Times*, October 24, 1989, 1, 14. For the speech, see FBIS-SOV, October 24, 1989.

[81] Author's interview with Zagladin.

[82] Eduard Shevardnadze, *The Future Belongs to Freedom* (New York: The Free Press, 1991), 47.

[83] Oberdorfer, "Afghanistan." See also Oberdorfer, *The Turn: From the Cold War to a New Era* (New York: Poseidon Press, 1991).

[84] On this last point, see Oberdorfer, "Afghanistan"; and Michael Dobbs, "Withdrawal from Afghanistan: Start of Empire's Unraveling," *Washington Post*, November 16, 1992.

the government in Kabul. Afghan president Babrak Karmal, installed in December 1979, apparently balked at the idea of the Soviets' departure. Riaz Khan, the Pakistani negotiator at Geneva, suggests that negotiations with the Afghan government and the Soviets had improved somewhat by 1985 but that the Afghan government was stalling on a time frame, thus prompting reformists in Moscow to push for a change of leadership in Kabul.[85] Boris Pyadishev, editor of *International Affairs*, implies that part of the reason that the Soviets engineered the dismissal of Karmal was that in October 1985, on a visit to Moscow, Karmal gave a negative response to Gorbachev's suggestion that he was thinking about "withdrawing the Soviet forces from Afghanistan."[86] Olivier Roy argues that Karmal was pushing exactly the type of state structure in Kabul that was being discredited by *perestroika* in Moscow, while his successor, Najibullah, was involved in the same type of power-consolidating strategies as Gorbachev such as coopting local leaders and giving them power at the local level.[87] The Soviet leadership needed a new Afghan president with whom to negotiate the withdrawal. By May 1986, the leadership of the PDPA changed hands from Karmal to Najibullah, and, at least in theory, the reformers in Moscow had in place a leader who would help bring about Soviet disengagement.

The official characterization of the war in Afghanistan had not yet changed. The opposition was still referred to as *"dushmany"* or bandits. The Soviet spokesmen continued to call for a cessation of outside interference.[88] Few details about the war were released, and restrictions on the press continued to be stringent. Behind the scenes, however, a rethinking of the war was already underway. The turning point in the withdrawal process, according to knowledgeable Soviets, appeared to come in late 1986 and 1987 with a thorough review of policy.[89] What had been a desire to withdraw emerged as a decision in principle to withdraw as it was placed on the political agenda. The number of consultations increased dramatically at that time, as did diplomatic efforts aimed at ending the war.

Despite U.S. policy toward the war in Afghanistan, reformist policy makers were occasionally able to use events in the international system to bolster their desire to withdraw. According to several sources, after the summit at Reykjavik in October 1986, Gorbachev and his advisors came to the conclu-

---

[85] Khan, *Untying the Afghan Knot*, 93; author's interview with Vladimir Snegirov, former Kabul correspondent for *Komsomolskaya Pravda*, November 11, November 20, 1990.

[86] Boris Pyadishev, "Najibullah, the President of the Republic of Afghanistan," *International Affairs* (Moscow), February 1990, 19.

[87] Roy, *The Lessons of the Soviet-Afghan War*, 28.

[88] See, for example, *Pravda*, statement by Ministry of Foreign Affairs (MFA) spokesman, March 25, 1987, in *CDSP* 39, no. 12 (1987): 10; and *Pravda*, statement by MFA spokesman, July 8, 1987, in *CDSP* 39, no. 26: 14.

[89] Author's interviews with Akhromeev; Arbatov; Borovik; Zagladin; Simoniia; and Valeri Sidorov, former aide to Alexander Yakovlev and Evgeni Primakov, November 15, 1990.

sion that the United States would not entertain seriously the idea of new political thinking until a Soviet withdrawal from Afghanistan was brought about.[90] Reformists argued that the success of reform relied heavily on cooperative conditions in the international environment. Efforts at creating such an environment would be greatly facilitated by better relations with the United States, which in turn were dependent on a number of Soviet concessions including pulling troops out of Afghanistan. Gorbachev, according to Kremlin archival documents, argued at a Politburo meeting on November 13, 1986, that "we have been at war in Afghanistan six years already. If we don't change our approach we will be there another 20–30 years. . . . We need to wrap up this process in the near future." Shevardnadze, at this meeting, proposed inviting Najibullah to Moscow for discussion regarding Soviet intentions.[91]

It is not possible to say definitively how this meeting differed from other Politburo meetings on the subject of Afghanistan. Moreover, it is unclear whether this was the first time Gorbachev urged withdrawal. But evidence suggests that even if it were not the first time, this discussion led to a different outcome. Policy began to change substantially after this meeting and a serious debate on withdrawal ensued. For example, during Najibullah's visit to Moscow in December 1986, Gorbachev told him that the Soviet commitment was limited and informed him that the Soviets would be withdrawing troops sometime between May 1988 and December 1988.[92]

By early 1987, with the internal balance of power in Gorbachev's favor, there were discernible changes in policy. For example, the notion of "national reconciliation" was introduced in mid-January 1987, following Najibullah's trip to Moscow. Under pressure from the Soviets, Najibullah agreed in principle to begin talks on sharing power with opposition forces. "National reconciliation" served the purpose of portraying the Kabul government as capable of handling the opposition without Soviet help. It laid the groundwork for troop withdrawal and bolstered the position of those policy makers in favor of withdrawal.[93]

The policy of *glasnost* directly affected the ability of reformers to get public support for a withdrawal from Afghanistan. The effects of the lack of re-

[90] Akhromeev (author's interview) accompanied Gorbachev to the summit as the senior Soviet arms control negotiator; author's interview with Zagladin.

[91] "Zasedanie Politburo TsK KPSS" (Session of the Politburo), Fond 89, Perechen' 11, dokument 56, November 13, 1986, Gorbachev statement, 25, Shevardnadze statement, 27–28.

[92] Pyadishev, "Najibullah." See also Oberdorfer, "Afghanistan," 31. He writes that "the end game would begin in the summer of 1987, according to an Afghan official who later defected to the west." In July 1987, Gorbachev stated, "We favor a short time frame for withdrawal." Philip Taubman, "Gorbachev Agrees to U.S. Suggestion for a Missile Ban," *New York Times*, July 23, 1987; and Doder and Branson, *Gorbachev*.

[93] Artyom Borovik, *The Hidden War* (New York: Atlantic, 1990), 198, quotes an Afghan army major complaining after the policy of national reconciliation had begun: "Tell me, why did we first call the enemy 'bandits,' then 'basmachi,' then 'terrorists,' then 'extremists,' and now the 'opposition'? It's impossible to fight with the opposition. Meanwhile, the enemy hasn't changed."

porting and knowledge about the war were not lost on Yakovlev, Shevardnadze, or Gorbachev. Yakovlev has been quite specific about how *glasnost* was
used to counter opposition to the withdrawal from Afghanistan:

> The difficulties, the maneuvering in the commission and the Politburo increased
> [with regard to the issue of withdrawal]. You could only guess what people were
> really thinking. . . . Suddenly, somebody had the idea of actually showing what
> was really happening. . . . Mikhail Sergeyevich [Gorbachev] came down firmly
> on our side. "Why not show it?" he said. "Why keep it all secret? Let's show it."
> On the whole, this process of *glasnost*—applied to the war—helped us a very
> great deal in bringing closer the withdrawal.[94]

One of the first and most important examples of *glasnost* applied to the war
came from Artyom Borovik and his articles published in *Ogonëk*, describing
for the first time the real war in Afghanistan. Soviet reporters in Afghanistan
for most of the war, even through 1987, had no notion of the number of Soviet troops in the country nor the number of casualties.[95] Journalists were not
permitted to refer in print to any military divisions or regiments. As one senior military officer who fought in Afghanistan remarked to Borovik after the
decision to withdraw was made, "our readers and television audiences got the
impression that Soviet fighting men were doing everything except fighting a
war."[96] The story behind the publication of Borovik's reports underscores the
internal battles that erupted around the decision to withdraw. Borovik claims
that there was high-level military and political support for publishing information directly from the field, but that there were dozens of other military
and political forces that interfered with publication. Without the help of Yuli
Vorontsov, "the highest Soviet official in the foreign office dealing with
Afghanistan" and later ambassador to Afghanistan, Borovik's forays into the
field and subsequent publication of articles would have been impossible.[97]

Borovik's articles were controversial because, even in the spring of 1987,
journalists generally did not leave Kabul and were not permitted to visit

[94] Central Television interview with Yakovlev, 4. While the general characterization of the war
remained unchanged in the press until the announcement of the withdrawal, the war—like all
Soviet policies—was analyzed in more realistic, critical tones after Gorbachev came to power.
See, for example, M. Gorbachev, "Speech in Vladivistok," *Pravda*, July 29, 1986, in *CDSP* 38, no.
30: 6; Gorbachev, "In Honor of Najib," *Pravda*, December 13, 1986, in *CDSP* 38 no. 50: 15.

[95] Despite *glasnost*, the number of casualties was not printed until August 1989, in *Pravda*.

[96] Borovik interview with Major General Kim Tsagolov, "Afganistan: predvaritel'nye itogi"
(Afghanistan: the preliminary results), *Ogonëk* no. 30 (July 1988): 25–27. The publication of this
interview, in which, for the first time a high-ranking military officer criticized the war, cost
Tsagolov his rank and his job as chief of the Department of Marxism-Leninism at the Frunze
Military Academy. Author's interview with Kim Tsagolov, January 4, 1991.

[97] Author's interview with Borovik. Korotich (author's interview) claims that Akhromeev and
Varennikov were helpful getting the articles past the censor. Newhouse, "Profiles from the
Chaos," 52–57. See also Hedrick Smith, *The New Russians* (New York: Random House, 1990),
102–104; Borovik, "Afganistan: Dvenik reportera" (Diary of a reporter), *Ogonëk* no. 29 (July
1987): 21–24; ibid., no. 30 (July 1987): 18–21; and in English, Borovik, *The Hidden War*.

troops, let alone write about their lives in the field. No one had published material on casualties or deaths, only on guarding buildings, constructing roads, or planting flowers. In contrast, beginning in 1987 and continuing through the end of the war, Borovik put on a soldier's uniform and travelled from unit to unit chronicling the fighting. As the the war wound down and withdrawal was firmly on the agenda, his stories became increasingly graphic and critical.

During the war, all dispatches had to go through the General Staff (GS) for clearance. In 1987, the GS refused to allow Borovik's articles to be published. Borovik went back to Vorontsov, newly appointed as first deputy foreign minister. Vorontsov "wanted to show what a 'democrat' he was," made 25 or 30 corrections, and said that he was in favor of publishing. Armed with Vorontsov's approval, Borovik did battle with the GS again ("It was a fight for every word") and eventually they arrived at a "compromise" and the accounts were published.[98]

Letters critical of the war began pouring into journals and newspapers. Mothers wrote that the graphic articles made their lives more difficult; it was easier to wait for their sons before they knew what was happening to them. This information, however, politicized many mothers of soldiers, who formed in the late 1980s one of the first civic organizations in the Soviet Union.[99]

Meanwhile, through 1987, Gorbachev and his circle grew more outspoken in their analysis of domestic problems. In the speeches and writings of Gorbachev and the specialist advisors, the crisis in society was linked not only to the stagnation of the 1970s but now also to the entire administrative command system imposed by Stalin. Gorbachev argued that the administrative command system had affected not only the economy, but all aspects of civil society. It had given rise to the attitude that while in theory, property belonged to the state and all its workers, in reality, it belonged to no one. This outspokenness influenced the political environment in which foreign policy decisions were made, helping to make reformist thinking about foreign policy appear connected to and consistent with other issues.

In February of 1987, before two different audiences, Gorbachev extended his critique of the policy process to foreign policy, indicating how the needs and interests of domestic politics influenced Soviet foreign policy. At a "Peace Forum," in front of cultural and intellectual figures from around the world, he noted the dependence of foreign policy on domestic policy: "Before my people, before you and before the whole world, I frankly say that our international policy is, more than ever before, determined by domestic policy, by

---

[98] Author's interview with Borovik. On the role of the media in creating a "groundswell" of protest against the war in 1987 and 1988, see Sallie Wise, "War Should Never Have Happened: Soviet Citizens Assess the War in Afghanistan," *Radio Liberty Research Bulletin* no. 23 (RL 226/88), June 1, 1988, 1–2.

[99] Author's interview with Borovik. "Mothers of Soldiers" is still one of the best organized nationally based non-governmental organizations in post-Soviet Russia.

our interest in concentrating on constructive work to improve our country."[100] Gorbachev and the new thinkers were reframing concepts of national security to fit domestic imperatives.[101]

A few days later, at a meeting of trade union leaders, Gorbachev linked the disintegration of détente to Soviet internal decline. Moreover, he provided a glimpse of the evolutionary process behind *perestroika* that supported the notion that a period was needed for power consolidation before wide-spread reform could begin. He said that the January 1987 plenum had been postponed three times because the policy makers needed to work out certain concepts in *perestroika* and determine what personnel changes needed to be made in order to enact the changes. "We had to deepen the analysis of the situation that had preceded [the] April [1985] plenary session of the Central Committee." The period from the April plenary session up through January 1987 was a time of "working out concepts of social and economic development."[102]

During this time of increasingly frank criticism of the system he had inherited, Gorbachev maintained regular contact with foreign and domestic specialists, writers, and experts who had been brought inside the party apparatus.[103] Meetings usually lasted several hours and were often followed by major policy shifts. Valeri Sidorov, an aide to Yakovlev and Primakov, reported that he was present at "every meeting with the intelligentsia. It is always a two-sided conversation. And Gorbachev tends to listen more."[104]

An example of specialist influence came in the changed policy toward the Third World. Optimistic official reports of the revolutionary process in the Third World had been replaced since the 27th Party Congress by much more restrained and somber evaluations. This shift from optimistic to pragmatic assessments followed nearly two decades of scholarly articles, reports, and conferences among Third World specialists at IMEMO and IVAN debating the merits of Soviet policy toward countries of "socialist orientation."[105]

[100] *Pravda*, February 17, 1987, *CDSP* 39, no. 7 (1987): 11.

[101] "Gorbachev's agitation for new political thinking on security is more a product of instrumental necessity than of military-strategic enlightenment." Stephen M. Meyer, "The Sources and Prospects of Gorbachev's New Political Thinking on Security," *International Security* 13, no. 2 (Fall 1988): 129, reprinted in Sean M. Lynn-Jones, Steven E. Miller, and Stephen Van Evera, eds. *Soviet Military Policy: An* International Security *Reader* (Cambridge, Mass.: MIT Press, 1989).

[102] *Pravda*, February 26, 1987, in *CDSP* 39, no. 8 (1987): 8.

[103] For example, see discussion of meeting in *Pravda*, February 14, 1987; cited in *CDSP* 39, no. 7: 6–8.

[104] Author's interview with Sidorov.

[105] For examples of work critical of Soviet Third World policy, see Georgii Mirsky, "Meniaiushchikhsia oblik 'tret'ego mira" (The changing face of "the Third World"), *Kommunist* no. 2 (1976): 106–115; Evgeni Primakov, "Nekotorie problemy razvivaiushchikhsia stran" (Some problems of developing countries), *Kommunist* no. 11 (1978): 81–91. See Elizabeth K. Valkenier, *The Soviet Union and the Third World: An Economic Bind* (New York: Praeger, 1983); and Jerry F. Hough, *The Struggle for the Third World* (Washington, D.C.: Brookings Institution, 1986).

In 1987 and 1988, the implications of the specialists' analyses were applied to Afghanistan by the leadership. Local conditions—specifically the indigenous resistance—were acknowledged to be important factors in the war.[106] The Americans were still blamed for fueling the war, but they were no longer classified as the source of the conflict. Once this occurred, the bipolar context of the conflict disappeared, along with concern about the Soviet reputation for strategic resolve. In this way, the changed image of the war facilitated the withdrawal process.

Sources in Moscow such as Valeri Sidorov, who worked for Yakovlev at the time, claimed that the decision to withdraw was reached in 1987. Yuri Gankovsky, perhaps the preeminent Afghan specialist in the Soviet Union, also claimed that the political decision to withdraw was taken in the spring of 1987, and that it was a unilateral move that had no connection to the Geneva accord process aimed at negotiating a settlement to the war.[107]

According to Nodari Simoniia, the frequency of consultations between government officials and Third World specialists increased dramatically in 1986 and 1987. Scholars had contact with people in the leadership, particularly with Brutents, first deputy director of the CCID; Zagladin; and Anatoly Chernyaev, Gorbachev's foreign policy aide. Ideas were quickly transmitted to the top, particularly through Primakov and Yakovlev, both former directors of IMEMO.[108]

On the larger political front, a victory of sorts regarding Afghanistan came by late December 1987, at the Washington summit, when Gorbachev stated publicly that the political decision to withdraw had been reached.[109] On February 9, 1988, he announced the impending withdrawal of troops from Afghanistan, devoting an entire speech exclusively to the war. He announced that the Soviets planned to begin withdrawal in May 1988 and that all Soviet troops would be out of the country by February 1989, a commitment that was met.[110]

The exclusive attention in the February speech to the war in Afghanistan is nearly unique; in all the leadership speeches in the period 1980–89, the only other time the war dominated a speech was when Brezhnev discussed the Soviet escalation in January 1980. Over the years, the Soviet leadership made vague comments concerning their intention to withdraw, but the comments had never been accompanied by any substantial change.[111]

---

[106] See for example, Gorbachev's comments on regional conflicts when he announced the withdrawal. *Pravda*, February 9, 1988, cited in *CDSP* 40, no. 6: 3.

[107] See Yuri Gankovsky, *At the Harriman Institute* 1, no. 13: "The political decision to leave Afghanistan was accepted in the beginning of 1987." For a first-hand account of the Geneva process which corroborates Gankovsky's statement, see Khan, *Untying the Afghan Knot*.

[108] Author's interview with Simoniia; corroborated by Gankovsky (author's interview).

[109] *Pravda*, December 12, 1987, 3–4, in *CDSP* 39, no. 50: 20.

[110] *Pravda*, February 9, 1988, in *CDSP* 40, no. 6: 1–3.

[111] Analysts agree that the withdrawal of six regiments in the fall of 1986 cannot be considered a significant change in Soviet policy toward the war, as these regiments were immediately

In the February 1988 speech, Gorbachev maintained that the withdrawal "was a reflection of our current political thinking, of our new, up-to-date vision of the world." Gorbachev used the metaphor of the bleeding wound once again, but this time its use suggested a new interpretation of the war and foreign policy in general. "If the arms race, which we are so insistently seeking to halt—with some success—is mankind's insane rush to the abyss, then regional conflicts are bleeding wounds capable of causing spots of gangrene on the body of mankind."[112]

Alexander Bovin, political correspondent for *Izvestiia*, noted a few months later that the Intermediate Nuclear Forces treaty and the Soviet withdrawal from Afghanistan were "symbol[s] of the overall restructuring and renewal in Soviet foreign policy."[113] Both represented a break in the chain of the past, a rolling back of Brezhnevian policies, as well as a symbol—political and psychological—of what cooperation between the superpowers could achieve.

On April 14, 1988, the Soviet Union, the United States, Pakistan, and Afghanistan signed the Geneva accord providing for withdrawal. The manner in which the Soviets announced the withdrawal in February and signed the accord in April suggested haste and the fear that domestic and foreign opponents of Soviet withdrawal could still derail the withdrawal. Gorbachev announced that the Soviets would withdraw despite the fact that various treaty issues had not been agreed to; there was no cease-fire agreement, and there was no pledge to stop sending supplies. The accord simply provided the Soviets with a legal face-saving device for an exit.

WITHDRAWAL ON THE AGENDA

The consequences of the accord on Afghanistan were considerable and varied. *Glasnost* hit the war in Afghanistan with full force after the announcement had been made. As a result, the foreign policy process that had led to decisions such as the escalation in Afghanistan was openly attacked and altered. Reactionary forces that remained inside the Party apparatus attempted to sabotage the withdrawal process. The Afghan government put pressure on the Soviets not to leave.

In February 1988, it became fully permissible to discuss the war in Afghanistan in print. Analysis of the decision making procedure that got the Soviets into the war was a common theme of the many articles published after the announcement. One of the first to comment was Aleksandr Prokhanov, a

---

and secretly replaced. See, for example, Alvin Z. Rubinstein, "Speculations on a National Tragedy," *Orbis* 30, no. 4 (Fall 1987): 589–608.

[112] *Pravda*, February 9, 1988, cited in *CDSP* 40, no. 6: 1, 3.

[113] A. Bovin, "Restructuring and Foreign Policy," *Izvestiia*, June 16, 1988, in *CDSP* 40, no. 24: 5–6.

Russian nationalist who, in the pages of *Literaturnaia gazeta*, blamed the specialists for the decision to intervene. "The experts who evaluated the situation in the country were mistaken; they were mistaken by specialists in Islam, by diplomats, politicians, and military men—since, I repeat, the basic goals simply have not been achieved."[114] In May 1988, Vyacheslav Dashichev, an Eastern Europe specialist, responded to Prokhanov's article. He discussed the impact of hegemony on the international system and specifically on U.S-Soviet relations and offered an explanation of Soviet foreign policy that seemed to come straight out of the American neorealist school: Soviet expansion had caused other states to balance against it. His criticism began with the complaint that there had been too little public discussion of foreign policy making. Hegemonic systems encourage states to balance against the major actor. Hegemonic tendencies in Soviet foreign policy were linked to "our centralization in domestic policy." The debacle in Afghanistan was a symptom of that method of policy making. "It is our conviction that the crisis was caused mainly by errors and the incompetent approach of the Brezhnev leadership to the accomplishment of foreign policy tasks."[115]

In July 1988, for the first time, a high-ranking military officer criticized the war. Artyom Borovik interviewed Major General Kim Tsagolov; Borovik contended that "there was not the slightest hint of socialism [in Afghanistan]. We were victims of our own illusions." Tsagolov responded, "That's true. For Afghan society, traditional relations are not a vestigial phenomenon. They are a powerful social stratum. . . . The repressive measures against eminent Islamic authorities . . . and instances of reprisals against certain mullahs right before the eyes of the believers played decisively into the opposition's hands."[116]

Artyom Borovik probed the changed image of the opponent; since the Soviets were withdrawing from Afghanistan, the war was no longer discussed in terms of a bipolar conflict and the diversity within the mujahideen was acknowledged. Tsagolov responded by giving the most sophisticated analysis in the press to date of what he referred to as the "Peshawar Seven," the seven major factions within the mujahideen. He noted that they were not a "unified

---

[114] Aleksandr Prokhanov, "A Writer's Opinion: Afghan Questions," *Literaturnaia gazeta*, February 17, 1988: 9; Porter, "The Military Abroad," 317, suggests that Prokhanov may have been expressing a view common among the military.

[115] Vyacheslav Dashichev, "The Search for New East-West Relations," *Literaturnaia gazeta*, May 18, 1988:14, in *CDSP* 40, no. 24: 4. Other discussions of the war published after the announcement include A. Bovin, "Afghanistan: A Difficult Decade," *Izvestiia*, December 23, 1988 in *CDSP* 40, no. 51: 10; the special issues of *SShA*, June and July 1989, with articles by Vladimir Lukin, Bovin, Tsagalov, Kremenyuk, and others; and Evgeni Primakov, *Pravda*, July 2, 1988: 8, in *CDSP* 40, no. 34: 13. Commenting on most of these articles is Cynthia Roberts, "*Glasnost'* in Soviet Foreign Policy: Setting the Record Straight?" *Report on the USSR*, December 15, 1989, 4–8.

[116] Borovik, "Afghanistan: the preliminary results," 25.

organically cohesive social force," although the Soviet press had consistently treated them as such. In closing, Tsagolov urged more discussion about the war: "In the early 1980s, Afghanistan was relegated to the category of so-called 'closed subjects.' . . . This is a graphic example of the lack of openness. . . . it is necessary to make up for the deficit in truth that has built up during the war."[117]

Gorbachev himself took full aim at the old thinkers with his criticism of the "command administrative method" at the 19th Party Conference in June 1988. He was even more specific about how domestic policies had affected the conduct of foreign policy than when he had linked the two in February 1987.

> While drawing lessons from the past, it must be admitted that command administrative methods did not bypass the foreign policy field. Sometimes even the most important decisions were made by a narrow circle of individuals, without a collective comprehensive discussion of analysis, and at times without the proper consultation with friends. This led to an inadequate reaction to international events and the policies of other states and even to erroneous decisions.[118]

Gorbachev's association of the command administrative system with errors in foreign policy decision making was echoed a few weeks later in a speech by Shevardnadze to foreign policy experts held at the Ministry of Foreign Affairs. He argued that "broad public participation in the formation of foreign policy is urgently needed."[119] Such criticism by the foreign minister amounted to a call to abandon the decision making methods that had been used by the top leadership for generations.

Shevardnadze's response to the growing criticism of the administrative command system was to organize scholarly councils at MID. These councils were meant to ensure regular contact between officials of MID and regional specialists recognized for their "special, professional knowledge."[120] Foreign policy had previously tended "to ignore professional recommendations about the nature, orientation and structure of international ties."[121] In addition, a "scientific coordinating center" was intended "to maintain constant ties with

[117] Ibid., 27. See also K. M. Tsagalov "Ne vse tak prosto" (Not everything is that simple), *SShA* 6 (1989): 62–68.

[118] Gorbachev's report to the 19th All-Union CPSU Conference, *Pravda*, June 29, 1988, in *CDSP* 40, no. 26: 11.

[119] Shevardnadze report to Ministry of Foreign Affairs, *Pravda*, July 26, 1988, in *CDSP* 40, no. 30: 13. "Nauchno-prakticheskaia konferentsiia MID SSSR XIX vsesoiuznaia konferentsiia KPSS: vneshnaia politika i diplomatiia," *Vestnik Ministerstva inostrannikh del* no. 12 (August 15, 1988): 27–46.

[120] 19th All-Union CPSU Conference, July 25, 1988, *International Affairs* (Moscow), October 1988, 12. Diligensky (author's interview) confirms that the contacts between regional experts and MID became very strong and generally eclipsed those with the CCID.

[121] "19th All-Union CPSU Conference," July 25, 1988, 13.

scientific [scholarly] centers in this country and abroad" on a range of issues.[122]

Just because the withdrawal was on the agenda did not mean that high-
level opposition to the withdrawal had ceased. According to Alexander
Yakovlev, in Politburo meetings, while no one decision maker openly objected
(in accordance with the accepted custom), several people made the withdrawal difficult.

> Whenever the question came up, Mikhail Sergeyevich [Gorbachev] said that So-
> viet troops should withdraw. Everybody agreed. But then the most terrible
> things started happening [pauses]. . . . The implementation was sabotaged. . . .
> The evacuation was hampered. The road was blocked, cut in two places. Then
> they found that a bridge had been blown up somewhere. Then it was said that
> the air force could not get through to Kabul. . . . Too much cargo had piled up.[123]

Yakovlev described a battle over the withdrawal between, on the one side,
Gorbachev, Shevardnadze and himself, and on the other side, Varennikov and
Akhromeev.

> The tactics of our adversaries were as follows. Okay, they would say, we are will-
> ing, ultimately, to fix a day. But everything will collapse. Afghanistan will quickly
> fall into the hands of the Americans, through Pakistan. Everything will collapse,
> everything will be lost, they said. We will have the real enemy on our
> doorstep. . . . The one thing that helped and saved us, was the fact that Mikhail
> Sergeyevich was on our side.[124]

Yakovlev claimed that there was debate up to the very end. Gorbachev eventually said, "Enough hesitation. . . . the troops must be withdrawn. That's all
there is to it. They must be withdrawn."[125]

Yakovlev's testimony directly contradicts the claims of some senior military
personnel that they supported the withdrawal.[126] Given available information, it is not possible to say definitively who is telling the truth, but there is
evidence to support both sides.[127] The reformers probably did encounter re-

---

[122] Ibid., 26.

[123] Central Television interview with Yakovlev, 3–4.

[124] Ibid., 4. Varennikov expressed rage at Shevardnadze in an interview with the author, which
suggests that Yakovlev was correct. In any case, Varennikov's interpetation of events was that Shevardnadze had colluded with the United States in ending the war and had betrayed the Soviet Union.

[125] Central Television interview with Yakovlev, 5. Another example of domestic battles over
reform include conservatives wanting to fire Korotich and Yegor Yakovlev at the 19th Party Conference. See Ed A. Hewett with Thane Gustafson and Victor H. Winston, "The 19th Party Conference," in Ed A. Hewett and Victor H. Winston, eds., *Milestones in Glasnost and Perestroyka:
Politics and People* (Washington, D.C.: Brookings, 1991), 112–131, esp. 118.

[126] For example, author's interview with Akhromeev.

[127] Senior military officers also claim that they objected to the intervention in 1979 (see Chapter 3) and that from the early 1980s they realized the situation was not winnable. What may actually have happened is that the military wanted a delay in the intervention, because they wanted
larger number of troops used and deployment would take time.

sistance from the military on the timing of the withdrawal; certainly there had been a long, drawn-out struggle to get the withdrawal on the agenda. Once this was achieved, the struggles may have intensified. The military's reaction may have been similar to that of Richard Nixon regarding Vietnam; there was a desire to get out but on one's own terms, that is, with victory. Ultimately, the group that supported the policy of withdraw-no-matter-what prevailed over the group pushing for withdraw-only-under-specific-conditions.

Despite this pressure, Gorbachev was able to do what his predecessors had been unable to do: to say "no" to client states. The Afghan government put pressure on the Soviets not to withdraw troops.[128] Yakovlev claims that from the summer of 1987 on, after Gorbachev had repeated to Najibullah that the troops would be withdrawn, Afghan objections escalated, deferring the departure date.[129] Borovik claims that Najibullah even approached the leadership of other Soviet client states such as Angola and Cuba, urging them to put pressure on the Soviets not to abandon them. Shevardnadze met with Angolan and Cuban representatives, but the withdrawal from Afghanistan signalled the first of many Soviet retreats.[130]

The Soviet withdrawal was carried out so as to cause maximum damage to the Afghanis. According to Reserve Major General L. Shershnev, Gorbachev "gave the order to use the whole might of the Soviet air force to carry out massive bombing and strafing strikes against Afghan villages which were believed to contain concentrations of rebels."[131]

The circumstances surrounding this particular decision are not clear: Artyom Borovik claims that in early January 1989, at a regular Politburo session, the last military operation in Afghanistan was discussed at length. Two pressures were bearing down on Gorbachev at that time: Najibullah was urging the Soviets not to leave (a plea that presumably carried weight with at least some Politburo members), and the first elections for the Congress of Peoples' Deputies were two months away. Borovik claims that Gorbachev was afraid that his political opponents, Boris Yeltsin and others, would use high casualty rates as a political weapon to win votes away from deputies sympathetic to Gorbachev. (This situation was paralleled six years later when President Yeltsin faced the parliamentary and presidential elections and the war in Chechnya.) "The leadership did not want coffins in any of the cities."[132]

To keep the Soviet casualty figures low, Gorbachev agreed to a major operation along the Salang highway as Soviet troops withdrew. The leadership authorized the military to offer information regarding the withdrawal to the mujahideen in return for a cease-fire. However, says Borovik, the Soviets broke their agreement, expecting that the mujahideen would do so. The mu-

---

[128] Author's interviews with Snegirov; Borovik.

[129] Central Television interview with Yakovlev, 4.

[130] Author's interview with Borovik.

[131] Russian television, January 28, 1992 in FBIS-SOV 92-024.

[132] Author's interview with Borovik.

jahideen did stay away from Soviet troops, but the Soviets opened fire on, reportedly, thousands of Afghan civilians.[133] Borovik was advised not to write
about these events. "Several days after the January operation, our political su-
pervisor in Kabul asked me what I knew about it; someone had told him that
I'd been there. Before I could answer, however, he gave me some friendly advice. 'Even if you do know something, you have forgotten it all already,' he
said. 'Right?'"[134]

Najibullah's reasons for objecting to the withdrawal were based on the fear
that there would be a bloodbath when the Soviets left: that mujahideen forces
would kill all Afghans who had worked with the Soviets. Many Soviets feared
this as well.[135] But in the end, the Soviets had succeeded in rebuilding the
Afghan army, and they had sharply increased their supply of arms as they
withdrew troops.[136] Soviet troop casualties were very low and overall the
event appeared to have a distinctly telegenic quality in contrast with what had
been a gruesome and frustrating war.

CONCLUSION

If the decision to withdraw had been considered in 1983 under Andropov,
why did it take until 1989 for the troops to come home? I argue that the outcome of this war was ultimately determined at home in Moscow, and not
abroad in Kabul, Geneva, or Washington, D.C. As with the United States in
Vietnam, the leadership waited until domestic pressure grew to such a degree
that there was no alternative. Unlike the American case, however, domestic
pressure to end the war in Afghanistan did not come from below, from
demonstrations in the streets or from voter discontent. Domestic pressure for
ending the Soviet war in Afghanistan came primarily from above, from progressive elements in the Gorbachev coalition and from their understanding
of economic and social realities.

In this chapter, I have detailed Gorbachev's strategies for shifting the in-

---

[133] Author's interview with Borovik. For more on the massacre, see "Telling the Truth," CBS
"60 Minutes" broadcast, October 29, 1989; and Borovik, *The Hidden War*, 252–256.

[134] Borovik, *The Hidden War*, 256. Although Borovik (author's interview) received help in
getting his stories published, many in the military wanted to keep him out of Afghanistan. In
1989, he was assigned a "guide" to accompany him on his trips around the country and to im-
pede his ability to talk to troops; no one would talk openly as long as it was presumed that a KGB
agent was tagging along. Borovik was, at other times, pulled off planes bound from the Soviet
Union to Kabul or made to wait in Tashkent for clearance, and he received vaguely threatening
telephone calls informing him that the Soviet military "couldn't guarantee his safety."

[135] Author's interview with Snegirov; Central Television interview with Yakovlev. Najibullah's
fears were partially realized in the end; he was publicly hung and castrated by the Taliban in
Kabul in September 1996.

[136] On the "success," see Roy, *The Lessons of the Soviet-Afghan War*, 24; and author's interview with Gankovsky.

ternal balance of power that enabled his coalition to force reformist policy issues, including the withdrawal from Afghanistan, onto the agenda.[137] These strategies included building up traditional bases of power such as the Central Committee, as well as alternative sources of support such as an expert community. The strategies for setting the foreign policy agenda involved empowering experts who publicized and legitimized the linkage of domestic reform with accommodation abroad.

The implementation of the reform agenda began on the home front with personnel changes, the restructuring of production relations, and increased openness on previously forbidden subjects. Gorbachev implemented the more dramatic changes only after he had made personnel changes in the ministries and the Politburo and engaged in political maneuvers with the various factions opposed to reform, and only after *glasnost* had begun to work its effect on society. Empowering the experts who articulated the need for reform also affected the political environment, making old policies like the war in Afghanistan increasingly out of step with new policies of reform.

---

[137] See John W. Kingdon, *Agendas, Alternatives and Public Policies* (Boston: Little, Brown, 1984). See also the discussion in Matthew Evangelista, "Sources of Moderation in Soviet Security Policy," in Philip Tetlock, et al., eds., *Behavior, Society and Nuclear War: Volume II* (Oxford: Oxford, 1991), 275–277.

CHAPTER SIX

Conclusion: The Importance of Ideas and Politics in Explaining Change

IN THIS BOOK, I have argued that internal political battles between old and new thinkers concerning the direction of domestic and foreign policy are central to understanding the long, withdrawing roar of the Soviet empire in the 1980s. Three periods—1979–80, 1982–84, and 1985–89—of the war in Afghanistan function as case studies that highlight the conditions necessary for change in policy: the articulation of reformist ideas by a wide range of experts, and a responsive leadership that turned the ideas into policy following a shift in the internal balance of power.

What was different about the 1985–89 period from earlier periods of the war, and from earlier attempts at reform by Khrushchev, was that the Gorbachev coalition gained control of political resources and succeeded in changing the internal balance of power in favor of reformists. The strategies used to alter the internal balance of power in the mid-1980s included significant personnel changes in the main institutions of power and the empowerment of expert communities as an alternative source of political support. When one of these conditions was present *without* the other—ideas without sponsorship, or reformist leadership without control of the agenda—major policy shifts did not occur. These conditions permitted "misfit" ideas—ones that directly and profoundly challenged traditional ways of thinking and behaving—to get on to the political agenda and become policies.

This explanation differs significantly from those that emphasize the role of the international system in shifting Soviet foreign policy, and by extension, in explaining the end of the Cold War.[1] New evidence from archival sources and my interviews with participants and observers of the policy process show that the international system played only an indeterminant role. Soviet policy makers responded in a variety of ways to events in the international system and particularly to U.S. foreign policy. U.S. rhetoric made the job of reformers in the Soviet Union more difficult, not less so. U.S. policy confirmed for many Soviet hardliners their perceptions that U.S. intentions were malign.

The domestic political context was the center stage upon which the drama

[1] See, for example, Daniel Deudney and G. John Ikenberry, "The International Sources of Soviet Change," *International Security* 16, no. 3 (Winter 1991/92): 74–118; Robert Legvold, "Soviet Learning in the 1980s," in George W. Breslauer and Philip E. Tetlock, eds., *Learning in U.S. and Soviet Foreign Policy* (Boulder: Westview, 1991), 684–732.

of radical policy change was played out. Pivotal in this drama were the strategies used by the leadership to alter the balance of power, particularly concerning the role of domestic and foreign policy experts. The domestic politics group agreed on the need to alter the relationship of the state to the people, to reduce the day-to-day involvement of the Party in the running of the country, and to assess critically past policy mistakes. In the arena of foreign policy, experts agreed on the need to develop a pragmatic, less ideological, foreign policy driven by cooperative rather than competitive notions of security, to alter relations with the West, and to question the viability of previous Soviet policies toward the Third World. Domestic and foreign policy experts were linked institutionally and intellectually by the concept that cooperation abroad, characterized by such policies as the withdrawal from Afghanistan, was necessary for reform at home.

One's position in the network determined to a large extent the amount and type of advice that was offered but not necessarily the level of pragmatism. Differences in influence in this case were not a result of some specialists saying what the leadership wanted to hear, but instead were largely the result of personal ties between Gorbachev and specific experts. The ties were developed during Gorbachev's time as secretary of agriculture, and additionally, as a consequence of the 110 reports requested by Andropov which influenced Gorbachev in the early 1980s.

My findings suggest that specialists played different roles in policy making at different times. The top echelon of the network was brought in on the issue of the war in Afghanistan as early as 1983, while the bulk of the specialists were not consulted until late 1986 and through the spring and summer of 1987. Given that the leadership's decision in principle to withdraw seems to have been reached in late spring and summer 1987, much of the network appears to have been involved in the policy process, but to different degrees. Soviet Afghan specialists served mainly to bolster a position on withdrawal that had been urged by the top echelon for some time. Nevertheless, it may be said that before, during, and after this decision, specialists advised policy makers on the war, as well as on improving relations with the United States. The timing of the advice on Afghanistan (and on many other subjects) shows that the top echelon was not confined simply to the mobilization of opinion but also initiated ideas.

If one compares the Soviet decision to intervene in Afghanistan with the decision to withdraw, one finds important differences but also a few similarities in both leadership style and the role of experts. By all accounts, the decision to intervene was highly centralized, involving just Gromyko, Ustinov, Andropov, and Brezhnev. The decision was announced, the policy implemented, and the public informed. This pattern was, to a certain extent, repeated with the decision to withdraw. According to high-ranking party officials, the ultimate "push" to withdraw came from above. The decision to withdraw seems in the end also to have been taken by a small group: Gorbachev, Yakovlev, and Shevardnadze.

The main difference in how the decisions to intervene and to withdraw were reached, however, lies in the fact that, in the case of the withdrawal, foreign and domestic policy specialists had been discussing the war with top leaders for several years. These specialists were continuously consulted on this topic. Indeed, Marshal Sergei Akhromeev, in stating that the push came from above, also said that a much larger group of specialists was consulted on the decision to withdraw than on the decision to intervene.[2] The consultations characterized Gorbachev's leadership style and the active role the expert community played in various policy initiatives. The use of these specialists in policy making was his attempt to open up the decision making process. In terms of foreign policy, by going outside the usual channels—the Politburo, the Central Committee, the KGB, military, and Ministry of Foreign Affairs—Gorbachev was attempting to build a more active and critical base. This effort was understandable, but it ultimately overwhelmed the process of reform in the Soviet Union.

As in many gripping dramas, the end of the Soviet story revolves around a tragic flaw. Gorbachev's flaw derived from the successful shift in power away from the Party, and the degree to which reform had spread throughout the empire. Neither he nor his government could control the political forces they had unharnessed. By late 1989 and early 1990, there was another, this time ultimate, shift in the internal balance of power away from Gorbachev.

Gorbachev's *perestroika, glasnost*, and new thinking mobilized protest not only in Eastern Europe, which by late 1989 was free of Soviet dominance thanks in part to Gorbachev's decision not to use force, but also in several Soviet republics. Proclamations of independence by the Baltic states, among others, instantly outpaced Moscow's conceptions of reform.[3] The power of mass politics as people took to the streets in Vilnius, Riga, Tallinn, Alma Ata, Baku, and Tbilisi, even Moscow itself, proved overwhelming to the Kremlin. A shift in power from the people back to the Soviet government would have required enormous force and a complete reversal of all that Gorbachev and his cohort had stood for. Instead, Gorbachev was left behind by the withdrawing roar that he had unleashed. He has apparently never understood the nature of nationalism or the demand for freedom that he encouraged.[4]

[2] Author's interview with Marshal Sergei Akhromeev, chief of the Soviet armed forces, 1984–88, and former senior military adviser to Gorbachev, January 3, 1990. Karen Brutents, first deputy directory of CCID, made the case also that scholars were important in the decision to withdraw. Author's interview, December 7, 1990.

[3] See Anatol Lieven, *The Baltic Revolution* (New Haven: Yale University Press, 1993).

[4] Gorbachev's memoirs strikingly demonstrate his failure to grasp the link between his actions and subsequent events. Mikhail Gorbachev, *Memoirs* (New York: Doubleday, 1996). For similar observations, see Jack F. Matlock, Jr., "Gorbachev: Lingering Mysteries," *New York Review of Books*, December 19, 1996, 34–40.

IDEAS AND POLITICS IN OTHER CASES

While change in Soviet foreign policy and the collapse of the Soviet Union are unique historical events, there are some lessons about the implementation of ideas and the influence of experts that may be applicable in other cases. The role of ideas and experts is highly dependent on the type of access that a community of experts has to the political leadership, and the degree to which ideas proposed by members of the community are salient to the leadership either because the leadership believes in the ideas or because the ideas help politically in some way. The leadership's ability to implement the experts' ideas is in turn determined by its ability to control political resources. Accordingly, turning ideas into policy is highly contingent.

These generalizations bear directly on the literature in international relations theory concerning the role of ideas and experts in foreign policy. Scholars writing on the role of ideas have tended to underplay the importance of politics in getting specific ideas on the political agenda. At the same time, scholars assessing policy change often see ideas and experts as no more than convenient hooks on which to hang policy initiatives driven by materialist goals. In contrast, I argue that both reformist ideas *and* the political strategies used by certain members of the leadership were necessary in implementing radical policy changes such as the reconceptualization of security in the Soviet Union and the withdrawal from Afghanistan.[5]

To get a sense of the extent to which ideas and politics, learning, or the international system each determine shifts in foreign policy, particularly those that represent radical departures from the status quo, additional cases should be examined. Cases should include states with different domestic political arrangements and variation in conditions in the international system. Knowledge is cumulative, and ultimately, the robustness of theoretical observations generated here may only be determined after an exploration of a wide variety of cases.

Comparative cases would provide answers to important aspects of expert-leadership relations not fully addressed by this study: do successful challenges to the status quo and subsequent shifts in policy follow similar patterns even when domestic political systems differ? What is the relationship of experts to power in other domestic systems? Can experts change the political agenda without the leadership's support? Or does the top leadership always determine the amount of influence that policy entrepreneurs have in the decision making process, even in, for example, liberal democracies?

---

[5] Also on ideas and politics, see Kathryn Sikkink, *Ideas and Institutions: Developmentalism in Brazil and Argentina* (Ithaca: Cornell University Press, 1991); and Judith Goldstein and Robert O. Keohane, eds., *Ideas and Foreign Policy: Beliefs, Institutions and Political Change* (Ithaca: Cornell University Press, 1993).

This book examined a major change in great power foreign policy: the shift from aggression to accommodation represented by the withdrawal from Afghanistan. It is worth comparing these findings with additional Soviet cases, most important of which would be the overall disengagement from Eastern Europe. Other cases involving withdrawal might include the French withdrawal from the wars in Indochina or Algeria, or the U.S. withdrawal from Vietnam.

The universe of cases, however, is larger than the collapse of empires or extraction from quagmires. The application of findings in this book need not be restricted to cases of security studies or even international relations. Withdrawal is merely one example of public policy change. Therefore, it is worth considering what this case tells us about the politics of ideas more generally in public policy, and specifically, in terms of the requirements of public policy change. Can we identify, for example, conditions necessary for radical change in health care policy? Environmental policy? Education policy?

President Clinton was asked, shortly after his election to a second term, what his biggest mistakes were in his first term. Among others, he pointed to his inability to get health care reform turned into policy.[6] The issue was clearly salient to the president. He had drawn on the ideas of various experts. But he had not paid sufficient attention to gaining the endorsement of the Congress. In short, he did not have control of the political resources necessary to get his ideas (and those of experts) turned into policy.

This example and the Soviet case point to the importance of understanding the mechanisms of policy change. Yet literature in political science and in other social science such as sociology that addresses change tends to lack explanations that take process and the politics of change into account. The literature instead focuses more on outcome and structure.[7]

This disparity can be illustrated by considering how sociology's "new institutionalism," an approach that explicitly addresses "organizational change," would account for change in Soviet foreign policy.[8] This approach borrows the concept "isomorphism" from natural science. Isomorphism acts as a constraint; "it forces one unit in a population to resemble other units that face the same set of environmental conditions."[9] A new institutionalist approach would explain Soviet behavior as an organizational isomorphic response to

[6] James Bennett, "Clinton's New Year's Eve: Looking Back," *New York Times*, January 3, 1997, 20.

[7] See Martha Finnemore, "Norms, Culture, and World Politics: Insights from Sociology's Institutionalism," *International Organization* 50, no. 2 (Spring 1996): 325–348; and Kathleen Thelen and Sven Steinmo, "Historical Institutionalism in Comparative Politics," in Sven Steinmo, Kathleen Thelen, and Frank Longstreth, eds., *Structuring Politics: Historical Institutionalism in Comparative Analysis* (New York: Cambridge University Press, 1992), 1–32.

[8] Paul J. DiMaggio and Walter W. Powell, "Introduction," in Walter W. Powell and Paul J. DiMaggio, eds., *The New Institutionalism in Organizational Analysis* (Chicago: University of Chicago Press, 1991), 1.

[9] Paul J. DiMaggio and Walter W. Powell, "The Iron Cage Revisited: Institutional Isomorphism and Collective Rationality in Organizational Fields," in ibid., 66.

Western institutions—that is, that increasing global interdependence led to a need to develop more adaptive bureaucracies and regulated rather than black markets. The Soviet Union would have then traded in its iron curtain for Max Weber's "iron cage."[10]

Like neorealism, this approach stresses systemic factors as a cause for unit-level change. As a result, it obscures the highly political and extremely contingent character of the changes and makes the reform-turned-revolution seem inevitable. As Martha Finnemore has noted in a general critique of new institutionalism, this approach tends to over-emphasize structure and underplay the role of agency.[11] New institutionalism emerges as particularly problematic in the Soviet case; the story told here is incomplete without a central focus on agency.

So what can be learned from the Soviet case for looking at public policy change in general? The answer is not tidy, and it is not unique. Ideas and how they interact with institutions (both new and old ones), as well as the political balance of power, simply matter a great deal in bringing about policy change.[12] External structures are part of the story, but not the most important part.

The Soviet experience of the 1980s was about the Gorbachev coalition's attempts to change the policy agenda by giving a voice to critical sources and by altering institutions that shaped the agenda. Just as important, it was about their attempts at changing the way political actors conceived of various issues, from relations with the West to relations between the Party and the people. To claim that change was a response to external structure (in this case, the international system), is contrary to the evidence.

THE POST-SOVIET ERA

On many levels, the world discussed in this book is different from today: the Soviet Union collapsed and the Cold War ended. Russia is in many respects as transparent as the Soviet Union was opaque. But vestiges of the old order live on in the new era. Russia inherited Soviet nuclear weapons, but not necessarily its adversarial relationship with the United States. The conceptual links between domestic reform at home and cooperation abroad grew out of those made famous by Mikhail Gorbachev and the expert community in the 1980s, but they have been altered in the 1990s.

---

[10] Ibid., 63 and 74. Some might argue that Russia has done exactly that. See Steven F. Cohen, "'Transition' or Tragedy?" *The Nation*, December 30, 1996.

[11] See Finnemore, "Norms, Culture, and World Politics."

[12] This approach is similar to that advocated by historical institutionalists in Steinmo, Thelen, and Longstreth, *Structuring Politics*, esp. Thelen and Steinmo, "Historical Institutionalism in Comparative Politics," 1–32; Peter A. Hall, "The Movement from Keynesianism to Monetarism: Institutional Analysis and British Economic Policy in the 1970s," 90–113; and Margaret Weir, "Ideas and the Politics of Bounded Innovation," 188–216.

Russian foreign policy five years into the post-Soviet period has been more talk than action; it has taken a back seat to the process of state-building.[13] All those involved in politics have been consumed by the revolution that is sweeping Russia, by the transformation and construction of the new state. The policy making machines, within the president's Security and Defense Councils, the ministries and the Duma, have lived and breathed three battles for the last several years: democratization, marketization, and the war in Chechnya. Even in the parliamentary and presidential elections of the mid-1990s, foreign policy issues played virtually no role.

To the extent that Russian foreign policy does exist, it has been mediated by domestic politics.[14] Authority-building and coalition-mobilizing strategies that were crucial to Gorbachev's ability to change the political agenda take on enhanced importance in the competitive arena of post-Soviet politics. Without the mobilization of constituencies, controversial policies that are seen as accommodationist towards the West (e.g., the second Strategic Arms Reduction Treaty, START II) will not get past a Duma with a substantially communist and nationalist composition.[15]

Expert communities continue to be dependent on the strategies that the leadership uses to get ideas on the political agenda. The institutes formerly subsidized by the Academy of Sciences have given way to a plethora of "think tanks" that operate independently of the state, often working for banks or Russian companies. The ability of any analytic center to influence policy making at the executive or legislative level tends to be determined, as with Gorbachev, by the personal connections between individuals in the analytical center and members of the leadership, and not by any formalized institutional mechanisms.[16]

[13] That said, Russian foreign policy, particularly toward the West, took on a more aggressive tone in 1996 and 1997 as Russian policy makers were confronted with the reality that NATO enlargement into Central Europe would go forward. See Dmitry Gornostaiev, "The First Year of Primakov's Diplomacy," *Nezavisimaia gazeta*, January 9, 1997.

[14] Questioning the relationship of domestic politics and Russian foreign policy is Michael McFaul, "Revolutionary Ideas, State Interests, and Russian Foreign Policy," in Vladimir Tismaneanu, ed., *Political Culture and Civil Society in Russia and the New States of Eurasia* (New York: M. E. Sharpe, 1995).

[15] In 1993, during what would later be seen as a honeymoon period with the West, Boris Yeltsin made the previously unimaginable decision to eliminate land-based multiple-warhead (MIRVed) missiles, which had been the backbone of the Soviet strategic nuclear arsenal. The Soviets and the Americans had made very different choices in the acquisition and deployment of their nuclear forces, and with START II, the Russian leadership agreed, essentially, to restructure their force posture contrary to the choices made by their predecessors and according to the choices made by their former opponent. In the political climate of 1997, when START II is due to come before the Duma, it lacks support.

[16] For details, see Oksana Antonenko, "New Russian Analytical Centers and Their Role in Political Decisionmaking," Strengthening Democratic Institutions Project, John F. Kennedy School of Government, February 1996; and Scott A. Bruckner, "Policy Research Centers in Russia: Tottering toward an Uncertain Future," *NIRA Review*, Summer 1996, National Institute for Research Advancement.

A major difference in the domestic context of policy making is the increased permeability of post-Soviet Russia. International institutions and a variety of actors in the international system have the opportunity to attempt to influence change in policy inside Russia. U.S. involvement in the democratization and marketization process of formerly communist states has been a cornerstone of U.S. foreign policy in the post-Soviet era.

The combination of transparency and integration with the international community suggests that actors outside Russia could have a greater effect on domestic reformist coalitions in Russia than they could during the Cold War. But the porousness (or opacity) of a state does not alone determine the ability of other states to influence policy. U.S. policy makers' abilities to affect policy outcomes continue to be constrained, as was made clear by Secretary of Defense William Perry's meeting in the fall of 1996 with a hostile Duma on START II ratification.[17] U.S. decision makers need to continue focusing on Russian domestic political conditions in order to anticipate potential reactions to U.S. initiatives.

As the struggle for the future of Russia and other new states in Eastern Europe takes shape, the process of state-building reveals how post-Soviet dynamics are affected by the legacy of the past. Foreign policy continues to be conditioned and mediated by the domestic political context more than the international one. The roar of the collapsing empire can still be heard.

[17] Pavel Felgenhauer, "Need Fresh Start to Ratify Treaty," *St. Petersburg Times*, November 18–24, 1996.

Index

Abalkin, Leonid, 83
Academy of Sciences of the Soviet Union (ANSSSR), 79, 84
access to leadership: by expert community, 66; specialists with, 12
Adler, Emmanuel, 30n.42, 33–34, 35n.61, 71n.22
Afghanistan: Andropov's position on, 65–66, 71–76; conditions permitting withdrawal from, 66; four phases of war in, 44; government response to planned Soviet withdrawal, 117, 121–22; incremental escalation in, 39–40, 43–44; mujahideen resistance within (1978–79), 45–54; size of Soviet military efforts in, 27; Soviet financial aid to, 26–27; Soviet war in, 67–68, 95–100. *See also* escalation in Afghanistan; intervention in Afghanistan; mujahideen; withdrawal from Afghanistan
Aganbegyan, Abel: contacts with Gorbachev, 86; as domestic policy specialist, 85; in expert community, 83, 84
Akhromeev, Sergei, xii–xiii; on Andropov's position on Afghan war, 74; on leadership opposition to invasion of Afghanistan, 56–57; memoirs, 14; planning of coup against Amin, 53; on Soviet foreign policy, 100; on specialists' role in withdrawal decision, 126; against war in Afghanistan, 101
Alexiev, Alexander, xiin.2, 27n.34, 96n.13, 99n.25
Amin, Hafizullah: as minister of foreign affairs, 45; ousting of, 44; requests for Soviet supplies and troops, 48
Amstutz, Bruce, 47n.27
Andrew, Christopher, 58n.84, 70n.21, 104n.56
Andropov, Yuri: anti-corruption campaign of, 74; approval of escalation, 53, 55, 59; assignments for Gorbachev, 13, 81, 87; as catalyst for new thinking, 65, 71–72; in decision to replace Amin government, 44; decision to send tanks into Afghanistan, 43; domestic agenda, 72; as Gorbachev's mentor, 77–78, 87; initial opposition to military force in Afghanistan, 58; leadership of, 65–66, 71–76; member of Com-

mission on Afghanistan, 48; perceptions of position on Soviet withdrawal, 74–76
Antonenko, Oksana, 78n.54, 130n.16
Arbatov, Alexei, 62, 83n.69
Arbatov, Georgii, 53nn.59 and 60, 58n.85, 60n.96, 71n.22, 72nn.27 and 30, 75n.40, 76n.46; on Andropov's position on Afghan war, 74; on Brezhnev's health, 55; contacts with Gorbachev, 88n.93; as director of USKAN, 57; on influence of military-industrial complex, 103; as member of expert community, 83, 84; on *perestroika*, 100; on U.S. arms build-up, 57, 70
arms build-up, U.S., 25, 70
Arnold, Anthony, 42
Arnold, Matthew, xi
Aven, Pyotr, 82n.66

Bachrach, Peter, 8n.10
balance of power, internal: among Communist Party entities, 100–104; factors in alteration of, 7–8; in Gorbachev's favor, 112; role in withdrawal from Afghanistan, 5; role of *glasnost* in, 108–9; shift away from Gorbachev, 126; shift in, 5, 11–12, 16–18, 66, 92, 95, 110; strategies to change, 13–14, 16–17, 108, 124; when dominated by old thinking, 41–64
Baratz, Morton, 8n.10
Basistov, Anatoly, 70
belief system: changes in core parts of, 24–25; role in complex learning, 24–25
Belyaev, Igor, 40n.6
Berman, Larry, 41n.8
Bertin, Gilles, 95n.11
Bessmertnykh, Alexander, 70
Betts, Richard, 41n.8, 56n.74
Blacker, Coit D., 34n.56
Blowpipes, 97–98
Blum, Douglas, 22n.12
Bogomolov, Oleg: on Andropov as catalyst, 75; protest against excalation in Afghanistan, 61
Borovik, Artyom, 15n.28, 27n.35, 40n.6, 88–89n.97, 101–2, 112n.93, 113–14, 118, 121–22
Bovin, Alexander, 117, 118n.115

About the Author

Sarah E. Mendelson is Assistant Professor of Political Science in the Graduate School of Public Affairs and Policy at the State University of New York at Albany. In 1997–98, she is a resident associate at the Carnegie Endowment for International Peace in Washington, D.C.